75 SCRIPTURES

– that will –

Living on a Higher Plane

J. David Eshleman, D.Min.

75 Scriptures That Will Amaze You

Living on a Higher Plane

Copyright © 2020
by J. David Eshleman, D. Min.

Library of Congress Control Number: 2020916486
International Standard Book Number: 978-1-60126-697-2

Published by

Masthof Press

219 Mill Road | Morgantown, PA 19543-9516

www.masthof.com

THIS WORK IS DEDICATED TO ALL
WHO HAVE A SINCERE DESIRE
TO BE MORE LIKE JESUS IN ORDER
THAT HIS WILL CAN BE BROUGHT
TO REALITY ON EARTH
AS IT IS IN HEAVEN.

PREFACE

Amazing Scriptures! We are greater than Abraham, Moses, David, and Elisha . . . we can do greater things than Jesus . . . we can do immeasurable more than all that we can ask or imagine according to His power that is at work within us . . . we have the same power in us that raised Jesus from the dead . . . all we need He has already given to us . . . we can ask what we want and it will be given . . . we are seated beside Christ . . . God, Jesus and the Holy Spirit are in us . . . we can do all things with Christ . . . we are reigning with Christ . . . we are more than conquerors . . . we will never hunger or thirst again . . . we are not to be anxious about anything . . . we are to rejoice and continue to rejoice . . . and live in perfect peace.

God's word is packed with amazing scriptures for all who will accept them by faith. This book contains more than 1,600 scripture references plus hundreds of biblical allusions. As you meditate on them your life will move to a new level.

Throughout my life—in childhood and youth, and during my fifty years of pastoral ministry—the scriptures have amazed, challenged and comforted me. My love for God's Word keeps growing. The Bible is God-breathed. The original Greek expresses it as stated in the Amplified Bible: "Every scripture is God-breathed–given by his inspiration–and profitable for instruction, for reproof and conviction of sin, for correction of error and discipline in obedience, and for training in righteousness [that is in holy living, in conformity to God's will in thought, purpose and action], so that the people of God may be complete and proficient, well fitted and thoroughly equipped for every good work" (II Timothy 3:16).

"The bible has done more to shape literature, history, entertainment, and culture than any book. Its influence on world history is unparalleled, and shows no signs of abating." (March 2007 edition of *Time*). "The bible has been a massive influence on literature and history, especially in the Western world, where the Gutenberg Bible was the first book printed using movable type. With estimated total sales of over 5 billion copies, it is considered to be the most influential and best-selling book of all time. As of the 2000s, it sells approximately 100 million copies annually." (Wikipedia). It's reported that the Bible outsells the top one hundred best sellers each year. Many monarchs have tried to destroy the Bible to no avail. Multitudes have died for owning just one page of this precious book.

The sacred writings of many other religions are not necessarily written for the common man. The Bible is for everyone, including children. On the other hand, every year the Bible is the focus of scores of doctoral dissertations.

The complete Bible has been translated into approximately 700 languages, while the New Testament has been translated into well over 1,500 languages. At least one part of the Bible has been translated into 3,312 of the 7,097 languages in our world.

The Bible consists of 66 books, written by more than 40 authors covering 16 centuries. No other book can claim such a broad expanse of history. It is divided into two main sections: The Old Testament written approximately 1450 to 400 B.C. and the New Testament written from approximately 55 A.D. to 95 A.D. It is often divided into sections: the Old Testament written before Jesus; Genesis through Deuteronomy, books of Moses; books of history, Joshua through Esther; books of poetry, Job through Song of Solomon; and books of prophecy, Isaiah through Malachi. The New Testament is divided into four Gospels setting forth the life and teachings of Jesus, followed by the history book of Acts of the Apostles, twenty-three letters directed to various churches, concluding with Revelation, a book of prophecy.

I have used different versions of the Bible to make God's Word more understandable. When there is no abbreviation after the scripture, it is from the NIV (*New International Version*), or if it is not a direct quote. Occasionally, I inserted words in the text for clarification, which appear in parentheses. Exceptions to this are quotes taken from the *Amplified Bible*, which incorporates both parentheses and brackets to expand the meaning of the original languages.

Other abbreviations of Bible versions employed are:

AMP	*Amplified Bible*
CEV	*Contemporary English Version*
KJV	*King James Version*
Msg.	*Message Bible*
NLT	*New Living Translation*
TLB	*The Living Bible*

This book is easily adaptable for individual or small group study. When some essays are short take two or three essays per session. Most of these 75 essays are self-contained, therefore, you can read beginning in any section and find them beneficial.

My prayer is for the Holy Spirit to use these pages, saturated with scripture, to help the reader walk intimately and joyfully with our Lord Jesus Christ and put into action its life-giving message. Unless we make disciples, who make disciples, God's Kingdom will not reverse our deteriorating moral slide in America. God has so much more for His children than we realize. May His Spirit open our eyes to His resurrection power for us. It's there! The question is will we use it?

Some of the names in the illustrations have been changed for sensitivity reasons.

TABLE OF CONTENTS

I.

OUR AMAZING GOD

GOD'S AMAZING CREATION
GENESIS 1:1

"In the beginning God created the havens and the earth" (Genesis 1:1). The Hebrew word for God used here is "*Elohim*" which is plural, which indicates the Father, Son and Holy Spirit. All three created the heavens and the earth. "The statement that God created the heavens and the earth is one of the most challenging concepts confronting the modern mind. The vast galaxy we live in is spinning at the incredible speed of 490,000 miles an hour. But even at this speed, our galaxy still needs 200 million years to make one rotation. And there are over one billion other galaxies just like ours in the universe." (Study notes from the *Life Application Study Bible*).

"God said, 'Let us make mankind in our image, in our likeness so that they may rule over the fish in the sea and the birds in the sky, over the livestock and all the wild animals, and over all the creatures that move along the ground'" (Genesis 1:26).

We have an estimated 70 trillion cells in our body. That is 70 followed by 12 zeroes. Most of these cells are one-tenth of the width of a human hair. Cells are made from water, proteins, lipids, carbohydrates and nucleic acids. "You formed my inward parts, you knit me together in my mother's womb. I will confess and praise you, for you are fearfully wonderful, and for the awful wonder of my birth! Wonderful are your works, and that my inner self knows right well. My frame was not hidden from you, when I was being formed in secret and intricately and curiously wrought (as if embroidered with various colors) in the depths of the earth [a region of darkness and mystery]. Your eyes saw my unformed substance, and in your book all the days of my life were written, before ever they took shape, when as yet there was none of them" (Psalm 139:13-16 AMP).

God's creation is light-years ahead of the most brilliant of human minds. We don't know the thousands of what goes on in the transformation of the chrysalis becoming a butterfly. This conversion is astronomically more complicated than anything man has developed including space travel, the science of robots, or advances in medical science as wonderful as all of these are.

God not only foreknows everything, He holds things together. (Colossians 1:17). It's interesting that medical science has found one cell that holds things together out of the approximately 70 trillion cells in our body. The name of that cell is laminin, and it is in the shape of a cross. The cross is God's plus sign that holds everything together. Jesus is the agent of creation: "For in him all things were created: things in heaven and in earth, visible and invisible . . . all things were created through him and for him" (Colossians 1:16). Satan has worked overtime to undercut Jesus as creator coming up with atheistic evolution. The angel "proclaimed . . . to every nation, 'Fear God and give him glory . . . Worship him who made the heavens, the earth, the sea and the springs of water'" (Revelation 14:6-7). Satan wants us to question and to limit the creation ability of our Lord.

Consider these few statistics. There are about 320,000 species of plants, of which the great majority, some 275 thousand, produce seeds. Green plants provide a substantial proportion of the world's molecular oxygen, and are the basis of most of the earth's ecosystems. Scientists estimate there are over a million described species of insect, and an estimated 6-10 million total species.

How can some birds, fish and turtles lay their eggs and travel a thousand miles or more and return year after year to where they were before and repeat this cycle?

It is estimated that there is an average of 100 billion stars per galaxy. This means there are about 1,000,000,000,000,000,000,000 (that's 1 billion trillion) stars in the observable universe! Estimates suggest there are between 200 billion and 2 trillion galaxies. Isaiah and the Psalmist both remind us that God calls each star by name. (Isaiah 40:26; Psalm 147:3).

The average star has a diameter of 1 million miles. Our earth's diameter is only 8,000 miles with a circumference of 25,000 miles. God told Abraham to look up into the sky and count the stars if he could. (Genesis 15:5). Then God promised, "I will surely bless you and make your descendants as numerous as the stars in the sky and as the sand on the seashore" (Genesis 22:17). Some scholars surmise that the number of grains of sand might be more or less than the number of stars in the cosmos. If my calculations are anything near reality there are millions, if not billions of heavenly bodies for every person who has ever lived.

Our God is amazing: Almighty, omniscience, omnipotent and omnipresent. Never doubt that He even knows our thoughts, which will be revealed on the Judgment Day. (Psalm 94:11). (I suggest you go to: "Creationworldview.org" for many more amazing insights on God's creation.)

GOD CHOSE YOU
BEFORE HE CREATED THE WORLD
EPHESIANS 1:4

"God chose us in Christ before the creation of the world to be holy and blameless in his sight" (Ephesians 1:4). You are no afterthought with God. Knowing God loved you before He created the world will enable you to live with a sense of awe at his greatness and your importance.

In the mind of God, Jesus was our means of salvation before the world was created. Revelation 13:8 NLT, "The Book of Life, which belongs to the Lamb, (Jesus), was killed before the world was made." "Jesus was chosen before the creation of the world, but was revealed in these last times for your sake" (I Peter 1:20). We were in God's mind before He created the world. That's how important you are to our Amazing God.

God's foreknowledge is something we cannot understand. "God has always known who his chosen ones would be. He had decided to let them become like his own Son, so that his Son would be the first of many children" (Romans 8:29 CEV). David writes: "Your eyes saw my unformed body, all the days ordained for me were written in your book before one of them came to be" (Psalm 139:16). The Lord said to Jeremiah, "Before I formed you in the womb, I knew you; before you were born, I set you apart; I appointed you as a prophet to the nations" (Jeremiah 1:5). (Isaiah 49:1).

"By Jesus all things were created, in heaven and on earth, visible and invisible, whether thrones or dominions or rulers or authorities— all things were created through him and for him. And he is before all things, and in him all things hold together" (Colossians 1:16-18). David writes, "Surely I was sinful at birth, sinful from the time my mother conceived me" (Psalm 51:8). Since Jesus is before all things, he could see us before we were conceived. How amazing is God!

God also created a specific work for us to do. "We are God's handiwork, created in Christ Jesus to do good works, which God prepared in advance for us to do" (Ephesians 2:10). The word, "handiwork" means a work of notable excellence. You are one of a kind! You are His masterpiece. Don't live another minute thinking you are an inferior person!

Roger was mentally challenged. He could not talk but a few words. His movements were jerky and erratic. But Roger brought life to many by his smile and desire to help everyone. Studies have shown that children who grow up with severe mentally challenged persons usually learn to be more kind, thoughtful, sympathetic, and loving than in the typical family. God never makes a mistake.

As someone wrote: "Would you have a second child if you knew that child would murder your first child?" We are God's second children. He chose to make us, and His first child chose to die for us. How amazing!

GOD'S AGAPE, SELF-SACRIFICING LOVE
I JOHN 3:16, 4:7-12

Dirk Willems exemplified God's agape love. He was imprisoned in the Netherlands in 1569 for propagating the Gospel. Dirk managed to escape, but one of the guards spotted and pursued him. Dirk, having lost weight on his prison diet, fled across an icy pond. His pursuer, however, went through the ice. Dirk heard the pursuer's call for help. He turned around and was able to help the man to safety. The pursuer wanted to release Dirk, but the authorities would hear nothing of it and had him burned at the stake. Choosing to heed the all-consuming love of God cost Dirk his life. What is God's love costing you?

Since God is love, love is central to our universe. The New Testament word for God's self-sacrificing love is "agape," which appears 60 times. Agape love is not romantic, sentimental or sexual love. It does not refer to family, brother/sister love; that word is *"philepa."* We know Philadelphia is the city of brotherly love, phileo love.

"We know what (agape) love is because Jesus gave his life for us. That's why we must give our lives for each other" (I John 3:16 CEV).

We are called to sacrifice our time and energy and our very life for others. God's agape love is not based on feelings. It is a joyful resolve to put the welfare of others above our own.

Dozens of times John admonishes us to love with God's agape love: "Let us love one another, for love comes from God. Everyone who loves has been born of God and knows God. Whoever does not love does not know God, because God is love" (I John 4:7-8). "God sent Jesus as an atoning sacrifice for our sins, turning aside God's wrath. Since God loves us, we also ought to love one another. If we love one another, God lives in us and his love is made complete in us . . ." (I John 4:10-12).

God loves, because love is His nature. He loves the unlovely and the unlovable, not because we deserve to be loved or because of any goodness in us. "God demonstrates his own love for us in this: While we were still sinners, Christ died for us" (Romans 5:8).

"Because of his great love for us, he made us alive with Christ even when we were dead in sin" (Ephesians 2:4-5). God's agape love is constantly seeking to benefit His children. "How great is the love the Father has lavished on us, that we should be called children of God! And that is what we are" (I John 3:1).

We are incapable of producing this self-sacrificing agape love, but God pours His love into our hearts enabling us to love our fellow believers or bitter enemies. Jesus said, "You must love each other, just as I have loved you" (John 13:34 CEV). He first loved us in order that we can love each other. God's love enables us to love the tramp, the prodigal in the pigpen or the CEO. You don't love Jesus any more than you love the person you love the least or the lowest of humanity. "If we say we love God and don't love each other, we are liars. We cannot see God. So how can we love God, if we don't love the people we can see?" (I John 4:20 CEV).

We love God by walking in obedience to His commands. (II John 6). Jesus says, "If you obey my commands, you will remain in my love, just as I have obeyed my Father's commands and remain in his love" (John 15:10). Obedience comes from faith. (Romans 1:5). "The Holy Spirit is given to those who obey him" (Acts 5:32). The first and primary quality of the Spirit is love. (Galatians 5:22).

Joy is another benefit of God's love. "I have told you to remain in my love, so that my joy may be in you and that your joy may be complete" (John 15:11). When we obey Jesus, our joy will be full. Jesus invites you to live in that fullness.

"Greater love has no one than that he lay down his life for his friends" (John 15:13). Love and obedience must be one action. "God's message of love is made known to all Gentiles so that they might believe and obey Christ" (Romans 16:26 NLT). Love, just like faith, by itself, if not accompanied by action, is dead . . . Do not merely say you love God, and so deceive yourselves. Do what God wants you to do. (James 1:17, 22). Remain in God's love, walk in obedience and experience His joy.

Obedience is God's love language. Jesus lived for others. Obeying Him expresses our love for Him. "For even Jesus did not come to be served, but to serve and to give his life as a ransom for many" (Mark 8:45). "Do nothing out of selfish ambition or vain conceit, but in humility consider others better than yourselves. Each of you should look not only to your own interests, but also to the interest of others" (Philippians 2:3-4). Constantly ask yourself, "Lord, what do you want me to do for others?" God will test your love by bringing people around you whom you do not respect. The good news is that He will give you His love for them. That's when life is exciting.

Too often we use our time to please ourselves and forget about the needs of others. "Try to find out what is pleasing to the Lord. Be careful how you live, not as fools but as those who are wise. Make the most of every opportunity for doing good . . ." (Ephesians 5:10, 17). If we are living in His love, the Lord will open our eyes to daily opportunities to share His love. He will bring creative ways to express His love that will amaze you.

Consider: There are millions in our prisons and in our nursing homes who never receive a visitor. There are tens of thousands of orphan and homeless children. Might God be calling you to provide a home for one? You say, "Our house is too small." Do you know the average size of today's house is two or three times larger than houses were 75 or 100 years ago? Can you imagine how our nation's problems would be decreased if Christians would adopt these children? The early church turned the Roman Empire upside down—really right side up. When parents abandoned their children, Christians adopted them. When contagious diseases hit their community, Christians cared for the sick and dying at their own risk often giving their life.

Prayer: Forgive us when we get so absorbed in our schedules that we don't take time for others. Enable us to hear their pain, their loneliness, and show them your love. May your agape love put a smile on your face, a spring in your step, and a song in your heart that overflows to others! Amen.

GOD'S ETERNAL LOVE
PSALM 136

God's love is endless and unchanging. "I have loved you with an everlasting love, I have drawn you with unfailing kindness" (Jeremiah 31:3). "Israel will be saved by the Lord with an everlasting salvation; you will never be put to shame or disgraced, to ages everlasting" (Isaiah 45:17). God says, "In a moment of anger, I turned my face away for a little while. But with everlasting love I will have compassion on you" (Isaiah 54:7-8 NLT). Moses writes, "The eternal God is your refuge, and underneath are the everlasting arms" (Deuteronomy 33:27). "For the Lord is good, his unfailing love continues forever" (Psalm 100:5 NLT). At the dedication of the temple, the people sang, "God is good . . . His love endures forever" (Ezra 3:11).

John Newton tries to help us envision eternity with these familiar words: "When we've been there ten thousand years, bright shining as the sun, we've no less days to sing God's praise than when we first begun." One pastor illustrated eternity by taking a long rope and winding it through the auditorium and out the back door where you could not see the end. He tied a thread at the beginning of the rope and asked the congregation to visualize the thread as their life and eternity as the "never-ending" rope. To help children understand eternity ask them to imagine a bird flying to another planet and then return in a thousand years. The bird takes a grain of sand and flies back and forth until all the grains of sand are removed from the earth. At that time eternity will just have begun.

At the Passover meal the Jews sang Psalms 113-118. (Matthew 26:30). The meal ended with Psalm 118 where each of the first four verses end with, "Give thanks to the Lord, for he is good! His faithful love endures forever." The Psalm ends with the same refrain, "His faithful love endures forever" (v. 29). Imagine how this must have encouraged Jesus, as he knew the cross and indescribable suffering were only a few hours away.

Since God's love is eternal it reaches from ages past through eternity. "Even before he made the world, God loved us and chose us in Christ to be holy and without fault in his eyes" (Ephesians 1:4 NLT). He had his eye on you long before you were born. Peter says, that we "were not bought from death with silver or gold but with the precious blood of Christ . . . He (Jesus) was chosen before the creation of the world, but was revealed in these last times for your sake" (I Peter 1:19-20).

In the Old Testament the Hebrew word for God's love is *"hesed"* which occurs approximately 125 times. In Psalm 126, *"Hesed"* is repeated 26 times. It's translated, "His love is eternal" in the *Holman Standard Bible*, while the *New Living Translation* reads: "His faithful love endures forever." "Give thanks to the Lord, for he is good! His faithful love endures forever. Give thanks to the God of gods. His faithful love endures forever. Give thanks to the Lord of lords. His faithful love endures forever. Give thanks to him who alone does mighty miracles. His faithful love endures forever . . ." (Psalm 136:1-4 NLT).

God's love is greater than the virtues of faith and hope because love will continue for eternity while faith and hope will have been fulfilled when the Lord returns. (I Corinthians 13:13). God's love is endless, unconditional and unchanging. Live with a consciousness of His love and you will live with joy.

Our rewards are eternal: Jesus said, "Store up your treasurers in heaven, where moths and rust cannot destroy them, and thieves cannot break in and steal them. Your heart will always be where your treasure is" (Matthew 6:20-21 CEV). The Pharisees' rewards were temporal—the applauds of men. (Matthew 6:1-2). Work for eternal rewards. Jesus said that giving a cup of water, or welcoming good and godly people who are serving him, you will be rewarded. (Matthew 10:40-42). If you are persecuted for Jesus you will receive a great reward. (Matthew 5:10-12).

Our greatest reward is seeing Jesus. "We know that when Christ appears, we shall be like him, for we shall see him as he is" (I John 3:2). Imagine! Our greatest desire must be to know Him, not just know about Him. (Philippians 3:10). Worship Him, speak to Him, love Him, serve Him, and meditate on His compassion, mercy, forgiveness, holiness and purity.

Since God's love for us is eternal this adds to the gravity of the decisions we make. Our life is like a vapor, (James 4:14) or a breath (Psalm 144:4). Be sure your "breath" is lived to honor God. The consequences last forever.

GOD'S EXTRAVAGANT LOVE
I JOHN 3:1

"What marvelous (incredible) love the Father has extended to us! We're called children of God! That's who we really are" (I John 3:1 Msg.).

Corrie ten Boom asks, "Why do we play around in the backyard mud puddle when we have a whole ocean of God's love for swimming?" The Nazis arrested her family because they hid Jews in their home in Holland. Only Corrie's sister survived the Holocaust. On returning to Germany she spoke at a church service. Jim Denison relates how she reacts to the former S.S. man who had stood guard at the shower door while she was at the processing center at Ravensbruck:

"And suddenly it was all there—the roomful of mocking men, the heaps of clothing, [my sister] Betsie's pain-blanched face. He came up to me as the church was emptying, beaming and bowing. 'How grateful I am for your message, Fraulein,' he said. 'To think that, as you say, he has washed my sins away!' His hand was thrust out to shake mine. And I, who had preached so often . . . the need to forgive, kept my hand at my side . . .

"Even as the angry, vengeful thoughts boiled through me, I saw the sin of them. Jesus Christ had died for this man; was I going to ask for more? Lord Jesus, I prayed, forgive me and help me to forgive him. I tried to smile; I struggled to raise my hand. I could not. I felt nothing, not the slightest spark of warmth or charity. And so again I breathed a silent prayer. Jesus, I cannot forgive him. Give me your forgiveness . . .

"As I took his hand the most incredible thing happened. From my shoulder along my arm and through my hand a current seemed to pass from me to him, while into my heart sprang a love for this stranger that almost overwhelmed me. And so, I discovered that it is not on our forgiveness any more than on our goodness that the world's healing hinges, but on His. When He tells us to love our enemies, He gives, along with the command, the love itself."

While we were still in our sins Jesus died to redeem us. (Romans 5:8). When we experience such extravagant, costly love, we can't help but joyfully surrender our life in humble service to Christ. The strength to serve God is not our strength but God's strength. "I can do all things through him who gives me strength" (Philippians 4:13). Live in God's amazing strength and grace so He can work through you and amaze you.

True revival happens when we fully realize the significance of God's love and grace being poured so undeservingly upon us. Jesus said, "He who believes in me – who cleaves to and trusts in and relies on me – as the scripture has said, 'Out from his innermost being springs and rivers of living waters shall flow (continuously)'" (John 7:38 AMP). Are you overflowing with living water? Whatever is blocking the Holy Spirit—His river of life—confess it as sin and receive His refreshing springs of living water. It's there for you.

We must learn, like Corrie and Paul that it is not our life, it's not your time, it's not your money, or your possessions, it's not your energy, it's not your desires or goals, it's not even your mind because we are to bring every thought into captivity and in line with Christ (II Corinthians 10:5). It's all His. He lives through you. You are dead. (Galatians 2:20). Your old sinful nature has been put to death. You die daily. (I Corinthians 15:31). Jesus said you must daily take up your cross (an instrument of death) and follow him if you are to be His disciple. (Luke 9:23). In your death the supernatural becomes natural as He lives His life through you. The joy you will experience is beyond description. (John 15:11). Jesus said a seed that is planted must die, and then it will bring forth a rich harvest. (John 12:24).

"In Christ we have redemption through his blood, the forgiveness of sins, in accordance with the riches of God's grace that he lavished on us with all wisdom and understanding" (Ephesians 1:7-8). His pure, holy love "has been poured out, (flooded), into our hearts through the Holy Spirit" (Romans 5:5, 8). This isn't a picture of a stingy sprinkling of love; this is an abundant dispensing of the only thing that completes us, the love of our Father, our Creator, and our King. He pours His love richly upon us through Jesus. (Titus 3:6 AMP). We can't live in His love and at the same time be a worrier or a complainer. His love gives us peace and joy that transcends our understanding. (Philippians 4:7).

We are all born with a sinful nature (Psalm 51:5). If you have your picture taken with a group, who is the first person you look for? If your picture is not what you feel it should be you don't want the picture. Our nature is to put ourselves first. The good news is, no matter how sinful we are, we are not beyond God's love and grace. "Christ died for sinners, the righteous for the unrighteous, to bring us to God" (I Peter 3:18).

Some of the more prominent Biblical characters fell into the most blatant sins. Jacob was a deceiver, Samson was a womanizer, Rahab was a harlot, David was a murderer and an adulterer, Matthew was a hated tax collector, Peter was a betrayer, Simon was a zealot, Paul was a blasphemer and murderer. We are all sinners in need of God's love and grace.

When we see our deceitful heart and how desperately wicked, we are – the worst sinner who has ever lived – that's when God's grace becomes real. When you come to Jesus in sincere repentance, God declares you righteous? (Romans 5:1). You get to start over again. You are a new person (II Corinthians 5:17). The attitude of your mind has changed. (Ephesians 4:32). Your sins are blotted out; you are set apart for special use and pronounced, "not guilty!" God says to Israel and to us, "All day long I have held out my hands to a disobedient and obstinate people" (Romans 10:21). He is holding out his hands to you in your situation. Accept his healing love. You will be delivered in your spirit. What amazing love!

Floyd McClung in his book, *The Father's Heart of God*, tells of "a young man whose parents gave him to his grandparents simply because they did not want him. His grandparents, in turn, put him in an orphanage at the age of five. There the director beat him every Sunday if he refused to go to church. Years later he committed his life to Christ through our work in Afghanistan, and then returned home to express his love and forgiveness to his parents with a gift. When his mother saw him, she cried out in rage and would not let him enter the house. He wept as he shared that he could never remember hearing the words 'I love you' from his lawyer father.' "Though my father and mother may forsake me, the Lord will rescue me" (Psalm 27:10).

There is an inseparable relationship between God's love and his mercy and grace. Our worst days are never so bad that we are beyond the reach of God's grace, and our best days are never so good that we are beyond the need of God's grace. Mark Batterson in his book, *All In*, page 25 writes "Mercy is not getting what you deserve – the wrath of God. Grace is getting what we don't deserve – the righteousness of Christ. Everything you've done wrong is forgiven and forgotten. Everything Christ did right – his righteousness – is transferred to your account. Then God calls it even." That's pretty amazing!

GOD'S LOVE FOR JESUS, EQUALS HIS LOVE FOR YOU
JOHN 17:23, 15:9

Can you imagine God's love for you is just as great as His love for Jesus? It's amazing that our great God who created the cosmos loves you and me as much as He loves His only Son Jesus. Jesus prays, "Father you have loved them, (his disciples) even as you have loved me" (John 17:23). Just as the Father loves Jesus, that's the extent of Jesus' love for us. Jesus says, "As the Father has loved me, so have I loved you. Now remain in my love" (John 15:9). Meditate on the depth of God's love and Jesus' love for you being the same as the love between God and Jesus, and we cannot help but be amazed.

Can you imagine giving your child to suffer and die the cruelest death of crucifixion for the cause of saving a person who has murdered multitudes of people, including your child? That's what we did to Jesus since we were all part of the crowd that screamed, "Crucify Him!" Jesus knows the worst about us but He loves us the most. One of the reasons we are not more passionate in our walk with God is that we forget His great love for us.

Isaac Watts expresses God's love in these words: "Were the whole realm of nature mine. That were a present far too small; Love so amazing, so divine, demands my soul, my life, my all."

The hymn by John Newton expresses it: "Amazing Grace, how sweet the sound that saved a wretch like me! I once was lost, but now am found, was blind, but now I see."

Fredrick Lehman expresses this love in the hymn: "The Love of God:" "The love of God is greater far than tongue or pen can ever tell. It goes beyond the highest star and reaches to the lowest hell. The guilty pair, bowed down with care, God gave his Son to win; his erring child he reconciled and pardoned from his sin. O love of God, how rich and pure! How measureless and strong! It shall forevermore endure—The saints' and angels' song . . .

"When hoary time shall pass away, and earthly thrones and kingdoms fall; when men who hear refuse to pray, on rocks and hills and mountains call; God's love, so sure, shall still endure, all measureless and strong; redeeming grace to Adam's race—the saints' and angels' song . . .

"Could we with ink the ocean fill, and were the skies of parchment made; were every stalk on earth a quill, and every man a scribe by trade; to write the love of God above would drain the ocean dry; nor could the scroll contain the whole, though stretched from sky to sky."

God's love is poured out on us. (Romans 5:5). The *Message Bible* reads: "We can't round up enough containers to hold everything God generously pours into our lives through the Holy Spirit!" That's why Paul after he lists his catalogue of sufferings, could say he is, "sorrowing yet always rejoicing" (II Corinthians 6:10). After being beaten at midnight, Paul and Silas sang in prison because they knew God's comfort, presence and love. (Acts 16:25).

God's people addressed God thousands of times in the Old Testament, but only a very few times was he addressed as Father. When Jesus gave us our model prayer, He said we are to begin: "Our Father in heaven" (Matthew 6:9). To those who are born again the name for God is Father. How blessed we are to have a Father who stands with outstretched arms to welcome us into His presence. (Isaiah 65:2).

Since God loves me to this extent how can I grumble at my circumstances in which God has placed me? Why am I ever distrustful, fearful or depressed? Why do I ever allow myself to grow cold or halfhearted in serving the God who loves me? Say with David, I will praise you seven times a day and arise at midnight and praise my Lord.

GOD'S TRANSFORMING LOVE
I CORINTHIANS 6:9-11

In 1725 Isaac Newton became the son of a ship commander. He went to sea at the age of eleven and eventually became the captain of a slave ship. His godly mother died when Isaac was a child. He had no religious convictions. However, during a violent storm, he called out, "Lord, have mercy upon us." He referred to this experience as his "great deliverance." Isaac Newton wrote 280 hymns, the most well known is "Amazing Grace." "Amazing grace, how sweet the sound that saved a wretch like me! I once was lost, but now am found, was blind, but now I see. Twas grace that taught my heart to fear, and grace my fears relieved; How precious did that grace appear the hour I first believed! Thought many dangers, toils and snares I have already come; Tis grace hath brought me safe thus far, and grace will lead me home . . . When we've been there ten thousand years, bright shining as the sun, we've no less days to sing God's praise than when we first begun."

His gravesite includes these words: "Isaac Newton, once an infidel, a servant of slaves in Africa, was by the rich mercy of our Lord and Savior Jesus Christ preserved, restored, pardoned, and appointed to preach the faith he had long labored to destroy." Isaac Newton greatly influenced the life of William Wilberforce who more than any other individual influenced the British government to outlaw slavery.

Isaac Newton, a slave trader, was transformed. "Do you not know that wrongdoers will not inherit the kingdom of God? Do not be deceived: Neither the sexually immoral nor idolaters nor adulterers nor men who have sex with men nor thieves nor the greedy nor drunkards nor slanderers nor swindlers will inherit the kingdom of God. And that is what some of you were. But (BUT!), you were washed, you were sanctified, you were justified in the name of the Lord Jesus Christ and by the Spirit of our God" (I Corinthians 6:9-11). No matter how evil a person may be, God's redemptive love is for everyone! "God is able to save completely those who come to God through him, because he always lives to intercede for them" (Hebrews 7:25). "God is not wanting anyone to perish, but everyone to come to repentance" (II Peter 3:9).

Andy came from a poor family who sent him to church. Since he said he didn't like the church, I asked him why he continued to attend. "They're the only people who loved me," he said. Andy went off to war in Vietnam and experienced indescribable horrors. Upon returning he became president of Hell's Angels, a motorcycle gang. I spent hours with Andy. He often repented on his knees. Andy married a beautiful woman, but because of his intense jealousy and fits of rage, she left him. He was furious and employed a hit man to kill his wife. Ironically, the hit man turned him in to the police. Andy has been behind bars for many years now. I have not seen Andy since we moved from the area, but I feel Andy is crying out to God for mercy. I have to leave people like Andy in God's hands. God is the final judge. I take comfort knowing that God is just and will make a fair decision.

"Come, all you who are thirsty . . . you who have no money, come, buy and eat! Come, buy wine and milk without money and without cost. Why spend money on what is not bread, and your labor on what does not satisfy? Listen to me, and eat what is good, and your soul will delight in the richest of fare" (Isaiah 55:1-2). Jesus said, "Come to me, all you who are weary and burdened, and I will give you rest. Take my yoke upon you and learn from me, for I am gentle and humble in heart and you will find rest for your souls. For my yoke is easy and my burden is light" (Matthew 11:28-30).

One of the most infamous persons who ever lived was Adolf Hitler. Jesus said, "God so greatly loved and dearly prized the world that he [even] gave up his only-begotten (unique) Son, so that whoever believes in (trusts, clings to, relies on) him may not perish – come to destruction, be lost – but have eternal (everlasting) life" (John 3:16 AMP). The "whoever" includes Adolf Hitler as well as you and me. We say we don't hate Jews. But if there is hatred in our hearts towards anyone, we have the same attitude that motivated Hitler. To deal with evil we must begin with ourselves.

Ask God to give you His love for your worst "enemy." His love can enable you to love those who raped and murdered your child. His love, not yours, but God's amazing love in and through you reaches out to everyone. Multitudes of people, especially women, are caught in human trafficking, millions are raped; God's transforming love can heal both perpetrators and victims.

"Does God love everyone or just Christians?" There is a sense in which God loves everyone. (John 3:16; Romans 5:8). This love is not conditional. God's love for everyone could be thought of as His merciful love. An example of God's inclusive, merciful love is expressed in Matthew 5:45, "Your Father in heaven . . . causes his sun to rise on the evil and the good, and sends rain on the righteous and the unrighteous."

God's merciful love for the world is also displayed in that God gives everyone many, even daily, opportunities to repent and come to Him: "The Lord is not slow in keeping his promise . . . Instead he is patient with you, not wanting anyone to perish, but everyone to come to repentance" (II Peter 3:9). "The wrath of God is being revealed from heaven against all the godlessness and wickedness of people, who suppress the truth by their wickedness, since what may be known about God is plain to them, because God has made it plain to them. For since the creation of the world God's invisible qualities – his eternal power and divine nature – have been clearly seen, being understood from what has been made, so that people are without excuse" (Romans 1:18-20). Whenever we think of the wrath of God we must think, not of God losing His cool but rather His wrath is His righteous reaction to sin.

God's love for everyone does not mean that everyone will be saved. (Matthew 25:46). God cannot ignore sin since He is a God of justice. (II Thessalonians 1:6). Sin cannot go unpunished forever. (Romans 3:25-26). If God simply disregarded sin and allowed it to continue to wreak chaos in creation forever, then He would not be a God of love. To ignore God's merciful love, to reject Christ, (II Peter 2:1) is to subject ourselves to God's wrath. (Ephesians 3:6).

Jesus said, "Whoever has my commands and keeps them is the one who loves me" (John 14:21). This love could be thought of as God's "covenant love." Covenant love is conditional, given to those who place their faith in Jesus for salvation. "Whoever believes in the Son has eternal life, but whoever rejects the Son will not see life, for God's wrath remains on them" (John 3:36).

Does God love everyone? Yes, He shows mercy and kindness to all. Does God love Christians more than He loves non-Christians? No, not in regard to His merciful love. Does God love Christians in a different way than He loves non-Christians? Yes, because believers have exercised faith in God's Son, they are saved. God has a unique relationship with Christians in that only Christians have forgiveness based on God's eternal grace. God is good to all in some ways and to some in all ways. The merciful love God extends to all people should bring everyone to faith in Him for salvation and thus to participate in His covenant love.

Will Thompson expressed God's love: "Softly and tenderly Jesus is calling. Calling for you and me; See, on the portals he's waiting and watching, watching for you and for me. O for the wonderful love he has promised, promised for you and for me! Though we have sinned, he has mercy and pardon, pardon for you and for me. Come home, come home. Ye who are weary come home; earnestly, tenderly, Jesus is calling, calling, O sinner, come home."

GOD'S LOVE IS SLOW TO ANGER
PSALM 86:15

"You, Lord, are a compassionate and gracious God, slow to anger, abounding in love and faithfulness" (Psalm 86:15; 103:8). The children of Israel "refused to listen and failed to remember the miracles you performed . . . They are stiff-necked . . . But you are a forgiving God, gracious and compassionate, slow to anger and abounding in love" (Nehemiah 9:17). "Return to the Lord your God for he is gracious and compassionate, slow to anger and abounding in love, and he relents from sending calamity" (Joel 2:13). "God passed in front of Moses, proclaiming, 'The Lord, is compassionate and gracious, slow to anger, abounding in love and faithfulness, maintaining love to thousands, and forgiving wickedness, rebellion, and sins'" (Exodus 34:6-7).

Each of these scriptures mentions a counterpart to God's love, which is God's anger. They all mention He is slow to anger but it's clear He has anger. So often we just focus on the parts of these passages that make us feel good. Don't yield to the temptation of separating God's love from His anger. If we do, we deliberately cut out parts of God's Word, resulting in an inaccurate understanding of God, which leads to anemic Christians and to false teaching.

It's so easy to be drawn into our culture that believes everyone is going to heaven because Jesus is compassionate. However, Jesus said, "Not everyone who says to me, 'Lord, Lord' will enter the kingdom of heaven, but only the one who does the will of my Father who is in heaven. Many will say . . . that they performed miracles in his name but he will tell them plainly, 'I never knew you. Away from me you evildoers'" (Matthew 7:21-23).

God's justice is perfect. He cannot simply overlook our sin. Sin demands payment. God's wrath toward evil was poured out, not on us but on His own Son. Jesus took our place on the cross. He suffered and paid the price for our sin. What He finished on the cross was God's plan to redeem our fallen world. When Jesus said, "It is finished," He was stating that He had successfully paid in full for every act of rebellion, past, present, and future.

Mary grew up around Christians and called herself a Christian. She wandered away from God choosing a life of drugs. When she had children they nearly died of hunger. When her son Randy was old enough to run the streets he stole food for himself and his little sister from a local grocery store. Although not proved, it seemed obvious Mary died from a drug overdose. I had Mary's funeral. We pray she had a "thief on the cross" last-minute conversion. Thank God I am not the judge. Her eternity is in God's hands.

Jesus told a parable concerning a man who planted a fig tree. For three years he looked for fruit on it but did not find any. He told the gardener to cut it down. The gardener asked for one more year to cultivate and fertilize it. "If it gives fruit next year, fine, if not cut it down," were his instructions. (Luke 13:6-9). Are you producing fruit for God? Jesus said, "If you do not remain in me, you are like a branch that is thrown away and withers; such branches are picked up, thrown into the fire and burned" (John 15:6). Disregarding and ignoring God's love has eternal consequences.

GOD'S LOVE AND HIS JUDGMENT ARE FAIR!
HEBREWS 4:13

While God's love is amazing, His judgments are at times shocking. There are few things stressed more strongly in the Bible than the fact of God's work as judge. Our loving God is a righteous judge. The Bible is very explicit in portraying God's wrath. The following is adapted from J. I. Packer's, *Knowing God*. "A study of the concordance shows that there are more references in scripture to the anger, fury and wrath of God, than there are to his love and tenderness." (A. W. Pink, *The Attributes of God*, p. 75). J. I. Packer quotes Leon Morris: "The doctrine of final judgment . . . stresses man's accountability and the certainty that justice will finally triumph over all the wrongs which are part and parcel of life here and now. The former gives a dignity to the humblest action, the latter brings calmness and assurance to those in the thick of the battle. . . . The Christian view of judgment means that history moves to a goal . . . Judgment protects the idea of this triumph of God and of good . . . Judgment means that evil will be disposed of authoritatively, decisively, finally. Judgment means that in the end God's will, will be perfectly done." (*The Biblical Doctrine of Judgment*, p. 72).

His justice was well defined from the beginning. God was clear, "You are free to eat from any tree in the garden; but you must not eat from the tree of the knowledge of good and evil, for when you eat of it you will surely die" (Genesis 2:16-17). The choice was Adam and Eve's. Without that choice they would have been robots. There can be no meaningful fellowship with inanimate robots.

When they ate, they died a spiritual death. For the first time they were afraid of God; their perfect relationship was broken. (Genesis 3:8). Because of God's love He did not destroy them physically. He provided an animal sacrifice as restitution for their sin, satisfying His justice. (Genesis 3:21). Later Jesus, the perfect Lamb of God became the substitute for our sin. (I Peter 3:18 AMP).

God judged the sinful world of Noah's day by sending the flood.

(Genesis 6-8). Moses killed an Egyptian and escaped to Midian where he lived for forty years. (Exodus 2:11-15). God judged the Egyptians by sending the ten plagues. (Exodus 7-12). Before God destroyed Sodom, Abraham asked, "Will not the judge of all the earth do right?" (Genesis 18:25). "God is a righteous judge, a God who expresses his wrath every day. If he does not relent, he will sharpen his sword. . . . He has prepared his deadly weapons; he makes ready his flaming arrows" (Psalms 7:11-13).

God is merciful but he will not leave the guilty unpunished. (Exodus 34:6-7). God judges those who worshipped the golden calf. (Exodus 32:26-35). He judged Achan for stealing. (Joshua 7). David says, "God is a God of justice" (Psalms 50:6). "Rise up, O God, judge the earth" (Psalm 82:8, 94:2, 75:7). "The sins of Judah made the Lord angry. He finally turned his back on them" (II Kings 24:19 CEV).

"The Lord will judge the peoples with equity. Let the heavens rejoice, let the earth be glad . . . He will judge the world in righteousness and the peoples in his truth" (Psalm 96:10-13). The rivers and mountains are to sing for joy; for he judges the world in righteousness. (Psalm 98:8-9).

All of the seventeen books of prophecy, Isaiah through Malachi, give clear words of God's warning and judgment as well as the promise of His blessing if the people gave their allegiance to Jehovah God. The prophets spent more time preaching judgment than they did predicting the coming of the Messiah! The one basic certainty underlying all discussion of life's problems in Job, Ecclesiastes and all the maxims of Proverbs is that, "God will bring every deed into judgment, including every hidden thing, whether it is good or evil" (Ecclesiastes 11:9, 12:14).

Isaiah describes judgment to all the nations. (chapters 13-39). God replies to Habakkuk's questions concerning God's punishment: "I am sending the Babylonians. They are fierce and cruel – marching across the land, conquering cities and towns . . . Their troops are faster than leopards, more ferocious than wolves . . ." (1:5-11 CEV). God says, "If you do not listen, and if you do not set your heart to honor my name . . . I will send a curse upon you . . ." (Malachi 2:1-2).

Coming to the New Testament God's judgment far from being reduced, is actually intensified. "Because of your stubbornness and your unrepentant heart, you are storing up wrath against yourself for the day of God's wrath when his righteous judgments will be revealed. God will repay each person according to what they have done. To those who by persistence in doing good seek glory, honor and immortality, he will give eternal life. But for those who are self-seeking and who reject the truth and follow evil, there will be wrath and anger . . . but glory, honor and peace for everyone who does good . . . for God does not show favoritism" (Romans 2:5-11).

Heaven's multitude shouted: "Hallelujah! Salvation and glory and power belong to our God, for true and just are his judgments . . ." (Revelation 19:1-8). "God is not unjust; he will not forget your work and the love you have shown him as you have helped his people and continue to help them" (Hebrews 6:10). "Anyone who does wrong will be repaid for their wrongs, and there is no favoritism" (Colossians 3:25, Acts 10:34).

Civilization is based on justice and civil laws. If you are late for work your employer will implement consequences. If you disobey the speed limit you will pay a fine. If you don't pay your taxes you will end up in jail. (Romans 13:1-7). Civil justice is not always fair. God never promised us a just life here on earth, but His love can heal all the pain of our unjust past.

A terrorist comes to your workplace killing many. He says he's sorry and would never do it again. The judge responds, "You're free to go." This is not justice. "The authorities do not bear the sword for nothing. They are God's servant; agents of wrath to bring punishment on the wrongdoer" (Romans 13:4).

God judges our thoughts. "You have searched me, Lord, and you know me. You know when I sit and when I rise; you perceive my thoughts from afar . . . Before a word is on my tongue you, Lord know it completely" (Psalm 139:1-4). "You perceive my thoughts from afar" (Psalm 139:2). "You know me, Lord; you see me and test my thoughts" (Jeremiah 12:3). Jesus knew people's thoughts and answered before they asked their questions. (Matthew. 9:4; 12:25).

I believe everything we have ever seen, heard or thought is recorded in our conscious or unconscious mind. "We must all appear before the judgment seat of Christ, so that each of us may receive what is due us for the things done while in the body, whether good or bad" (II Corinthians 5:10). When we come to God's judgment all God will do is place our thoughts before us and we will be silent except to say, "Lord, be merciful to me, I am a sinner."

John heard the angel's song: "Just and true are your ways, King of the ages . . . All nations will come and worship before you, for your righteous acts have been revealed" (Revelation 15:3-4).

How blessed we are there is no other judge who can condemn us when we are under the protection of Jesus. "There is no condemnation for those who are in Christ Jesus" (Romans 8:1). "Christ suffered once for sins, the righteous for the unrighteous, to bring you to God" (I Peter 3:18). I'm glad God is my judge. He paid the price by giving me Jesus to cover anything that is not in line with His perfect will.

"God has clothed me with garments of salvation and arrayed me in a robe of his righteousness" (Isaiah 61:10). This chorus has been a comfort to me over the years: "I'm covered over with the robe of righteousness that Jesus gives to me. I'm covered over with the precious blood of Jesus and he lives in me. What a joy it is to know my heavenly Father loves me so and gives to me, my Jesus. When he looks at me, he sees not what I used to be but he sees Jesus." Hallelujah!

"Let us fearlessly and confidently and boldly draw near to the throne of grace – the throne of God's unmerited favor [to us sinners] and find grace to help in good time for every need – appropriate help and well-timed help, coming just when we need it" (Hebrews 4:16 AMP). If you don't know Jesus, call to Him in sincere repentance. He loves you and will give you an overflowing life. (John 3:16; Romans 10:9-10; John 7:39).

II.

OUR "AMAZING" FALL

WHERE DID EVIL ORIGINATE?[1]
ROMANS 8:20-21

God created us with freedom to choose. That's risky! We get to choose to accept or reject God's love. Without that risk there is no genuine love. We love our children. If we do not give them the freedom to disobey then there is no love relationship. There can only be a love relationship if they choose to love us. If they reject us, we have deep pain. Our God has deep pain when we reject Him. But if we return in repentance, like the Prodigal, God welcomes us, forgives us without condemning us and even has a celebration. (Luke 15). Love is worth taking the risk. Just as we permit our children to choose our love, God permits us to choose His love. When we reject Him evil results. When we accept Him good results. We receive His forgiveness and restored relationship.

"If God is all-good and if he created only good things, then where did evil come from? How can evil come from what is perfectly good?" St. Augustine answered this by saying one of the good things God made was free choice. It is good to be free. But if it is good to be free, then evil is possible. We cannot be free to love God unless we are also free not to love Him. We cannot be free to praise God unless we are also free to curse Him. So evil began when a free creature (Lucifer) used his freedom of will what he felt was good over the good of the Creator. . . .

"What caused Lucifer to use his freedom to sin against God?" It wasn't God, since he tempts no one. (James 1:13). Further, there was

---

1. Most of the above was adapted from Dr. Normal L. Geiser, professor of apologetics at Veritas Evangelical Seminary in Murrieta, California.

no other sinful being in existence, tempting him to sin. Neither was his nature imperfect, for God made every creature good. (Genesis 1:31-2:1). Lucifer himself was the cause of his sin. A free action is one that is self-caused. It can't be caused by another, for in that case they would be responsible for the sin. Nothing cannot be the cause of something. Sin originated in Lucifer's prideful act of rebellion against God. (I Timothy 3:6)

"As for why God has permitted so much evil for so long, we can only ask: Who would know better than an all-knowing Being?" As for us finite creatures, we must be content to know: "The secret things belong to the Lord our God" (Deuteronomy 29:29). But we do know that the all-loving and all-powerful God is also all-knowing and that he sees the end from the beginning. (Isaiah 46:10). In our waiting, "God is longsuffering, not willing that any should perish but that all should come to repentance" (II Peter 3:9).

"Why does God permit such horrible disasters? There were no earthquakes, tornados, or hurricanes in the Garden of Eden, and there will be none in the new heaven and new earth. The reason there are such things in between Paradise Lost and Paradise to Come is that 'sin entered the world by one man [Adam] and death by sin,'" (Romans 5:12).

"The created world can hardly wait for what's coming next. Everything in creation is being more or less held back. God reins it in until both creation and all the creatures are ready and can be released at the same moment into the glorious times ahead. Meanwhile, the joyful anticipation deepens" (Romans 8:20-21 Msg.).

God never wastes a tragedy. Joseph said to his brothers who had sold him to Egypt as a slave, "You meant evil against me, but God meant it for good, to bring about that many people should be kept alive" (Genesis 50:21). C. S. Lewis said, "God whispers to us in our pleasures, speaks in our conscience, but shouts in our pains; it is his megaphone to rouse a deaf world." Although God does not cause the evil, nonetheless, He is working in the evil to bring about a greater good.

This is not the best of all possible worlds, but it is the best of all possible ways to reach the best of all possible worlds. The truth is that we can't get to the Promised Land without going through the wilderness. God permits evil in order to defeat evil. He allows lower evil to produce the higher good. As Oswald Chambers says, "If God can accomplish his purpose in this world through a broken heart, then why not thank him for breaking yours?"

THE WORST VERSE IN THE BIBLE
GENESIS 3:6

"When the woman saw that the fruit of the tree was good for food and pleasing to the eye, and also desirable for gaining wisdom, she took some and ate it. She also gave some to her husband, who was with her, and he ate it" (Genesis 3:6).

God placed Adam and Eve in paradise. Everything was picture-perfect. God walked and talked with them. Their every need was met. Relationships were a pure delight. The environment was clean and wholesome. There was no death, no weeds, no insects, no arguments, or anger. Life could not have been better. However, there was one restriction: They were not to eat of the tree in the middle of the garden.

Satan, crafty as he was, coming in the form of a serpent, persuaded them with a lie to taste the fruit from the forbidden tree. Since God gave them everything they needed to enjoy, why did they disobey? Give a child everything you can possibly conceive to make their life perfect with the instruction, it's all yours to enjoy except this one toy. That's the one they want. Everyone wants what is forbidden. Never blame Adam and Eve for the pain we experience because we would have made the same mistake.

While we may say it is naïve to blame everything on this one act it is this one act that reveals a rebellious spirit found in all humankind. "The heart is deceitful above all things and desperately wicked" (Jeremiah 17:9). The deceit that lodges in our heart is so complicated and so diverse, that it is impossible to trace it in all its aspects. We know so little of what's in our heart. Jeremiah says in the next verse; "I the Lord search the heart, and examine the mind, (thoughts), to reward each person according to their conduct, according to what their deeds deserve."

Jesus said, "It is from within, out of a person's heart, that evil thoughts come – sexual immorality, theft, murder, adultery, greed, malice, deceit, lewdness, envy, slander, arrogance and folly. All these evils come from inside and defile a person" (Mark 7:21-23). "When tempted, no one should say, 'God is tempting me.' For God cannot be tempted by evil, nor does he tempt anyone; but each person is tempted when they are dragged away by their own evil desire and enticed. Then after desire has been conceived it gives birth to sin, and sin when it is full-grown, gives birth to death" (James 1:13-15).

It's because of our sin that we are in the condition we are in. The Greek word for sin means to miss the mark or get off the track God has designed for us. By the time of Noah, "The Lord saw how great the wickedness of the human race had become on the earth and that every inclination of the thoughts of the human heart was only evil all the time" (Genesis 6:5). Because of their self-centered heart they had not learned to obey God's instructions and went their own way. Jesus said, "As it was in the days of Noah, so it will be at the coming of the Son of Man. For in the days before the flood, people were eating and drinking, marrying and giving in marriage, up to the day Noah entered the ark; and they knew nothing about what would happen until the flood came and took them all away. That is how it will be at the coming of the Son of Man . . . Therefore, keep watch, because you do not know on what day your Lord will come" (Matthew 24:37-42).

We inherited a self-centered nature, a nature that says "no" to a pure, holy and perfect God. We can't blame others, no matter how wicked they are. We are no better. As one person who was continually raped as a child and treated worse than we can imagine says, "When we see the terrible wickedness of humans hurting others, we need to remember we have sinned against a holy God more than others have sinned against us, therefore we need to own our own sin that fills us with remorse, not the sin of others who sin against us."

Ruth Paxton in her book, *Rivers of Living Water,* gives this portrait of our human condition: "The natural person is four-square: self-will, self-love, self-trust, and self-exaltation; and upon this foundation is reared a superstructure that is one huge capital 'I.' Self-centeredness, self-assertion, self-conceit, self-indulgence, self-pleasing, self-seeking, self-pity, self-sensitiveness, self-defense, self-sufficiency, self-consciousness, self-righteousness, self-glorying – this is the material out of which the building is fashioned." When we are tempted to think how important we are just ask your child about your grandfather. We are two generations of being forgotten.

When the awfulness of our own sin truly amazes us and we see our heart as God sees it, we begin to understand the source of all tremendous pain and suffering in our world today.

DESTROY THE AMALEKITES AND CANAANITES
I SAMUEL 15:2-3

Since God's love is so extravagant, why did He command the extermination/genocide of the Canaanites—men, women and children? Why did God command Saul and the Israelites: "This is what the Lord Almighty says: 'I will punish the Amalekites for what they did to Israel when they waylaid them as they came up from Egypt. Now, attack the Amalekites and totally destroy everything that belongs to them. Do not spare them; put to death men and women, children and infants, cattle and sheep, camels and donkeys'" (I Samuel 15:2-3). God ordered similar actions when the Israelites invaded the Promised Land. (Deuteronomy 2:34; 3:6; 20:16-18).

We are incapable of fully understanding our sovereign God. God's ways are higher than our ways and his thoughts are higher than our thoughts. (Isaiah 55:9; Romans 11:33-36). We have to trust God's heart even when we do not understand His ways.

God knows the future. If Israel did not carry out God's orders to eradicate the Amalekites, they would come back to trouble the Israelites. Saul claimed to have killed everyone except the Amalekite King Agag. (I Samuel 15:20). Saul lied. There were enough Amalekites to take David and his men's families captive. (I Samuel 30:1-2). David's life was threatened because of Saul's disobedience. If Saul had fulfilled what God had commanded this never would have occurred. Later, a descendant of Agag, Haman, tried to have the entire Jewish people exterminated (see the book of Esther). Saul's disobedience almost resulted in Israel's destruction. God knew this would occur, so He ordered the extermination of the Amalekites ahead of time.

In regard to the Canaanites, God commanded, "In the cities of the nations the Lord is giving you: . . . completely destroy them – the Hittites, Amorites, Canaanites, Perizzites, Hivites and Jebusites. . . . Otherwise, they will teach you to follow all the detestable things they do in worshiping their gods, and you will sin against the Lord" (Deuteronomy 20:16-18). What God said would happen, happened. (Judges 2:1-3; 14:24; II Kings 16:3-4). God did not order the extermination of these people to be cruel, but to prevent even greater evil in the future. Joshua 12:7-24 lists 31 kings who were also destroyed because of their wickedness.

Even more troubling is: Why would God order the death of innocent children? These children would have likely grown up as adherents to the evil religions and practices of their parents. They would naturally have been resentful of the Israelites and later sought to avenge the "unjust" treatment of their parents. Children are not innocent, "I was sinful at birth, sinful from the time my mother conceived me" (Psalm 51:5). "Even from birth the wicked go astray, from the womb they are wayward, spreading lies" (Psalm 58:3). This does not mean that a child will be accountable for his or her sin because they do not know right from wrong. Jesus said, "Let the little children come to me, and do not hinder them, for the kingdom of heaven belongs to such as these" (Matthew 19:14).

As we study God's Word, He gives us insight into most questions that trouble us. Read the prophets, Isaiah through Malachi. For example, take an hour and read Hosea. You will appreciate the overwhelming love our heavenly Father has for His people. You will see the terrible and consistent rebellion of God's children. They were constantly in a cycle of allegiance and rebellion. No matter what God did, they turned their back on Him. His punishment was severe and rightly so.

Jesus' new covenant, which transcends the old covenant, helps us see more clearly the heart of God. The scriptures are not flat. By that I mean God reveals Himself in a progressive way. Hebrews 1:1-3 help us understand this: "In the past God spoke to our ancestors through the prophets at many times and in various ways, but in these last days he has spoken to us by his Son, whom he appointed heir of all things, and through who also he made the universe. The Son is the radiance of God's glory and the exact representation of his being, sustaining all things by his powerful word." "Jesus has become the guarantor of a better covenant" (Hebrews 7:22).

As Christians we interpret the Scriptures through the lens of Jesus Christ. Five times in Matthew 5 Jesus says, "You have heard it said, but I say unto you." "You have heard it said, 'Love your neighbor and hate your enemy.' But I tell you, love your enemies and pray for those who persecute you.'" (v. 43). Jesus taught that loving enemies, not killing them was God's way. Jesus' teaching surpasses the Law and the Prophets. "Truly I tell you, among those born of women there has not risen anyone greater than John the Baptist, yet whoever is least in the kingdom of heaven is greater than he" (Mathew 11:11). (John 1:17-18).

Jesus speaks clearly of God's wrath, which helps us bridge the Old Testament commands to kill with the New Testament covenant of love. We know John 3:16 but forget 3:36: "Whoever believes in the Son has eternal life, but whoever rejects the Son will not see life, for God's wrath remains on them." "Anyone who is angry with his brother will be subject to judgment. . . . Anyone who says, 'You fool!' will be in danger of the fire of hell" (Matt. 5:22). In half of Jesus' parables, He speaks of judgment. (e.g. Luke 19:27).

"Do not take vengeance but leave room for God's wrath . . . 'It is mine to avenge, I will repay,' says the Lord" (Romans 12:19). All of us followed our fleshly desires and "were by nature deserving of wrath" (Ephesians 2:3). "The wrath of God is being revealed from heaven against all . . . wickedness of people who suppress the truth by their wickedness . . ." (Romans 1:18). "The people tried to hide from the wrath of the Lamb" (Revelation 6:16). "Our God is a consuming fire" (Hebrews 12:29). Jude says, "These incidents (of rebellion) serve as an example of those who suffer the punishment of eternal fire" (v. 7).

Ron Sider writes, "There is not a single Christian author before Constantine who said killing or joining the military by Christians is ever legitimate. Whenever the surviving Christian texts mention killing – whether in abortion, capital punishment or war – they always say Christians must not do it. When Constantine issued the decree in 313 that ended persecution and made it legal to be a Christian, Christians entered a dramatically new era. In spite of the teaching of Christian authors, a substantial number of Christians had joined the army in the two decades before 313. After Constantine's conversion, vastly more Christians joined the Roman army. Within 100 years, only Christians could serve in the Roman army. . . .

"From the 5th century to the present the just-war theory has been accepted by most Christians. The Anabaptist, however, insisted that we are to love our enemies. The Quakers became a pacifist voice in the 17th century. Several evangelical denominations and a majority of Pentecostal denominations embrace pacifism in their early years. At some point 13 of 21 Pentecostal groups formed by 1917 give evidence of being pacifist. Wesleyan Methodists, the Church of God (Anderson) the Churches of Christ, the Church of God (Cleveland, Tennessee) and the Assemblies of God were all initially pacifist. The Assemblies of God were officially pacifist until 1967. The Church of God in Christ – the largest African American denomination, with more than 6 million members – has been officially pacifist since it began. Dwight

L. Moody and Charles Spurgeon were also pacifists. Since World War II the Catholic Church affirms pacificism."

God is just, holy, loving, merciful, and gracious. How his attributes work together can be a mystery to us. (I Corinthians 13:12). Even though we cannot fully understand His way we know that He will work all things out for the good of those who trust Him.

THINGS CAN'T
GET WORSE CAN THEY?
DEUTERONOMY 28

I hear people ask: "Can things get worse?" With our technology we hear or see devastation and tragedies every day. We live with crisis fatigue. Jesus said, "Because of the increase of wickedness the love of most will grow cold" (Matthew 24:12).

From beginning to end the scriptures are clear, sin results in death. (James 1:13-15). Scores of times in the first five books of Moses God states through His prophet what He expects from His people. He proclaims blessing for their obedience and curses for their disobedience. Deuteronomy 28:1-68 begins with fifteen blessings (vv. 1-14). The remaining 54 verses set forth God's curses. Some are so horrendous they are hard to imagine.

God promises blessings before He announces the consequences of disobedience. Before He gave the Ten Commandments, He reminds His people that He is the one who delivered them from slavery in Egypt. (Exodus 20:2). God always extends His grace before He asks us to obey Him. He never asks us to do anything that He does not provide strength for us to do. (Philippians 4:13).

Listen to His promised blessing in Deuteronomy 28:1-14: "If you fully obey the Lord . . . I will set you high above all the nations of the earth . . . The fruit of your womb will be blessed, the crops of your land and the young of your livestock . . . The Lord will grant that the enemies . . . will be defeated before you . . . The Lord will send a blessing on your barns and on everything you put your hand to . . . All the peoples on earth will see that you are called by the name of the Lord and they will fear you. The Lord will grant you abundant prosperity . . . The Lord will open the heavens . . . to send rain on your land in its season . . . You will lend to many nations but you will borrow from none. The Lord will make you the head, not the tail . . . you will always be at the top, never at the bottom."

If they disobey, note the contrast: "All these curses will come on you. They will pursue you and overtake you until you are destroyed because you did not obey the Lord your God and observe the commands, he gave you . . . Because you did not serve the Lord your God joyfully and gladly in the time of prosperity, therefore in hunger and thirst, in nakedness and dire poverty you will serve the enemies the Lord sends against you. He will put an iron yoke on your neck until he has destroyed you . . .

"Because of the suffering that your enemy will inflict on you during the siege, you will eat the fruit of your womb, the flesh of the sons and daughters . . . Even the most gentle and sensitive man among you will have no compassion on his own brother or the wife he loves or his surviving children, and he will not give to one of them any of the flesh of his children that he is eating. It will be all he has left because of the suffering your enemy will inflict on you during the siege of all your cities. The gentler and more sensitive woman among you . . . will begrudge the husband she loves and her own son or daughter the afterbirth from her womb and the children she bears. For in her dire need she intends to eat them secretly because of the suffering your enemy will inflict on you during the siege of your cities" (28:45-57).

Many will read this and think, that was three thousand years ago; it can't get worse than that. But Jesus reminds us: "Many will come in my name . . . and will deceive many. You will hear of wars . . . nation will rise against nation . . . there will be famines and earthquakes . . . You will be hated by all nations . . . Many will turn away from the faith and will betray and hate each other . . . Because of the increase of wickedness, the love of most will grow cold . . . Let those who are in Judea flee to the mountains . . . How dreadful it will be for pregnant women . . . There will be great distress, unequaled from the beginning of the world until now – and never be equaled again. If those days had not been cut short, no one would survive, but for the sake of the elect those days will be shortened" (Matthew 24:1-25). "When the Son of Man comes will he find faith on the earth?" (Luke 18:8). May these sobering scriptures give us a passion to rescue others from the judgment of God that is coming upon the earth.

Jude, Jesus' brother warns us that we are to save others by snatching them from the fire. (v. 22). "Our God is a consuming fire" (Hebrews 12:29). We need to have a holy reverence and godly fear to serve Him

ple will deliberately forget that long ago by God's word
ne into being and the earth was formed out of water
y these waters also the world of that time was deluged
and destroyed. By the same word the present heavens and earth are
reserved for fire, being kept for the Day of Judgment and destruction
of the ungodly" (II Peter 2:5-7). Today people are deliberately forgetting God's warnings.

The good news from Jesus is: "Do not be afraid of those who kill
the body and after that can do no more. But I will show you whom you
should fear: Fear him who after your body has been killed, has authority to throw you into hell. Yes, I tell you, fear him. Are not five sparrows sold for two pennies? Yet not one of them is forgotten by God.
Indeed, the very hairs of your head are all numbered. Don't be afraid;
you are worth more than any sparrows" (Matthew 10:28-30). God has
said, "'Never will I leave you; never will I forsake you.' So, we say with
confidence, 'The Lord is my helper; I will not be afraid. What can mere
mortals do to me?'" (Hebrews 13:5-6).Jesus concludes his commission
to us; "Surely, I am with you always to the very end of the age, (every
day until he returns)" (Matthew 28:20).

Pope John Paul II was shot by Ali Agca. He went to visit Ali in
his prison cell to extend forgiveness to Ali. Extending God's forgiveness will help to bring healing to our world. Let's get better, not bitter.
God is not willing that any perish but that all come to repentance. (II
Peter 3:9). We are ministers of reconciliation. (II Corinthians 5:18).
Focus on extending God's kingdom. "Knowing the terror of the Lord,
we persuade men" (II Corinthians 5:11 KJV). May the Lord give us a
passion to "snatch them from the fire" (Jude 23).

WHO IS RULING OUR WORLD?
I JOHN 5:19

"We know that we are children of God, and that the whole world
is under the control of the evil one" (I John 5:19). Three times Jesus
calls Satan the prince of this world. (John 12:31; 14:30; 16:11). The
Amplified Bible translates "prince" as the "evil genius or ruler."

Paul reminds the Ephesians they used to live following the ways
of the world and the ruler of the kingdom of the air. (2:2). "Our struggle is not against flesh and blood, but against the rulers, against the

authorities, against the powers of this dark world and against the spiritual forces of evil in the heavenly realms" (6:12). Ours is not a Sunday afternoon walk in the park. This is open-face warfare with Satan, a battle to death itself.

According to George Barna's research (www.barna.com) only about 35% of Americans believe Satan is real. Paradoxically their research reveals that about 60% of Christians believe a person can be under the influence of spiritual forces, such as demons or evil spirits. Many of these same people indicate they believe Satan is merely a symbol of evil. Throughout scripture Satan is referred to 140 times with different names: Satan (53), Devil (33), Dragon (14), Serpent (12), Evil one (12), Beelzebub (7), Prince of demons (3), Prince of the World (3), The father of lies (1), Secret Power of Lawlessness (1), Ruler of the kingdom of the air (1).

Since most Christians do not believe in Satan it's not surprising that most do not believe in the Holy Spirit as a living force. "If anyone does not have the (Holy) Spirit of Christ, they do not belong to Christ" (Romans 8:10). Many believe that the Holy Spirit is a symbol of God's power or presence but is not a living entity. Interestingly, about half (49 percent) of those who agreed that the Holy Spirit is only a symbol but not a living entity, agreed that the Bible is totally accurate in all of the principles it teaches. We are not consistent in our thinking.

Hollywood has made evil accessible and tame. This makes Satan and demons out to be less troublesome than the Bible indicates. Satan is a roaring lion seeking to devour the whole world. (I Peter 5:8). "The great dragon was hurled down – that ancient serpent called the devil, or Satan, who leads the whole world astray. He was hurled to the earth, and his angels with him" (Revelation 12:9). Satan also masquerades as an angel of light. (II Corinthians 11:14). With this secret guise he deceives multitudes both inside and outside the church.

Perhaps Satan's greatest trick is to get people to believe he does not exist. This trick works because we repress the truth and choose to believe in Satan. "God's [holy] wrath and indignation are reveled from heaven against all ungodliness . . . of men, who repress the truth and make it inoperative. For that which is known about God is evident to them and made plain in their consciousness, because God has shown it to them . . . in his creation" (Romans 1:18-20 AMP).

Satan's power is limited to the extent God allows him to operate. Satan came to Job (1:9) and accused God of not allowing him to tempt Job, so God gave Satan the permission to tempt Job but put a limitation on Satan, that is, he was not given permission to touch Job's body. Satan failed to cause Job to sin even though he removed Job's children and possessions. Satan then requested to afflict Job's body. God gave His permission. Job suffered horrendously but still Job did not sin. No wonder the Bible refers to him as one who was "blameless, upright; he feared God and shunned evil" (Job 1:1).

Jesus says in Luke 10:18-19, "I saw Satan fall like lightning from heaven. I have given you authority to trample on snakes, scorpions and to overcome all the power of the enemy, nothing will harm you." Jesus conquered Satan: "Having disarmed the powers and authorities, he made a public spectacle of them, triumphing over them by the cross" (Colossians 2:15). This is the imagery of Jesus marching His captives in a victory parade just as a victorious army general would march his captives to show the world his victory. "He rescued us from the dominion of darkness and brought us into the kingdom of the Son he loves, in whom we have redemption, the forgiveness of sins" (Colossians 1:13-14).

"We are more than conquerors through Christ who loved us . . . neither death nor life, angels nor demons . . . nor any powers . . . will be able to separate us from the love of God what is in Christ Jesus our Lord" (Romans 8:37-39). John reminds us, "Greater is he who is in you (God's Holy Spirit) than the one who is in the world" (I John 4:4).

God's in charge of the nations. "God changes times and seasons; he deposes kings and raises up others" (Daniel 2:21). "The holy ones declare the verdict, so that the living may know that the Most High is sovereign over all kingdoms on earth and gives them to anyone he wishes and sets over them the lowliest of people" (Daniel 4:17). God punished King Nebuchadnezzar so that he had to live in the wilderness until he acknowledged that the Most High God was sovereign over all kingdoms on earth and sets over them anyone he wished. (Daniel 5:21). "The nations are like a drop in a bucket; they are regarded as dust on the scales; he weighs the islands as though they were fine dust . . . Before him all the nations are as nothing; they are regarded by him as worthless and less than nothing" (Isaiah 40:15-17).

"He is the God who judges: he brings one down, and exalts another" (Psalm 75:7). "Coming out of Jesus' mouth is a sharp sword with which to strike down the nations. He will rule them with an iron scepter" (Revelation 19:15-16). God shakes all the foundations of the earth. (Psalm 82:5).

A huge army surrounded Elijah and his servant. The servant

asked, "What shall we do?" "Don't be afraid," the prophet answered. "Those who are with us are more than those who are with them." Elisha prayed, "Open the servant's eyes. He looked and saw the hills full of horses and chariots of fire all around Elisha" (II Kings 6:15-17ff). God is in charge of all His angels. David reminds us the angels are encamped around us. (Psalm 34:7).

"The earth is the Lords, and everything in it, the world and all who live in it" (Psalm 24:1). "He (Jesus) is the ruler of the kings of the earth" (Revelation 1:5). "The eyes of the Lord run to and fro throughout the whole earth, to give strong support to those whose heart is blameless toward him" (2 Chronicles 16:9). Is your heart blameless?

WHY DOESN'T GOD CHANGE THINGS?
II CHRONICLES 7:14

In the Garden of Eden, God walked with Adam and Eve. They chose to break that relationship when they ate of the forbidden fruit. Their offspring, Cain murdered Abel. Things went from bad to worse: "The Lord saw how great the wickedness of the human race had become . . . and that every inclination of their thoughts was only evil continually" (Genesis 6:5). God wiped out the human race with a flood. He spared Noah who was righteous. In total disregard of God, it wasn't long before Noah's posterity had no respect for God. They decided to build a tower to make a name for themselves in total disregard of God. (Genesis 11:4).

God is like a parent who wants a relationship with His children. But His children rebel time after time. Of course, He could create a people who would obey Him but they would not be like Him in character. They would be robots. Robots would be similar to our relationship with inanimate objects like we relate to a hammer or screwdriver. We could be surrounded with a million tools but would be dreadfully lonely. God longs to have a vital relationship with us. God's wants a family. God's wants children who love Him. He tries again and again every way possible to get them to love and obey Him.

God says, "When I shut up the heaven so that there is no rain, or command locusts to devour the land or send a plague among my people, if my people, who are called by my name, will humble themselves and pray and seek my face, (crave my face), and turn from their wicked ways, then I will hear from heaven, and I will forgive their sin and heal their land. If you walk before me faithfully . . . and do all I command, and observe my decrees and laws, I will establish your royal throne, as I covenanted with David. . . . But if you turn away and forsake the commands and go off to serve other gods and worship them, I will uproot you from my land . . ." (II Chronicles 7:13-20).

When descendants of Abraham, later known as Judah, reject God's kindness choosing instead to team up with the pagan nations, God punishes them. (Isaiah 8:6ff). "Lean on, trust and be confident in the Lord with all your heart and mind, and do not rely on your own insight or understanding. In all your ways know, recognize and acknowledge him, and he will direct and make straight and plain your paths. Be not wise, in your own eyes; reverently fear and worship the Lord, and turn away from evil. It shall be health to your nerves, and sinews, and marrow and moistening to your bones" (Proverbs 3:5-8 AMP).

"They made their hearts like flint and would not listen to the words of the Lord Almighty . . . so the Lord Almighty was very angry" (Zechariah 7:12).

Like Israel, God's chosen people, we tend to forget God has many attributes; two of which are His love and His wrath. Rejecting His guidance results in sin and invites His wrath. We must realize the consequences of our choices. What we sow, we reap. (Galatians 6:7). God wants to protect us from bad choices, but He gives us the freedom to make those choices. He says, "All day long I have held out my hands to a disobedient and obstinate people" (Romans 10:21). If God would simply go ahead and right our wrong choices, we could not have a meaningful relationship with Him. If God would change things without our cooperation there would be no such things as love, no fellowship, no joy, or family. Because God is love, romance is at the heart of the universe.

But because there are a few who choose to follow the way of the Lord, who choose to love Him with all their heart, soul, mind and strength He uses those few to carry out his work. "God crowned us with glory and honor. He made us rulers over the works of his hands" (Psalm 8:5-6), God works through humans, not independently of them. This is why things get messed up. He is waiting on us to do our part. God wanted to spare His people from judgment but Jeremiah reports He could not find one honest man. "Go up and down the streets of Jerusalem, look around and consider, . . . If you can find but one person who deals honestly and seeks the truth, I will forgive this city" (Jeremiah 5:1). Ezekiel reminds us that God limits Himself to the intercession of His people. "I looked for someone among them who would build up the wall and stand before me in the gap on behalf of the land so I would not have to destroy it, but I found no one. So, I will pour out my wrath on them and consume them with my fierce anger, bringing down on their own heads all they have done, declares the Sovereign Lord" (Ezekiel 22:30-31).

Habakkuk is a model for us. He can't understand why God would use Babylonia, a nation more wicked than Judah, to punish Judah for their sins. Finally, he concludes admitting that even though he can't understand God's working he trusts God and states his faith: "I trembled when I heard this . . . I will wait quietly for the coming day when disaster will strike the people who invade us. Even though the fig trees have no blossoms, and there are no grapes on the vine; even though the olive crop fails, and the fields lie empty and barren; even though the flocks die . . . yet I will rejoice in the Lord! I will be joyful in the God of my salvation. The Sovereign Lord is my strength! He will make me as surefooted as a deer and bring me safely over the mountains" (Habakkuk 3:17-19). Will we be people of faith as Habakkuk models for us? We are meant to live on the heights.

God will change things if His people will follow His ways. He will right our wrongs after His return. Consider these statistics from the Internet. Note that every one of these is brought on primarily by our sinful, self-centered living: Nearly 1/2 of the world's population lives on less than $2.50 a day. More than 1.3 billion live in extreme poverty—less than $1.25 a day. One billion children worldwide are living in poverty. According to UNICEF, 22,000 children die each day due to poverty, 805 million people worldwide do not have enough food to eat, more than 750 million people lack adequate access to clean drinking water. Diarrhea caused by polluted drinking water, sanitation, and hand hygiene kills an estimated 842,000 people every year—that's 2,300 people per day.

God will change things as He creates a new heaven and a new earth. In the meantime, our responsibility is to do to others, as we would have them do to us and to pray as Jesus taught us: for His will to be done on earth as it is in heaven. (Matthew 6:10).

YOUR GENEALOGY CAN'T BE THIS BAD
MATTHEW 1:1-17

"This is the genealogy of Jesus the Messiah, the son of David, the son of Abraham" (Matthew 1:1).

All of us have looked at our ancestry and felt embarrassed and humiliated by one of our relatives. There are no perfect families. We have all blamed our weakness and sins on our genes. No matter how appalling you believe your mother or father or grandparents or distant relatives were, Jesus' ancestry was far, far from perfect.

Jesus' genealogy is inundated with infamous persons—some are despicable. Twice Abraham distorted the truth by calling Sarah his sister. Sarah blamed others for her faults. Isaac showed favoritism to Esau. He alienated his wife, Rebecca. Rebecca deceived her husband. Judah suggested they sell their brother Joseph into slavery. He had sex with a woman he thought was a shrine prostitute. It turned out the woman was his daughter-in-law, Tamar. Tamar had disguised herself as a prostitute, which tricked Judah. Ruth was a Moabite, a descendant of Lot, born in an incestuous relationship with Lot's oldest daughter. Rahab was a prostitute. David committed adultery. He murdered Uriah to try to cover up his sin. He could lead an army but could not manage his own children. Rehoboam abandoned the worship of God and allowed idolatry to flourish. Ahaz and Manasseh both sacrificed their children in the worship of Baal.

No matter what our family and relatives have done, Jesus understands our pedigree. Never cease to be amazed and awed at what our holy and righteous Almighty God designed for His Son Jesus, to be humiliated and punished for our sin so we could be redeemed and brought into His family and His very own children! We can never use the excuse: I have come from the worst family in town so why would God accept a person like me?

We must forgive our parents, relatives and everyone who has offended us. We are to forget what is behind and strain forward to what is ahead. (Philippians 3:14). God's love will break down every wall of resentment that Satan would erect in our minds. Jesus said, "When you pray, if you hold anything against anyone, forgive them, so that your Father in heaven may forgive you your sins" (Mark 11:25). "If you do not forgive others your Father will not forgive your sins" (Matthew 6:15). It's that serious! All of us need to forgive.

One in every three women and one in every five boys or men has been sexually assaulted. More than one half of our children do not have the same live-in father growing up. Divorce affects more than one half the homes in our nation. Pain is in everyone's family. Forgive your parents and extended family. When we don't forgive we hurt ourselves far more than the one we refuse to forgive.

Jesus came to his own people but they rejected Him and condemned Him to be crucified. (John 1:11). He understands your background. He was tempted in all points as we are – yet He did not sin. (Hebrews 4:15). Throw you pain and broken heart on Him. (I Peter 5:7). It's been said, "Don't go to the phone, go to the throne." He is anxious to heal your hurts! He has lavished His love upon you. Now you can forgive and love as He loved you. His love covers and forgives multitudes of hurts and sins including yours. (I Peter 4:8). Thank Him continually for His love—so wonderful no words can do it justice.

HEART PROBLEMS
JEREMIAH 17:9

If you doubt the evil in your heart, I suggest you analyze your dreams. Have you ever said or did anything in your dreams that if known would cause you to be mortified? What is the source of these thoughts? Dementia is another mystery. Do you know good people who in their older years suffer from dementia? Not all, but a sizeable percentage say and do things that they would never have considered saying or doing when they had healthy mental faculties. Where do these thought and actions originate?

"The heart is deceitful above all things and beyond cure. Who can understand it?" (Jeremiah 17:9). Jesus said, "Out of the heart (out of the recesses of our mind), come evil thoughts – murder, adultery, sexual immorality, theft, false testimony, slander. These are what defile a person" (Matthew 15:19). We can't begin to understand dementia or dreams although we are making progress concerning dementia.

When you hear of horrendous or hideous acts of others, do you find yourself thinking you would never do such things. Why are they so cruel? However, as we reflect on our thoughts of anger and revenge, as we engage in introspection and soul-searching, we begin to realize we too are capable of thinking and doing the same things even though we hate to admit it. Do you ever think, "Why don't we just love each other and get along together in peace?"

We inherited a sinful, self-centered nature. Solomon writes: "The hearts of people are full of evil and there is madness in their hearts while they live" (Ecclesiastes 9:3). "All have sinned and fallen short of God's glorious standard" (Romans 3:23 NLT). "There is none righteous, not even one" (Romans 3:10). "All our righteous acts are as filthy rags" (Isaiah 64:6). Don't be amazed that you could be guilty of the same things that are appalling to you when others do them. Once we realize who we really are we can cast ourselves on Jesus, thanking Him for forgiveness. A broken and contrite heart He will not despise. (Psalm 51:17).

Consider David's experience. Sent by the Lord, Nathan approached David with this parable: There was a rich man and a poor man. The rich man had a large number of sheep but the poor man had nothing except one little lamb. It grew up with him and his children and even slept in his arms. When a traveler came to the rich man, he stole the lamb from the poor man to provide a meal for the traveler. "David burned with anger against the rich man and said to Nathan, 'As surely as the Lord lives, the man who did this must die! He must pay for that lamb four times over because he did such a thing and had no pity." Then Nathan said to David, "You are the man!" (II Samuel 12).

God had given David the kingship of Israel and Judea. Nathan said, "Why did you despise the word of the Lord by doing what is evil? You struck down Uriah with the sword and took his wife (Bethesda) to be your own. You killed him with the sword of the Ammonites. Now the sword will never depart from your house because you despised me and took the wife of Uriah the Hittite . . . Then David said, 'I have sinned against the Lord.' Nathan replied, 'The Lord has taken away your sin. You are not going to die. But because by doing this you have shown utter contempt for the Lord, the son born to you will die'" (II Samuel 12:7-14).

Like David, we must have a repentant heart. Repentance, being truly sorry before God for our sins, is the pathway to restoration. Jesus said, "He who comes to me I will never drive away" (John 6:37). However, consequences of our sins are great just as in David's experience. Not only did his son die, and the sword never depart from his house, Nathan reported, "Before your very eyes I will take your wives and give them to one who is close to you and he will sleep with your wives in broad daylight. You did it in secret, but I will do this thing in broad daylight before all Israel" (II Samuel 12:11-12).

How could Judas Iscariot walk with Jesus for three years and then betray him? (Mark 14:10). Peter, the leader of Jesus' disciples denied Jesus. (Mark 14:66:72). When the soldiers came to arrest Jesus, "everyone deserted him and fled" (Mark 14:50). How many who claim to walk with Jesus will deny Him? One survey claimed that 50% who attend church attend out of habit or to meet friends. How many share their faith? Jesus said, "If anyone is ashamed of me and my words in this adulterous and sinful generation, the Son of Man will be ashamed of them when he comes in his Father's glory with the holy angels" (Luke 8:38).

Prosperity has blinded our eyes: We are conscious of our tremendous scientific achievement in the area of medicine and material wealth. We have allowed these advancements to give a high opinion of ourselves. We view material wealth as more important than moral character. Even though we have two and one-half million prisoners, even though we have far more bars and nightclubs than churches and spend more on our pets than we give to feed the hungry we feel we are pretty good. "We imagine God as a magnified image of ourselves . . . The thought of ourselves as creatures fallen from God's image, rebels against God's rule, guilty and unclean in God's sight, fit only for God's condemnation, never enters our heads . . . Dale Carnegie's, *How to Win Friends and Influence People* has become our bible . . . We believe we can repair our own relationship with God by putting God in a position where he cannot say no anymore." (J. I. Packer, *Knowing God*, pp. 130-131). The devil is delighted with our blindness.

We are warned not to put our trust in ourselves. People are not perfect. Multitudes have been hurt when their pastor was unfaithful or money came up missing from the church treasury. Never cease to be amazed at the sinfulness and fickleness of the human heart. Pray with David, "Search me, God and know my heart; test me and know my anxious thoughts. See if there is any offensive way in me, and lead me in the way everlasting" (Psalm 139:23-24). "Test me, Lord, and try me, examine my heart and my mind" (Psalm 26:2). "Examine yourselves to see whether you are in the faith" (II Corinthians 13:5). "No matter how deep the stain of your sin, I can remove it. I can make you as clean as freshly fallen snow. Even if you are stained as red as crimson, I can make you as white as wool" (Isaiah 1:18 NLT).

NO EASY STEPS TO SALVATION
JOHN 14:6, ACTS 4:12

A child can understand the steps to salvation but these steps are not easy. What do I mean? Salvation is a commitment to Messiah Jesus who performs such a radical change that Jesus refers to it as the new birth. (John 3:3). It's described as "If anyone is in Christ, the new creation has come: The old has gone, the new creation is here!" (II Corinthians 5:17).

First: The first step to being saved is to recognize we are sinners; we are destitute and need to repent. (Matthew 5:3). (See the next essay for a more detailed explanation of repentance). Confession and repentance are against our human nature. Confess means to agree with God concerning our sins. Peter reported that when the Holy Spirit was given to the gentiles, they praised God, "So then even to Gentiles God has granted repentance that leads to salvation" (Acts 11:18).

To repent means we change our direction in life, from self-centeredness to Christ-centeredness. "If we confess our sins (repent) God is faithful and just and will forgive us our sins and purify us from all unrighteousness" (I John 1:9). Our ego rebels. Ego exaltation is the most dangerous and deadly of sins. It doesn't die easily. Our pride gets in the way. That's why there are no easy steps to salvation.

A tax collector and a Pharisee went to the temple to pray. The proud Pharisee thanked God that he was not sinful like other people. The tax collector prayed, "God have mercy on me, a sinner" (Luke 18:13). Jesus assures us the humble tax collector's prayer was heard and he was justified.

A few verses later a rich ruler came to Jesus asking what he must do to inherit eternal life. (Luke 18:18-25). Jesus listed several of the Ten Commandments. His response was that he kept them from his youth. Jesus said, "You still lack one thing. Sell everything you have and give to the poor, and you will have treasure in heaven. Then come, follow me." He was sad since he was very wealthy. Jesus looked at him and said, "How hard it is for the rich to enter the kingdom of God! Indeed, it is easier for a camel to go thought the eye of a needle than for someone who is rich to enter the kingdom of God."

Compare Jesus' encounter with Zacchaeus, a wealthy tax collector. Zacchaeus, who was short of stature, was desperate to see Jesus. He humbled himself and climbed a tree. Jesus invited Zacchaeus to come to him. Apparently, they talked. "Zacchaeus stood up and said to the Lord, 'Look Lord! Here and now I give half of my possessions to the poor, and if I have cheated anybody out of anything, I will pay back four times the amount.'" "Jesus said to him, 'Today salvation has come to this house, because this man, too, is a son of Abraham. For the Son of man came to seek and to save the lost'" (Luke 19:1-10). The rich ruler shut himself out of the kingdom since his wealth was more important than following Jesus, while Zacchaeus humbled himself and received Jesus' gift of salvation.

Jesus in his Sermon on the Mount says the first step into God's Kingdom is to be poor in spirit (destitute) for they will receive entrance into God's Kingdom. (Matthew 5:3). C. S. Lewis said, "If you think you are not conceited, it means you are very conceited indeed." To receive salvation, we must see ourselves in need of God's mercy.

Jesus shocked a large crowd and shocks us as well by saying, "If anyone comes to me and does not hate father and mother, wife and children, brothers and sisters – yes, even their own life – such a person cannot be my disciple. And whoever does not carry their cross and follow me cannot be my disciple" (Luke 14:26-27). What did Jesus mean? He helps us to understand in the next verses by using a metaphor concerning a man who builds a house without first counting the cost. He is saying we must count the cost of being Jesus' follower. (Luke 14:28-30).

To be Jesus' disciple our loyalty requires commitment to Him above our loyalty to our family. Jesus' command to "hate father and mother" requires us to prioritize our relationship with Jesus over our relationship with parents, siblings, and other family members. We know from many other scriptures that it is right to love our family members. Jesus confirmed the fifth commandment that we honor our fathers and mothers. The Pharisees were following their traditions instead of helping their parents. (Mark 7:9-13). Paul warned "anyone who does not provide for their relatives, and especially for their own household, has denied the faith and is worse than an unbeliever" (1 Timothy 5:8).

In the same breath Jesus says we are to hate our own life. Jesus is not teaching a hatred of our parents any more than He is teaching self-hatred. We are to love ourselves. (Matthew 22:39). He explains further by adding the phrase that we must carry our own cross. (v. 27). The NLT reads: "If you want to be my disciple, you must hate everyone else by comparison" (Luke 14:26, NLT). The *Amplified Bible* says that a follower of Christ must "hate" his family members "in the sense of indifference to or relative disregard for them in comparison with his attitude toward God." It is "hatred" by comparison, not an absolute hatred.

The word "hate" in Luke 14:26 is used in the other contexts to indicate preference. Deuteronomy 21:15 KJV speaks of two wives, one beloved, and another hated. Other translations referred to the "hated" wife as "unloved." Romans 9:13, "Jacob I loved but Esau I hated." (See also Malachi 1:2-3).

We may not have to make the choice between family and following Christ, since our family will likely support our allegiance to Christ. In scores of other nations, Christians face shunning, disowning, or persecution from their families when they choose Christ. Jesus calls us to acknowledge His lordship over all earthly ties. "We must go through many hardships to enter the kingdom of God" (Acts 14:22). Those who must sacrifice earthly relationships have this promise: "Truly I tell you, no one who has left home or brothers or sisters or mother or father or children or fields for me and the gospel will fail to receive a hundred times as much in this present age: homes, brothers, sisters, mothers, children and fields – along with persecution – and in the age to come eternal life." (Mark 10:29-30).

Second: After we recognize we are a sinner, we must believe, i.e. trust, cling to and rely upon the fact that Jesus is the only way to eternal life. "God so greatly loved and dearly prized the world that he [even] gave up his only begotten (unique) Son, so that whoever believes in (trusts, clings to, relies on) him may not perish – come to destruction, be lost – but have eternal (everlasting) life" (John 3:16 AMP). Jesus said, "I am the way and the truth and the life. No one comes to the Father except through me" (John 14:6). "There is salvation in no one else, for there is no other name . . . given to mankind by which we must be saved" (Acts 4:12). "There is one God and one mediator between God and men, the man Christ Jesus" (I Timothy 2:5). Jude says that Jesus is the only God our Savior. (Jude 25). To agree with these words, society will likely label you as narrow-minded, egotistic, even dangerous.

Third: The third step is to realize that Jesus is Lord. "If you acknowledge and confess with your lips that Jesus is Lord and, in your heart, believe (adhere to, trust in and rely on the truth) that God raised him from the dead, you will be saved. For with the heart a person believes (adheres to, trusts in and relies on Christ) and so is justified (declared righteous, acceptable to God), and with the mouth he or she confesses – declares openly and speaks out freely their faith – and confirms [their] salvation" (Romans 10:9-10 AMP). Only a few Christians are declaring opening and speaking freely about their walk with Jesus. One study reveals only six percent share Jesus and the Good News. Have you confessed Jesus with your mouth the past month? Jesus said, "If anyone is ashamed of me and my words, the Son of Man will be ashamed of him when he comes in his glory . . ." (Luke 9:26).

It seems apparent that only a few of those who say they want to accept Jesus has a wholehearted commitment to follow him. I say this because my observation has been that few have a love for God's word, a passion to see others come to the Savior or an energetic motive to serve their Lord in whatever way they can. To be born again clearly implies a radical change. "If any person is (engrafted) in Christ, the Messiah, he is (a new creature altogether) a new creation; the old (previous moral and spiritual condition) is passed away. Behold the fresh and new has come!" (II Corinthians 5:17 AMP). Peter adds we are given a new nature. (II Peter 1:4). "No one who is born of God will continue to sin (make a practice of sinning because God's nature lives in them). (I John 3:9). The *Amplified Bible* reads: "No one born of God [deliberately and knowingly] habitually practices sin, for God nature abides in them."

Fourth: We must open our heart and our life, to Jesus. "To as many as receive and welcome him, he gave the authority [power, privilege, right] to become the children of God, that is, to those who believe in – adhere to, trust in and rely on – his name" (John 1:12 AMP). "If we walk in the light . . . the blood of Jesus, God's Son, purifies us from all sin" (I John 1:7). Don't overlook the little word "if" in this verse.

One of the controversial teachings today, is that a person can accept Christ and decide later if they want to be His disciple. If this should be the case, I feel sure it isn't, but if it is these people miss out on the abundant life Jesus has provided for His followers. They only taste the good things of Jesus and seldom experience His joy and resurrection power in their daily living. They live on milk, not meat. (Hebrews 5:12-14). However, if they are wrong, believing they don't need to take up their cross daily then they are deceived and will spend eternity in hell. Don't even consider this choice. Give your life completely to Him, be His disciple and He will acknowledge you on the judgment day and welcome you into His eternal kingdom.

If these steps are believed and prayed sincerely from the heart, we are born into God's kingdom. Jesus said, "I assure you, most solemnly I tell you, that unless a person is born again (anew, from above), he cannot even see – know, be acquainted with [and experience] the kingdom of God" (John 3:3 AMP). After we are born again, we grow in our walk with Jesus by applying our faith just as we did when we were saved. (Colossians 2:6).

III.

OUR AMAZING SALVATION

IS REPENTANCE NECESSARY?
LUKE 13:3-4

When is the last time you used the word or even heard the word, "repent" or the concept of repentance? We can preach, "God loves you" but a message that does not include repentance will not lead people to salvation. Jesus said, unless you repent you will perish. (Luke 13:3-4). There is no forgiveness without repentance since anything short of repentance is a claim of our innocence before God. Jesus did not come to call the righteous, i.e. the self-righteous or the proud but those who recognize they are sinners. (Luke 5:31-32). "All have sinned" (Romans 3:9-18). "If we say we have no sin, we are only fooling ourselves and refusing to accept the truth" (I John 1:8 NLT).

Repentance is being remorseful to the extent you resolve by an act of your will to change your mind and your actions. Grief without repentance can lead only to despair. When Judas betrayed Jesus he was remorseful and hung himself, but he was not repentant. (Matthew 27:3-5). "Godly sorrow brings repentance that leads to salvation and leaves no regret, but worldly sorrow brings death" (II Corinthians 7:10). Peter was truly repentant as he wept bitterly [that is, with painfully moving grief], after betraying Jesus. (Luke 22:62 AMP).

We avoid repentance because it demands death to our ego. (Matthew 5:3). David expresses it: "A broken and contrite heart, O God, you will not despise" (Psalm 51:17). Repentant Christians willingly accept reproof. Repentance means to make a 180-degree turn. Some compare it to a chrysalis that crawls on the dirt and then begins the transformation into a beautiful butterfly.

Godly repentance enables us to call upon the Lord and receive His free gift of eternal life. (Romans 10:13). God does not leave us to despair in our brokenness but offers us the comfort of forgiveness and love, so that when we cry out to God in faith, He willingly forgives us and saves us. (Acts 2:21).

John the Baptist's message was preaching "a baptism of repentance for the forgiveness of sins . . . 'You brood of vipers! Who warned you to flee from the coming wrath? Produce fruit in keeping with repentance . . . If you do not repent you will be thrown into the fire'" (Luke 3:3, 7-9).

Jesus began His public ministry preaching, "Repent and believe the good news!" (Mark 1:15). Notice, Jesus places repentance before belief. Jesus sent His disciples: "they went out preaching that people should repent" (Mark 6:12). He says, "I tell you . . . there will be more rejoicing in heaven over one sinner who repents than over the ninety-nine who need no repentance" (Luke 15:7, 10, 17-20). The Prodigal, before he left home said to his Father, "give me," but when he returned, he said in a humble, repentant attitude, "make me." Like the Prodigal we must learn to say to our Father, not "give me" but "make me." (Luke 15:12-19).

In Luke 13:1-5 Jesus says that the persons on whom the tower of Siloam fell were no more guilty than the other people and the ones Pilate murdered were no worse sinners than all the other Galileans. Then He adds: "Unless you repent you too will all perish" (vv. 3 and 5). Lazarus, the rich man, who was in hell begged for someone to warn his brothers so they would repent and not suffer torment like he was. (Luke 16:30).

Just before Jesus ascended to heaven He said to His disciples, "This is what is written: 'The Christ will suffer and rise from the dead on the third day, and repentance and forgiveness of sins will be preached in his name to all nations'" (Luke 24:46-47). Jesus saw repentance as an absolute necessity to enter His Kingdom.

On the day of Pentecost Peter declared that Jesus is the fulfillment of the prophet's message. "God has made this Jesus, whom you crucified, both Lord and Christ. When the people heard this, they were cut to the heart and said to Peter and the other apostles, 'Brothers, what shall we do?' Peter replied, 'Repent and be baptized, every one of you, in the name of Jesus Christ for the forgiveness of your sins. And you will receive the gift of the Holy Spirit'" (Acts 2:36-38). Paul says, "In the past God overlooked such ignorance, but now he commands all people everywhere to repent" (Acts 17:30).

Paul writes to Timothy, "The Lord's servant must gently instruct, (them) in the hope that God will grant them repentance, leading them to a knowledge of the truth, and that they will come to their senses and escape from the trap of the devil, who has taken them captive to do his will" (II Timothy 2:25-26). Until we have a spirit of repentance, we will be proud, self-centered, self-righteous Pharisees. (Luke 18:9-14). Peter's final words: "God is patient with you, not wanting anyone to perish, but everyone to come to repentance" (II Peter 3:9).

When Jonah preached repentance the response of the wicked city of Nineveh was amazing. They proved their repentance by praying, fasting and obeying God. The revival spared the city for the next one hundred years.

Repentance and obedience need to be linked as one action. Paul testified to King Agrippa, "I preached that they should repent and turn to God and prove their repentance by their deeds" (Acts 26:20). "Remember what you have received and heard, obey it, and repent" (Revelation 3:3). A repentant heart hates sin and loves righteousness.

The churches in Revelation 2 and 3 were established in the fifties and sixties of the first century. The main theme of Jesus' message to these thirty plus year-old churches was, "repent." Even though we may be followers of Christ for thirty or more years just as these people were, repentance is necessary throughout our life because we are never perfect. (I John 1:8 and 10).

The goodness of God is meant to lead us to repentance. (Romans 2:4). Our response to God's goodness needs to be: Lord we are unworthy servants. Thank you for your blessings. Too often prosperity causes us to focus on the earthly "blessings." These blessings take our time, our energy, our money, and even our heart! On the other hand, when God sends punishment for our sins, we often fail to repent. "The rest of mankind who were not killed by these plagues still did not repent of the work of their hands; they did not stop worshiping demons, and idols of gold, silver, bronze stone and wood. Nor did they repent of their murders, their magic arts, their sexual immorality and their thefts" (Revelation 9:20-21).

Half-hearted repentance is not genuine repentance. Whenever you hear, "If I was wrong, I am sorry" or "maybe I did make a mistake but you have to admit it was your fault, too," you know this is not genuine repentance. Blaming the other person for the wrong usually indicates we do not own our part in the dispute. Even if we believe we are only one percent in the wrong we need to repent of that one percent. Jesus taught us to pray: "Forgive us for doing wrong, as we forgive others . . . If you forgive others for the wrongs, they do to you, your Father in heaven will forgive you. But if you don't forgive others, your Father will not forgive your sins" (Matthew 6:12, 14-15 CEV). Lack of repentance has eternal consequences.

You meet people every day who have no desire to repent. Some wear shirts that say, "I don't care what you think. I am my own boss." Love them and pray that their eyes will be opened to their self-centered living before it is too late.

THE GATE IS NARROW
MATTHEW 7:13-14

How counter culture is the concept of a narrow gave? Satan has blinded our eyes to the fact that we will all be accountable to God. Can you find one page in your Bible where accountability and judgment are not implied? "Enter through the narrow gate. For wide is the gate and broad is the road that leads to destruction, and many enter through it. But small is the gate and narrow the road that leads to life and only a few find it" (Matthew 7:13-14). The contrast of Jesus' words to the mainstream culture of America is amazing. Our culture believes everyone is going to heaven except a very few who are especially wicked. If you question that most people, including pastors, believe we are all going to heaven then attend a few funerals and listen to the message.

The Bible is clear. Jesus said, "To all who did receive him, to those who believed in his name he gave the right to become children of God – children born not of natural descent, not of human decision or a husband's will, but born of God" (John 1:12-13). "No one comes to the Father except through me" (John 14:6).

"Not everyone who says to me, 'Lord, Lord,' will enter the kingdom of heaven, but only the one who does the will of my Father who is in heaven. Many will say to me on that day, 'Lord, Lord, did we not prophesy in your name and in your name drive out demons and, in your name, perform many miracles?' Then I will tell them plainly, 'I never knew you. Away from me, you evildoers" (Matthew 7:21-23). Verse 21 in the NLT: "Not all people who sound religious are really godly. They may refer to me as 'Lord,' but they still won't enter the Kingdom of Heaven. The decisive issue is whether they obey my Father in heaven." Jesus' message to the foolish virgins who did not prepare for the coming of the bridegroom is that they will be turned away from the wedding banquet. (Matthew 25:1-13).

Jesus said: "Make every effort to enter through the narrow door, because many, I tell you will try to enter and will not be able to. Once the owner of the house gets up and closes the door, you will stand outside knocking and pleading, 'Sir open the door for us.' But he will answer, 'I don't know you or where you come from.' Then you will say, 'We ate and drank with you and you taught in our streets.' But he will reply 'I don't' know you or where you come from. Away from me, all you evildoers!' There will be weeping there, and gnashing of teeth, when you see Abraham, Isaac, and Jacob and all the prophets . . . but you yourselves thrown out" (Matthew 13:24-28). "Only a remnant will be saved" (Romans 9:27).

When God speaks of redemption, He frequently contrasts the few with the many. God chose Israel to be a light to the nations of the world not because they were more numerous than other nations; in fact, they were the fewest of all people. (Deuteronomy 7:6-8). "Many Gentiles will come from all over the world and sit down with Abraham, Isaac, and Jacob at the feast in the Kingdom of Heaven. But many Israelites – those for whom the Kingdom was prepared – will be cast into outer darkness, were there will be weeping and gnashing of teeth" (Matthew 8:1-12). The number of those with faith at the Lord's return will be so small that Jesus asks: "When the Son of Man comes will he find faith upon the earth?" (Luke 18:1-8). We must be careful not to take this to the point that we overlook the faithful Christians. Elijah thought he was the only faithful one left but Obadiah hid one hundred prophets and provided for them.

There are seventeen catalogues of sin found in the New Testament. In several it is clearly stated that anyone practicing these sins will not enter the Kingdom of Heaven. Since these sins are found so broadly in the human race one can deduct that the majority will not enter heaven. "The acts of the flesh are obvious, sexual immorality, impurity and debauchery, idolatry and witchcraft; hatred, discord, jealousy, fits of rage, selfish ambition, dissensions, envy, drunkenness, orgies and the like. I warn you as I did before that those who live like this will not inherit the kingdom of God" (Galatians 5:19-21).

"There should not be even a hint of sexual immorality or any kind of impurity or of greed, because these are improper for God's holy people. Nor should there be obscenity, foolish talk or coarse joking, which are out of place, but rather thanksgiving. For of this you can be sure: No immoral or greedy person – such a person is an idolater – has any inheritance in the kingdom of Christ and of God. Let no one deceive you with empty words, for because of such things God's wrath comes on those who are disobedient. Therefore, do not be partners with them" (Ephesians 5:3-7).

"Do you not know that the unrighteous and the wrongdoers will not inherit or have any share in the kingdom of God? Do not be deceived (misled); neither the impure and immoral, nor idolaters, nor adulterers, nor those who participate in homosexuality, nor cheats – swindlers and thieves; nor greedy graspers, nor drunkards, nor foul-mouthed revilers and slanders, nor extortionists and robbers will inherit or have any share in the kingdom of God. And such some of you were. But you were washed clean [purified by a complete atonement (covering) for sin and made free from the guilt of sin]; and you were consecrated (set apart, hallowed); and you were justified (pronounced righteous, by trust) in the name of the Lord Jesus Christ and in the (Holy) Spirit" (I Corinthians 6:9-11 AMP)

While is it clear that only a minority will inherit God's Kingdom it is God's passionate desire that everyone be saved: He does not want "anyone to perish but for everyone to come to repentance" (II Peter 3:9). He wants to see you enter His Kingdom that He died to make it possible for you to do so. God loved the world so much that He gave His very best, His only Son that whoever puts their trust in Him, will not be lost but have eternal life. (John 3:16).

Paul shares the same message: "God wants all people to be saved and to come to a knowledge of the truth. For there is one God and one mediator between God and mankind, the man Christ Jesus, who gave himself as a ransom for all people" (I Timothy 2:4). Revelation 7:9 reminds us that there will be a great multitude in heaven that no one can number. Apparently, this multitude as great as it is, is small compared to those who choose the broad way that leads to destruction. Do all you can to help people find the narrow way.

WHO IS INTOLERANT?
ISAIAH 5:20

A news commentator endorsed the statement that any religion that believes others need to accept its message or face damnation is egotistical, intrusive, invasive, and intolerant. He is convinced that we should oppose such religions as vehemently as he does. Those who believe the "gay" lifestyle often accuse those who believe the Bible's position that marriage between one man and one woman and all sexual activity outside of marriage is sinful are labeled as intolerant. "Woe to those who call evil good and good evil, who put darkness for light and light for darkness" (Isaiah 5:20).

Was Jesus Intolerant? Tolerance has become America's idol. Our attitude is, "I'll do what I want. It's none of your business." Jesus message flies in the face of this self-centered lifestyle. Jesus came not to call the righteous but sinners. (Luke 5:32). Jesus loved the rich young ruler but let him walk away because he was not willing to do what He asked; to sell his possessions and give the money to the poor. (Mark 10:21-23). To the woman at the well Jesus made it clear that the man she was living with was not her husband. (John 4). He did not condemn the woman caught in adultery but said, "Go now and leave your life of sin" (John 8:11). He called Matthew the tax collector—a man hated by society—and transformed him into a faithful disciple. (Matthew 9:9).

Jesus says, "Do you suppose that I have come to bring peace to the earth. I did not come to bring peace (tolerance) but a sword. For I have come to turn a man against his father, a daughter against her mother, a daughter-in-law against her mother-in-law . . . Anyone who loves his father or mother, son or daughter more than me is not worthy of me; and anyone who does not take his cross and follow me is not worthy of me" (Matthew 10:34-38). Later He said, "Do you think I came to bring peace on earth? No. I tell you, but division. From now on there will be five in one family divided against each other, three against two and two against three" (Luke 12:51-53).

In the Sermon on the Mount, Jesus said, "Anyone who is angry with his brother will be subject to judgment . . . Anyone who says, 'You fool!' will be in danger of the fire of hell" (Matthew 5:22). "Do not give dogs what is sacred; do not throw your pearls to pigs" (Matthew 7:6). Jesus called Herod a fox. (Luke 13-32). "Small is the gate and narrow the road that leads to life, and only a few find it. Watch out for false prophets" (Matthew 7:14-15). "Not everyone who says to me, 'Lord, Lord,' will enter the kingdom of heaven, but only he who does the will of my Father who is in heaven. Many will say to me on that day, 'Lord, Lord' did we not prophesy in your name and in your name drive our demons and perform many miracles? Then I will tell them I never knew you. Away from me, you evildoers!" (Matthew 7:21-23).

In the parable of the ten servants Jesus called one man a wicked servant and had him killed because he hid his money instead of investing it. (Luke 19:11-27). In Matthew 25:30 the man who buried his talent is to be thrown into darkness, where there will be weeping and gnashing of teeth. In Matthew 23, Jesus calls the Pharisees "blind fools," and seven times He calls them "hypocrites."

We are to exercise patience and forbearance, but there are many things Jesus cannot tolerate. In Mark 5, the Pharisees wanted to accuse Jesus because He was breaking the Sabbath by healing the man with a crippled hand. Verse 3, "Jesus looked around them in anger and deeply distressed at their stubborn hearts . . ." He scolded the disciples for their little faith. (Mark 4:40). Paul lists more than a dozen specific sins stating that those who do these things will not enter God's Kingdom. (Galatians 5:19-21).

Don't let people intimidate you when they call you intolerant or bigoted. As God's children we love everyone but we must not accept the deliberate and brazen sinfulness and wickedness of our culture. As pastor, everyone was welcome to my church but I would not give the platform to those living in flagrant sin. Jesus reminds us, "All men will hate you because of me" (Mark 13:13; John 15:18-27). After describing people practicing many different sinful lifestyles Paul writes, "Do not be partners with them" (Ephesians 5:7).

Our culture says, "Mind your own business." Yet if your neighbor is giving drugs to children you cannot tolerate this. We need to speak out against prejudice because of skin color or racial identity. If you become aware of human trafficking you need to do all you can to eliminate it. We must follow the Holy Spirit's leading as when to speak and when to be silent, but it is clear we have a responsibility to warn those who call evil good and good evil. God's people are too often shy or afraid to do what Jesus calls us to do.

There are seventy-six "one another" occurrences in the New Testament. We have responsibility for each other. We are to love, pray, encourage, teach, counsel, admonish, warn, submit, serve, honor, accept, bear with one another and also bear another's burdens. Paul writes: "If someone is caught in a sin, you who live by the Spirit should restore that person gently. But watch yourselves, or you also may be tempted" (Galatians 6:1-2). "If you brother or sister sins against you rebuke them; forgive them. Even if they sin against you seven times in a day and seven times come back to you saying, 'I repent,' you must forgive them" (Luke 17:3-4).

Our culture says, tolerate, overlook, or just ignore sin. Jesus loved people enough to set boundaries. May the Lord give us wisdom to know what and when to tolerate and when to confront one another in the spirit of "agape" love.

NO LATCH ON THE OUTSIDE OF THE DOOR
REVELATION 3:15-22

Jesus said, "I stand at the door and knock. If anyone hears my voice and opens the door, I will come in and eat with that person, and they with me" (Revelation 3:20). This verse has often been used as an invitation to those who have never said, "yes" to inviting Jesus to be the Lord of their life. Using it in this way has been influential to bring many to salvation in Christ, however in its context it's an invitation for those who claim to be saved but have backslidden. They claim to need nothing, but Jesus said He would spit them out of His mouth unless they repent. (v. 16).

He continues: "I know your deeds, that you are neither cold nor hot. I wish you were either one or the other! So, because you are luke-warm – neither hot nor cold – I am about to spit you out of my mouth. You say, 'I am rich; I have acquired wealth and do not need a thing.' But you do not realize that you are wretched, pitiful, poor, blind and naked. I counsel you to buy from me gold refined in the fire, so you can become rich; and white clothes to wear, so you can cover your shameful nakedness; and salve to put on your eyes, so you can see. Those whom I love I rebuke and discipline. So be earnest and repent. Here I am! I stand at the door and knock. If anyone hears my voice and opens the door, I will come in and eat with that person, and they with me. To the one who is victorious, I will give the right to sit with me on my throne, just as I was victorious and sat down with my Father on his throne" (Revelation 3:15-21).

The lukewarm condition of these rich Laodiceans is a worse witness than if they would have denied Jesus. As Christians let's be grateful that Jesus rebukes and disciplines us to get us out of this lukewarm or halfhearted, unenthusiastic state. He commands us to be in earnest and repent. He knocks on your heart to let Him take control. The Laodiceans were blind to their lukewarm state. It is so easy to feel secure and proud. Pride is the president of hell. Jesus can't stand a cocky and indifference attitude. Indifference is the hardest of all barriers to break. According to Jesus there is no category as a neutral Christian.

Indifference often has a direct relationship with wealth. Like Laodicea the American church is wealthy. Being wealthy often blinds us to our need for God. When He knocks and we do not open, we are poor, wretched, pitiful, blind and naked.

Jesus confronts this problem with rebuke and discipline. (Revelation 3:19). "Faithful are the wounds of a friend" (Proverbs 27:6 AMP). "The Lord corrects and disciplines every one whom he loves, and he punishes, even scourges, every son whom he accepts and welcomes and cherishes. You must submit to and endure [correction] for discipline. God is dealing with you as with sons; for what son is there whom his father does not train and correct and discipline? If you are exempt from corrections and left without discipline then you are illegitimate offspring and not true sons. Moreover, we have had earthly fathers who discipline us and we yielded and respected them . . . For our earthly fathers disciplined us for only a short period of time and chastised us as seemed proper and good to them, but he (Jesus) disciplines us for our certain good, that we may become sharers in his own holiness. For the time being no discipline brings joy but seems grievous and painful, but afterwards it yields peaceable fruit of righteousness . . ." (Hebrews 12:6-11 AMP). We are disciplined by the Lord, "so that we will not be finally condemned with the world" (I Corinthians 11:32).

James writes: "The judge is standing at the door" (James 5:9). Jesus standing at the door and knocking pictures the imminence or nearness of Christ's coming. We must always be ready since we do not know when He will return. (Matthew 25:13).

Hallman Hunt painted a picture depicting Jesus knocking at the door to illustrate Revelation 3:20. He made a point by deliberately not putting a latch on the outside of the door. Jesus is a gentleman. He knocks at the door of each one of us. He does not force Himself on us. Jesus seeks us. (Luke 19:10). He calls to us, "Come to me" (Matthew 11:28). He begs us: "All day long I have held out my hands to a disobedient and obstinate people" (Romans 10:31). He loves us: "God did not send his Son into the world to condemn the world but to save the world through him" (John 3:17). Jesus knocks, we can answer or refuse. He will not break in; He must be invited in. Everyone is lord of the house of their heart, their fortress, he or she must open the door. If they refuse, they are miserable conquerors in their "castle."

The Greeks had three meals each day: breakfast was no more than a piece of dried bread dipped in wine. For the midday meal one did not go home; it was like a picnic snack eaten by the side of the road under a shade tree, a meal eaten in the passing. Jesus chose the word for the evening meal, the main meal of the day; people lingered and sat long and talked over it. The day's work was done. Now there was time for unlimited and unhurried fellowship. The one who created our world desires our intimate friendship. What an amazing offer. Unless you accept His offer to fellowship with Him you are in great danger of being lukewarm and facing judgment. Will you take time to enjoy His company or will you let Him keep knocking at your door?

WHAT ARE YOU WORTH?
I PETER 1:18-21

Do you ever feel worthless, useless? Listen to I Peter 1:18-21: "It was not with perishable things such as silver or gold that you were redeemed from the empty way of life handed down to you from your ancestors but with the precious blood of Christ, a lamb without blemish or defect. He was chosen before the creation of the world but was revealed in these last times for your sake. Through him you believe in God who raised him from the dead and glorified him, and so your faith and hope are in God."

You are so valuable that Jesus gave His life to redeem you. (Matthew 20:28). When you put your faith in Jesus, i.e. trusted Him and relied on Him you were born again. (John 3:16). You are now part of God's family. (John 1:12-13). God is your Father and Christians are your brothers and sisters. This relationship is so important that Jesus said, if you call your brother or sister a fool, you are in danger of hell fire. (Matthew 5:22). When you trust in Christ, it's proof that God has chosen you and adopted you as His child. (Ephesians 1:4). You were marked by the Holy Spirit with a seal. (Ephesians 1:13). When God puts you in Christ Jesus, Jesus "becomes your righteousness, holiness and redemption" (I Corinthians 1:30). Even though we don't deserve it, God puts righteousness to our account. (Romans 4:24).

In *Stories for a Woman's Heart* Alice Gray writes: "A tourist strolling through a European village stopped to observe a master craftsman of gold filigreed porcelain. He watched as the craftsman took an exquisite vase, and carefully examined it. After a few minutes, a faint smile of satisfaction touched the corners of the artist's mouth . . .

"The workmanship was perfect. The artwork was intricate and delicate. Then he took a hammer and smashed it into a thousand pieces. Why? The craftsman looked at the tourist and explained. 'You see the value of this vase is not in its perfection. Not in the artwork, or form or shape. The value lies in the fact that I am now going to put these pieces back together again – with gold!' . . .

"So, it is with our lives. The value of our lives lies not in our perceived perfection, or in what we have done or left undone, not in how hard we've worked, not in the hope that we get a second chance to redeem ourselves. No, our value lies in the fact that God wastes nothing. He takes all the pieces, even the imperfect ones, shattered fragments and puts them back together again with His blood, which is infinitely more precious than gold."

No matter how painful, broken and shattered your past it is not beyond redemption. If your parents rejected you, and told you were not wanted, if you went through a hurtful divorce, if you were abused in every way imaginable, if you like millions were homeless, hungry and cold no matter what addictions you lived with or how terrible your life—God will redeem it if you bring it to Him. Because of these horrendous experiences you are now equipped to help other who are suffering like you have suffered.

Let Him put you together with gold—with His precious blood, which is infinitely worth more than gold. "God comforts us in all our troubles, so that we can comfort those in any trouble with the comfort we ourselves receive from God. For just as we share abundantly in the sufferings of Christ, so also our comfort abounds through Christ. If we are distressed, it is for your comfort and salvation; if we are comforted, it is for your comfort, which produces in you patient endurance of the same sufferings we suffer. And our hope for you is firm, because we know that just as you share in our sufferings, so also you share in our comfort" (II Corinthians 1:4-7).

Someone wisely observed, "Our wounds are not taken away but become visible sources of hope for others." Our ministry often grows out of our pain. If we have gone through the pain of rejection, divorce, abuse, etc., we are more equipped to help others with similar pain.

When Frank accepted Christ as a youth his dad threw him down the steps and told him never to come back. They even had a funeral for him and put up a gravestone. Frank went on to be a faithful pastor for our Lord and is in heaven today. Millions of others have a powerful testimony concerning the remaking of their lives, put together with Jesus' precious blood.

God put us together at great cost. Our worth in Christ Jesus is beyond our comprehension just as the worth of your child is beyond anything you can comprehend. Jesus has entrusted His work to you and me. We are His ambassadors, His soldiers in Christ's victorious army. (II Corinthians 5:18-20; II Timothy 2:3). He gives us all authority in heaven and on earth to make disciples by teaching them everything He has commanded us. (Matthew 28:19-20). We are His hands and feet to carry His message to the ends of the earth. God is amazing and you become amazing as He works through you doing more than you can imagine. (Ephesians 3:20-21). See yourself loved by God who gave His Son for you. You are made whole by the precious blood of Jesus. You are valuable. You are esteemed. Live in the joy of Jesus' resurrection power!

MOVE FROM ONE-HALF MILE TO SIDE-BY-SIDE JOSHUA 2:3-4

Before Joshua led the Children of Israel across the Jordan River, he gave these instructions: "When you see the ark of the covenant of the Lord your God, and the Levitical priests carrying it, you are to move out from your positions and follow it. Then you will know which way to go, since you have never been this way before. But keep a distance of about 2,000 cubits between you and the ark; do not go near it" (Joshua 2:3-4). Two thousand cubits is more than half a mile. From that distance they could barely see the ark, which was only about 4 foot by 2 foot by 2 foot.

The people were glad to obey because of their previous experience with approaching God. "When the people saw the thunder and lightning and heard the trumpet and saw the mountain in smoke, they trembled with fear. They stayed at a distance and said to Moses "'Speak to us yourself and we will listen. But do not have God speak to us or we will die'" (Exodus 19:28-19).

Now blessed we are. We are invited to, "Come near to God and he will come near to you" (James 4:8). Hebrews 4:16-17 encourages us to come boldly or fearlessly and confidently to God's throne to find help in our time of need. Some Christians come humbly with heads hung low, afraid to ask God to meet their needs. This often indicates a lack of faith. Others pray frivolously, giving little thought to what they say, which reveals their shallowness.

Come with reverence because we are coming to Almighty God who proved His love for us. He is our King. But come with bold assurance because He is your Friend. Jesus said, "You are my friends if you do what I command you. I no longer call you servants, because a servant does not know his master's business. Instead, I have called you friends, for everything that I have learned from my Father I have made known to you" (John 15:14-15). Note the condition to having Jesus as our friend. You are my friends if—that little word is crucial—if you do what I command you. It's up to us; we can be as close to God as we want to be.

Someone said, "We first know God as our Creator, then we know Him as our Savior, and grow to serve Him as our Lord. Over time, our personal relationship with Him deepens as we experience Him as Father. But few of us know Him as Friend." A friend is someone who takes time to understand me and love me. Do you know Jesus as your friend? So many who would identify themselves as Christians know about Him, but don't know Him.

Jesus said, "The sheep listen to the gate keeper's voice. He calls his own sheep by name and leads them out . . . He goes on ahead of them, and his sheep follow him because they know his voice" (John 10:3-4). Again, Jesus said, "Come to me, all you who are weary and burdened, and I will give you rest. Take my yoke upon you and learn from me, for I am gentle and humble in heart, and you will find rest for your souls. For my yoke is easy and my burden is light" (Matthew 11:28-30).

"The Spirit you received does not make you slaves, so that you live in fear, rather the Spirit you received brought about your adoption to sonship. And by him we cry, 'Abba, Father'" (Romans 8:15). We cry Daddy, Daddy! We are adopted into His family which means Jesus is our older brother. (Hebrews 2:11). Jesus said, "Whoever does the will of my Father in heaven is my brother and sister and mother" (Matthew 12:50).

"There is no fear in love. But perfect love drives out fear, because fear has to do with punishment. The one who fears is not made perfect in love" (I John 4:18). We love Him because He first loved us. Live in His amazing love. How blessed we are that we live after Pentecost rather than before when God's people could barely see the ark. Live in this intimate relationship with Jesus.

"The Lord is near to all who call upon Him, to all who call upon Him in truth" (Psalm 145:18).

IV.

OUR AMAZING POSITION IN CHRIST

THE TRINITY LIVES IN US
JOHN 14:8-17

Can there be anything more amazing than the fact that the triune God lives in us? It seems impossible. In our culture it's becoming common to doubt there is a god or if people believe there is a god, they believe there are many ways to God. Muslims pray to their god. Buddhists pray to their many gods. Hindus have hundreds of gods.

It's interesting that more than half of those who call themselves atheists, who say there is no god, or agnostics who say we can't know if there is a god, more than half of these persons admit they pray to someone. We are born with an innate desire to give allegiance to God. When we see His creation, it points clearly to a creator.

Speaking of Jesus' entrance into the world John says, "The true light that gives light to everyone was coming into the world" (John 1:9). We are all made in the image of God. (Genesis 1:27). This means we have the breath of life and are eternal beings. (Genesis 2:7). "God has set eternity in the human heart" (Ecclesiastes 3:11). There is restlessness in everyone until we find rest in God. (Isaiah 26:3).

The Psalmist says: "As the deer pants for streams of water, so my soul pants for streams of water, my soul pants for you, my God. My soul thirsts for God, for the living God" (Psalm 42:1-2). "I open my mouth and pant, longing for your commands" (Psalm 119:131). "Your statutes are my heritage forever; they are the joy of my heart" (Psalm 119:111). "My whole being longs for you. Earnestly I seek you" (Psalm 63:1). "Your face, Lord I will seek" (Psalm 27:4). "Seek him while he may be found, call upon him while he is near" (Isaiah 55:6). "You will seek me and find me when you seek me with all your heart" (Jeremiah 29:13).

We are exceedingly blessed to live after the coming of Jesus. It is much easier for me to identify with God when I realize Jesus is God. "Jesus moved into our neighborhood" (John 1:14 Msg.). He understands since he walked where we walked. This realization is possible because the Holy Spirit makes real to me what Jesus and the Father have done for me.

Jesus is not only with us, around us, over us, upon us but IN us. Listen to these wonderful words; just a few hours before Jesus went to the cross He said to Philip: "I will send you another comforter, the Spirit of truth, he will be with you forever" (John 14:16). We can't imagine what those words must have sounded like to Philip. Jesus says to Philip, you will know the comforter because he will live with you and will be in you. Amazing, Jesus and His Spirit living in Philip. Shocking, unimaginable, Jesus' Spirit is living in you! (John 14:17). Jesus promised Philip, and the disciples, I will never leave you as orphans. Jesus is saying to Philip, when Pentecost comes, you will realize that I am in my Father and you are IN me and I am IN you! Someone has said, "So nigh, so very nigh to God, I cannot nearer be, for in the person of his Son, I am as near as he."

Just before the cross Jesus said, "I assure you, most solemnly I tell you, if anyone steadfastly believes in me, he will himself be able to do the things that I do; and he will do even greater things than these, because I go to the Father" (John 14:12 AMP). That happened at Pentecost when 3,000 people came into God's kingdom. It is happening every day around the world.

Are you aware that Jesus is IN you; living through you this very moment and that you are IN Him? You may say, "I have heard that hundreds of times." But are you conscious of Jesus living IN you? Have you thought about it today? Being conscious of Jesus living IN you will affect your thoughts, your attitude, and your speech. It will show in your face. Yes, it will even show in how you walk. You can't hide it. Jesus IN you will transform you!

Jesus did only what the Father did and said only what the Father told Him to say. We have the same Holy Spirit Jesus had so claim these promises for yourself. (John 5:19 & 12:49). Stop making excuses but believe. He wants to tell us what to say and how to say it. In this world we are like Jesus. (I John 4:17).

Jesus said, anyone who loves Me, will obey Me. My Father will love them and WE, WE will come to them and make our home IN them. Not only is Jesus living in us but God, our Father is living in us.

Jesus and His Father are one, therefore if one is in us, so is the other. If only we would remember that Jesus and God are in us, life would be a constant adventure. Dare I let God be to me all that the Scripture says He is to me?

A glove can do nothing. But put your hand in the glove and it can do whatever you can do. We are the glove. Apart from Jesus we can do nothing. (John 15:5). When Jesus is in us, we can do whatever Jesus can do. In fact, Jesus said we can do greater things than He did. (John 14:12). "If we live in him, we must live as Jesus lived" (I John 2:6).

We are told 216 times in the New Testament that we are IN Jesus and He is IN us. We still forget. It's one of the most difficult truths to remember. Colossians 3:3, is one of my favorite scriptures: "Your life is now hidden with Christ in God." "Anyone who loves me will obey my teaching. My Father will love them and we will come to them and make our home with them" (John 14:23).

First John 2:23-25, if you abide by what you heard – if you obey my teachings you will remain IN the Son and IN the Father and you will have eternal life. "If anyone acknowledges that Jesus is the Son of God, God lives IN them and they in God" (I John 4:15). Reading these verses, it's easy to see why John is Jesus' beloved disciple. (John 20:2). Oh that we would believe as John believed.

Can you imagine anything overcoming you since you are both in Jesus Christ the Messiah and in God our Heavenly Father? Could there be any place more secure? Can you imagine a person worrying about their situation if they know they are hidden in Christ and in God, the Father and Creator of the universe? God proves His loving care for you by giving His Only Son to pay for your sin.

Now let God's promises amaze you even more: Not only are we IN the Son and IN the Father but we are IN the Holy Spirit. It seems more appropriate to say, the Holy Spirit is IN us but both are true. "You, as Christians, are not in the flesh, you are in the realm of the Holy Spirit. If anyone does not have the Holy Spirit of Christ, they do not belong to Christ. But if Christ is IN you, then even though your body is subject to death because of sin, the Holy Spirit gives life . . . And if the Holy Spirit of God who raised Jesus from the dead is living IN you, God who raised Christ from the dead will also give life to your mortal bodies, because of the Holy Spirit who lives IN you" (Romans 8:9-11).

Most Christians live with a Holy Spirit deficit disorder. It is simpler to understand God the Father and Jesus living in us because we can picture them in our minds. The Holy Spirit is more mystical. I thank God often throughout the day for His Spirit that directs my steps guiding me to the people I need to meet. I pray often for the Holy Spirit to direct my mind and my tongue. "This is what we speak, not in words taught us by human wisdom but words taught by the Spirit, explaining spiritual realities with Spirit-taught words" (I Corinthians 2:13). Acts 1:8 is critical for our daily living: "You will receive power when the Holy Spirit comes on you; and you will be my witnesses . . . If anyone speaks, they should do so as one who speaks the very words of God" (I Peter 4:11).

Whenever I announced the attendance in a church I pastored a dear saint made it a habit to remind us that there were three more present than the number announced: Father, Son and Holy Spirit.

Let's pray for each other as Paul prayed for the Galatians: "My dear children, for whom I am again in the pains of childbirth until Christ is formed IN you" (Galatians 4:19). Christ in us is so basic and necessary that Paul agonizes and suffers as one going through birth pains to see that Jesus is formed in them.

I pray that this teaching will help you remember that you are IN Jesus and Jesus is IN you, you are IN God and God lives IN you, you are IN the Holy Spirit and the Holy Spirit lives IN you. Can there be anything more amazing! Thank and praise the triune God today and throughout eternity for the Father, Son and Holy Spirit: all three living in you. No wonder you are a new creation in Christ Jesus.

THE AMAZING WORD "IN"
JOHN 15:1-17

In no other passage in Jesus' teaching is their repetition like in John 15. Repetition indicates emphasis and importance. Jesus uses the same Greek word, (*meno*), 11 times in verses 4-11 to describe our relationship with Him. It's translated different ways in various versions: abide in Jesus, remain in Jesus, dwell in Jesus, stay in Jesus, be vitally united with Jesus, live your life in Jesus, make your home in Jesus and grow in Jesus.

Can anything be more important or more intimate? How did Jesus remain in the Father? If we can discover how Jesus remained in the Father it will help us to understand how we can remain in Jesus.

Jesus said, "The Son can do nothing by himself; he can do only what he sees his Father doing, because whatever my Father does the Son also does" (John 5:19). "I do nothing on my own but speak just what the Father has taught me . . . I always do what pleases him" (John 8:28-29; 2:49-50; 14:31).

For years I have prayed daily that I would say and do only what my Father wants me to say and do. I am far from perfect but it is exciting to experience the intimate relationship that Jesus had with His Father.

The key to abiding in Jesus is stated in John 15:10: "If you obey my commandments, you will remain in my love, just as I have kept my Father's commands and remain in his love." It's repeated in 14:15, "If you love me, keep my commands." Jesus is clear, obeying His commands is how we remain in His love and remain in Him.

Constantly examine yourself, "Am I doing things Jesus does not want me to do, or am I not doing what I know I should be doing?" If you are not doing what you know you should be doing or doing things you know you shouldn't be doing confess them as sin, receive His forgiveness and vow to be obedient. Never excuse your "little sins," or your idiosyncrasies by saying, "I can't help it, that's just who I am." There is no such thing as partial obedience—it's only when all we have is Christ that we can really know Christ.

I grew up with a motto hanging on the wall of my bedroom, which had a great influence on my life: "Say nothing you would not want to be saying when Jesus comes. Do nothing you would not want to be doing when Jesus comes and do not be where you should not be when Jesus comes." This motto helps me to be conscious that no matter what I say or do Jesus is there. It is even more helpful to put the motto in positive terms: Say only what you should be saying when Jesus comes, do only what you should be doing when Jesus comes and be where you should be when Jesus comes.

Jesus says in John 15:2, "The Father cuts off every branch in me that bears no fruit, while every branch that does bear fruit, he prunes so that it will be even more fruitful." If orchards are left un-pruned the harvest is very disappointing. We need pruning daily because we have thoughts that are not lined up with our Father's will. Do we love God with all our heart? What about loving our neighbor or our enemy as Jesus commands?

Jesus says, (vv. 1-2), "I am the true vine, and my Father is the Gardner, he cuts off every branch in me, – the me refers to Jesus, – he cuts off every branch in me that bears no fruit, while every branch that does bear fruit, he prunes so that it will be even more fruitful." You may be surprised that the Father pruned Jesus. (v. 2). If Jesus needed to be pruned how much more do you and I need to be pruned! Hebrews 5:8 verifies the Father's pruning, "Jesus learned obedience from what he suffered." Learning is a process. Pruning is an ongoing painful process. Since Jesus experienced pruning He can understand every temptation we will ever face. He is truly our sympathetic priest, representing us to our Father. (Hebrews 4:14-16).

When did the Father prune Jesus? I believe Jesus experienced pruning when He, "often withdrew to lonely places and prayed" (Luke 5:16). Pruning frequently occurs in our prayer closet. After walking with Jesus for 70 years I still need pruning.

In John 15:7 Jesus gives us an incredible promise: "If you remain in me and my words remain in you, ask whatever you wish and it will be done for you." It's crucial to understand that He will give us what we wish, only if we remain in Him and His words remain in us. Is God's Word remaining in you? Ask God to give you a hunger for His word.

For God's Word to dwell in us a verse a day read from a 3 x 5 card stuck to your mirror will not suffice. Saturate your mind with God's Word until you can recall the essence of it throughout the day. Read long passages of the Bible. On the other hand, meditating on a single verse can impact your life. Your goal is to know Jesus, not simply to know about Him. Pulling a verse out here and there is fine but you will never develop maturity unless you saturate your mind with God's living word applying it to your life 24/7. What did Jesus do when He was tempted? He quoted the Word of God. Many scholars believe He memorized the complete Torah or five books of Moses.

As a mentor I met with Joe for about eighteen months. Joe is a very successful Christian businessman with many employees. It is disappointing to report that Joe would spend far more time digesting the daily news than digesting God's Word. Joe will never find the joy and peace that awaits him until he makes Jesus and His word a higher priority.

Paul instructs Timothy: "Study to be eager to do your upmost to present yourself to God approved, a working who has no cause to be ashamed, directing, analyzing and accurately dividing – rightly handling and skillfully teaching the word of truth" (II Timothy 2:15 AMP). When we are full of God's Word, we can't help but declare praise to God who called you out of darkness into His wonderful light. (I Peter 2:9).

We do not worship a book. We worship a person, Jesus! Jesus said to the Pharisees, "You diligently study the scriptures because you think that by them you possess eternal life. These are the scriptures that testify about me, yet you refuse to come to me to have life" (John 5:39-40). I'm sure there are pastors like the Pharisees as well as many Christians who know the facts of the word but they don't know Jesus.

The word must dwell in us so our lives line up with God's will, then we can ask what we want and God will give it to us. (John 15:7). The key is we only ask what is His will. There will be times when we think we know His will but the timing is not God's timing. Other times the situation is beyond our understanding and we learn to trust Him knowing that all things will work for good. (Romans 8:28). In every dark valley of life, when the answerer is delayed, God will grant us peace because we have learned to trust Him when we don't understand Him. When we can't see His hand, we can trust His heart.

Praying continually and abiding in Jesus are two sides to the same coin. Talk to God just as you talk to yourself. "Be alert and always keep on praying for all the Lord's people" (Ephesians 6:18).

The early church joined together constantly in prayer. (Acts 1:14). Today so few meet together to pray because we do not have a burden for the lost, or the faith to believe your prayers will be answered. We have allowed the devil to rob us of our passion, which is to love God and others with all our heart. For what shall we pray? There are always obvious needs: Ask God to raise up the leaders He wants in office, and to bring down the leaders He doesn't want in office. (I Timothy 2:1-2). Two billion people have never heard the name of Jesus. Jesus commands us to pray for workers to bring in the harvest. (Matthew 9:37). Pray for the Bible to be translated in their language. Millions are being persecuted in over 100 countries. Pray for the multitudes that need clean water and healthy food.

The devil will bring 101 things to your mind so you forget to pray. Many of the things he brings to mind may be good but they are not what is God's best for you at the moment. The devil may convince you that working overtime, playing a game, putting a puzzle together, watching the TV, or reading a good book is more important than meeting with a few followers of Jesus to pray for the needs of our world.

If we learn that a close friend has been in an accident and is in intensive care or our grandchild is in the hospital with a life-threatening illness we will pray. However, might it be just as important to pray for lost family members, neighbors and those who do not know Jesus? The Apostle Paul says, "For I could wish that I myself were cursed and cut off from Christ for the sake of my people" (Romans 9:2-3). With the disciples we say: "Teach us to pray!" (Luke 11:1-13).

ONE STEP BELOW THE ANGELS
PSALM 8:6-9

Are you aware of angels? There are over 280 verses in the Bible that directly mention angels. There are probably at least that many more that speak of angels indirectly by calling them by another name such as seraphim and cherubim, archangels, mighty ones, and living creatures.

"You have made us a little lower than the angels, and crowned us with glory and honor. You made us rulers over the works of your hands, you put everything under our feet: all flocks and herds, and the animals of the wild, the birds in the sky, and the fish in the sea, all that swim the paths of the seas. Lord, our Lord, how majestic is your name in all the earth!" (Psalm 8:6-9).

John says in Revelation, "I heard around the throne the living creatures and the elders the voice of many angels, numbering myriads of myriads and thousands of thousands." (5:11).

In a similar passage in Hebrews 12:22-23, angels join us in worship: "we have come to Mount Zion and to the city of the living God, the heavenly Jerusalem, and to thousands upon thousands of angels in joyful assembly, to the church of the firstborn whose names are written in heaven . . ." Can you imagine being in a choir of millions of angels and millions of our brothers and sisters who love the Lord? Just to imagine being in that multitude should send chills up and down our backs. That's much greater than being surrounded by 75,000 sports fans at a stadium.

"To which of the angels did God ever say, 'Sit at my right hand until I make your enemies a footstool for your feet?' Are not all angels ministering spirits sent to serve those who will inherit salvation?" (Hebrews 1:13-14). Angels serve us. Angels long to look into things that pertain to our salvation. (I Peter 1:12). We are compared to the heavenly being that surround God's throne. (Isaiah 6:2-3; Revelation 4:6-

9). Isaiah saw the seraphim calling to one another, "Holy, holy, holy is the Lord Almighty; the whole earth is full of his glory." Paul was aware of the authority of angels as he, "charges Timothy, in the sight of God and Christ Jesus and the elect angels to keep these instructions on Christian living without partiality" (I Timothy 5:21).

What do angels do for us? Hebrews 1 says angels are ministering spirits sent to serve those who will inherit salvation. One night I was driving in torrents of rain. My car hydroplaned. I was headed straight into a tractor-trailer. The brakes seemed to speed up the car instead of slowing it. I shouted, "Jesus! Jesus! Jesus!" The car miraculously was moved several feet avoiding a collision. How thankful I am for angels. I believe this is one of the numerous times God's angels have protected and guided me. I feel certain the Lord's angels watched over me as I drove considerable distances after dark on wet, even icy roads. I praise God for His guarding angels.

Children are important to God. Jesus said, "Let the little children come to me, and do not hinder them, for the kingdom of heaven belongs to such as these" (Matthew 19:14). Children have angels watching over them. Jesus said, "See that you do not despise one of these little ones. For I tell you that their angels in heaven always see the face of my Father in heaven" (Matthew 18:10-11). What a contrast to our culture where children are often not wanted and even aborted. Many children are caught in the crossfire of adults expressing their anger in their homes and on the streets.

Before there were seatbelts, as a small child I was standing between the front and back seat of our car. As the car went around a curve, I fell against the car door handle. Instantly my father reached over the seat and grabbed me before I landed on the road. I believe God's guarding angel kept me from injury.

Jesus said, "there will be more rejoicing in heaven over one sinner who repents than over ninety-nine righteous persons (self-righteous) who do not need to repent" (Luke 15:7, 10). Apparently, the angels and those who have gone before us can see us or why would they be able to celebrate when we repent? That should encourage us in our daily walk.

When Peter and the Apostles were put in prison for preaching the Gospel an angel of the Lord opened the doors and brought them out so they could "tell the people all about this new life" (Acts 5:19-20). Again, in Acts 12:7-10, when Peter was in prison because of preaching the Gospel the angel woke him up, removed his chains and opened the doors of the prison setting him free.

Angels excel in strength. "Praise the Lord, you mighty ones who do his bidding, who obey his word" (Psalm 103:20). David prays: "May those who seek my life be disgraced and put to shame . . . May they be like chaff before the wind with the angel of the Lord driving them away; . . . with the angel of the Lord pursuing them" (Psalm 35:4-6). The Egyptian pharaoh finally released the Children of Israel after 430 years of slavery because the angel struck down the firstborn of the Egyptians, both humans and animals while passing over God's people who placed the blood of the lamb on the sides and top of their door-frame. (Exodus 12:23, I Corinthians 10:10). The common estimates of the number of persons who came through the Red Sea are between four and six million people. A conservative estimate of the firstborn Egyptians who were killed would be ½ million to a million.

Another sign of their power occurred against the Assyrians who tortured their prisoners for entertainment. God sent the angel of the Lord who put to death 185,000 Assyrians in one night. (II Kings 19:35).

After David's sin of pride led him to take a census of his military resources 70,000 people died. Then the angel stretched out his hand to destroy Jerusalem but the Lord relented stopping the angel. (II Samuel 24:16). King Nebuchadnezzar made an image of gold but the three Hebrew children, Shadrach, Meshach and Abednego refused to bow to the image. The king had them thrown into the fiery furnace. The next morning the king found them alive since God sent His angel to rescue them. (Daniel 3:28). When King Darius had Daniel thrown into the lion's den because he would not bow down to the king the angel delivered Daniel from the lions. (Daniel 6:22).

We are encouraged to minister to others who may be "angels" of whom we are "unaware." (Hebrews 13:2). Angels frequently appear in the form of adult men. Abraham did not recognize the men who appeared to him as angels. (Genesis 18:1-8; v. 22; 19:1-3). He had a servant bring water for them to wash their feet and relax while his household prepared a meal for them to eat. Apparently, they have a heavenly body like Jesus who also ate after he had arisen. (John 21:10-13). The angels left Abraham, and went on their way to destroy Sodom but not before they rescued Lot and his family. (Genesis 18:22; 19:1-3).

Angels carried God's message to Jacob. "Jacob left Beersheba and set out for Haran to escape from Laban. He stopped for the night and took a stone, put it under his head and lay down. He had a dream in which he saw a stairway resting on the earth, with its top reaching to heaven, and the angels of God were ascending and descending on it. There above it stood the Lord, and he said: 'I am the Lord. . . . I will give you and your descendants the land on which you are lying. . . . All peoples on earth will be blessed through you and your offspring'" (Genesis 28:10-15).

The Old Testament Law was given through angels. (Galatians 3:19). "Since the message spoken through angels was binding, and every violation and disobedience received its just punishment, how shall we escape if we ignore so great a salvation?" (Hebrews 2:2-3).

We do not worship angels. When John was about to worship an angel, the angels said: "Don't do that! I am a fellow servant with you . . . worship God" (Revelation 19:10). Angels are intelligent and have moral discernment. However, there are also many evil angels, Jude 1:6, "The angels who did not keep their positions of authority . . . he has kept in darkness, bound with everlasting chains of judgment of the great Day." Apparently, we will judge these (evil) angels. (I Corinthians 6:3).

Each church in Revelation 2 and 3 had an angel who carried the message to the church. Since these seven churches had an angel over them, I believe our churches today have angels watching over them.

Angels play a prominent role in God's judgment. Angels appear 80 or more times in the Book of Revelation. Could it be that God uses His angels to carry out judgment because they have never experienced salvation? They were in heaven before we were created and therefore cannot understand the great love God has for us and His creation here on earth. When they see the sin of humanity, they cannot imagine how anyone could possibly turn their backs on God's great love and blessings. Therefore, they have no mercy when God assigns them to carry out His wrath and judgment. On the other hand, angels delight to minister mercy, protection and assistance to God's faithful children because they see how Jesus loves His children.

When Jesus returns, "he shall send his angels with a loud trumpet call, and they shall gather the elect from the four winds, from one end of heaven to the other" (Matthew 24:31).

David lived with a consciousness of the presence of angels. "He will command his angels concerning you to guard you in all your ways" (Psalm 91:11). "The angel of the Lord encamps (guards NLT) around those who fear him and he delivers (rescues) them" (Psalm 34:7). How blessed we are to know that angels guard us in all our ways.

YOU ARE GREATER THAN ABRAHAM AND MOSES
MATTHEW 11:11

Matthew 11:11 is one of the most "unbelievable" verses in the Bible. This verse more than any other prompted me to write this book. Jesus said, "Truly I tell you, among those born of women there has not risen anyone greater than John the Baptist, yet whoever is least in the kingdom of heaven is greater than he." I lived with an inferiority complex: I stuttered as people laughed. Anyone with an inferiority complex needs to ask the Holy Spirit to open his or her eyes to see what this verse is saying. You will never be the same.

Can you imagine that you are greater than Abraham, Isaac, Jacob, Moses, David, Isaiah, Daniel and all the Old Testament prophets? It sounds blasphemous to even think that the least significant person in God's New Testament Kingdom is greater than all these Old Testament prophets. For instance, Elijah is known as a great man of prayer resulting in many amazing miracles but James reminds us, Elijah was a human being just like us. (James 5:17-18). How could I be greater than Elijah who stood up against 850 prophets of Baal and caused it to rain following a three-year drought? (I Kings 18:38).

How could we be greater than Moses who led his people, several million strong, through the Red Sea or spoke face to face with God on Mount Sinai, or David who slew the nine-foot giant and destroyed the opposing army or Daniel who survived the lion's den?

This scripture is possible because through the death and resurrection of Jesus and the coming of the Holy Spirit, God lives in us continually. At Pentecost God sent His Holy Spirit to make real for us what Jesus did for us. The Old Testament prophets, as well as John the Baptist, did not have the continual abiding presence of God's Holy Spirit as we do in the New Testament. Jesus underscored the truth of this scripture when He said, "Whoever believes in me will do the works I have been doing, and they will do even greater things than these, because I am going to the Father" (John 14:12). We are in him and he in us. (John 15:4-8). This was not true for those before Christ. Now he will never leave us or forsakes us. (Hebrews 13:5).

John the Baptist was a friend of the bridegroom (John 3:29) while we are a participant with the bridegroom. (Ephesians 5:25-27, 30, 32). We are engaged now but at the Lord's return we will be married to Him. In ancient Jewish culture a man initiated the process of getting married by pledging his life to his prospective bride on the condition that she will accept his offer and reciprocate his love and pledge. This is what God does for us in Christ. Jesus' incarnation, ministry and death on our behalf is God's declaration of love toward us. How can we not love and serve Him?

John the Baptist lived under the Old Covenant, which could not take away sin. We have the marvelous privilege of living under the New Covenant, which is far superior because it is found on the finished work of Messiah Jesus who is the perfect sacrifice for our sins and the sins of the world. (John 1:29). "Jesus guarantees the effectiveness of this better (New Testament) covenant" (Hebrews 7:22 NLT).

After listing "God's Hall of Faith" in Hebrews 11 the author writes: "These were all commended for their faith, yet none of them received what had been promised, since God had planned something better for us so that only together with us would they be made perfect" (v. 40). At the final judgment God will reward both the Old and New Testament saints together. God will not reward us until the final judgment because the fruit of all of our works will not be known until that Great Day! This should give us tremendous incentive to serve our Lord with zeal until our dying breath. (Romans 12:11).

Since we are greater than the Old Testament saints it should buoy our spirits and raise our faith level enabling us to be a powerful witness for our Lord serving Him with all our heart, soul, mind, and strength. Consider the message of these following verses, which were veiled from the eyes of the Old Testament saints. "He has brought you back as his friends. He has done this through his death on the cross in his own human body. As a result, he has brought you into the very presence of God, and you are holy and blameless as you stand before him without a single fault" (Colossians 1:22 NLT). "May he strengthen your hearts so that you will be blameless and holy in the presence of our God and Father when our Lord comes with all his holy ones" (I Thessalonians 3:13). "May God sanctify (made you holy), through and through. May your whole spirit, soul and body be kept blameless at the coming of our Lord Jesus Christ. The one who calls you is faithful, and he will do it" (I Thessalonians 5:23-24).

"If the old covenant which brings condemnation was glorious how much more glorious is the new covenant, which makes us right with God! In fact, that first glory was not glorious at all compared with the overwhelming glory of the new covenant. So, if the old covenant which has been set aside was glorious, then the new covenant, which remains forever, has far greater glory. Since this new covenant gives us such confidence, we can be very bold. We are not like Moses, who put a veil over his face so the people of Israel would not see the glory fading away . . . This veil can be removed only by believing in Christ. Yes, even today when they read Moses' writing, their hearts are covered with that veil and they do not understand. But when anyone turns to the Lord, then the veil is taken away. Now the Lord is the Spirit, and whenever the Spirit of the Lord is, he gives freedom. And all of us have had the veil removed so that we can be mirrors that brightly reflect the glory of the Lord. And as the Spirit of the Lord works within us, we become more and more like him and reflect his glory even more" (II Corinthians 3:9-18 NLT).

The moonlight is wonderful, the old covenant was wonderful but when the sun, representing the new covenant comes out, the moonlight is overpowered by the sunlight. We live in the sunlight (Sonlight) of God's presence so we are blessed beyond Moses and all the Old Testament heroes. Live in the Sunlight (Sonlight) and come boldly and with confidence to God's throne of grace. Cast all your anxiety, fears, cares, troubles, and disturbing thoughts on the Lord. "Our faces show the bright glory of the Lord, as the Lord's Spirit makes us more and more like our glorious Lord" (II Corinthians 3:18 NLT).

BETTER THAN A BOX SEAT
EPHESIANS 2:6-7

Not only does God save us because of His mercy, not only are we greater than Abraham and all the Old Testament saints, but God "raised us up with Christ and seated us with him in the heavenly realms in Christ Jesus, in order that in the coming ages he might show the incomparable riches of his grace expressed in his kindness to us in Christ Jesus" (Ephesians 2:6-7). I remember vividly sitting in a seminary classroom some 60 years ago when I became conscious of what this verse was saying. It has fascinated and mesmerized me ever since. Seldom does a day go by that I don't meditate on this verse.

The *Amplified Bible* makes it even more dramatic: "God raised us up together with Jesus and made us sit down together – giving us joint seating with Him – in the heavenly sphere [by virtue of our being] in Christ Jesus, the Messiah the Anointed One. He did this that he might clearly demonstrate through the ages to come the immeasurable (limitless, surpassing) riches of His free grace in kindness and goodness of heart toward us in Christ Jesus" (Ephesians 2:6 AMP).

"To the one who is victorious. I will give the right to sit with me on my throne, just as I was victorious and sat down with my Father on his throne" (Revelation 3:15-21).

We have absolutely no right to this seat beside Christ; it is a gift from God because of what Jesus has done for us. Just as we can't understand our new life in Christ, (Ephesians 2:4-5), we can't comprehend the invitation to sit beside Christ in the heavenly realms. Can you imagine sitting beside the President of the United States? Sitting beside the President is not worth comparing to sitting beside Jesus the Messiah.

"Jesus was taken up into heaven and he sat at the right hand of God" (Mark 16:19). You are in the seat beside Christ. Knowing and believing this will enable you to do and be what He wants you to be. Exercise your faith. Ask Jesus to give you the faith to see yourself and imagine yourself beside Jesus looking Him in the eye. Then take any questions, any situation that is frustrating you and thank Him for the fact that He is in control of all things and that He will make them work out for your best.

In this seat beside Christ we are, "one with him in spirit" (I Corinthians 6:17). We have the mind of Christ, (I Corinthians 2:16), the attitude of Christ, (Philippians 2:5), we are friends of Christ, (John 15:15). We are co-crucified, co-raised and co-exalted with Christ. (Romans 6:1-7). How can we take this seat and worry or be depressed? Worry is unbelief. Confess unbelief as sin and determine with God's grace to put it aside. If the issue keeps coming back, as it will, take it back to Jesus as often as it comes. (James 4:8). Don't let Satan trick you by condemning yourself. When we sit beside Jesus there is no room for worry, feeling insecure or feelings of worthlessness.

Today when the judge takes his seat observers in the courtroom can take their seat. When the judge is seated it indicates authority and power. Matthew included this phrase just before he records Jesus' Sermon on the Mount in Matthew 5-7: "When Jesus saw the crowds, he went up on a mountainside and sat down" (Matthew 5:1). Jesus sitting adds to the authority of His teaching. This teaching has proved to be one of the most controversial portions of scripture through the centuries. Never dismiss this scripture to be applied to another time. It's for today. Because many have not taken Jesus' Sermon on the Mount seriously, we have an anemic faith and an insipid Christianity. Jesus said, "love your enemies and do good to those who hate you . . . pray for those who mistreat you . . . If anyone takes your coat do not withhold your shirt from them. . . . give to everyone who asks you . . ." (Luke 6:27-30). We need to take Jesus' message seriously and live by it daily. He would never ask us to do anything He will not empower us to do.

Seated beside Christ is a position of power. In humility and in boldness sit down beside Jesus and let Him give you whatever you feel you need. Claim Philippians 4:19, (*Amplified Bible*), "My God will liberally supply (fill to the full) your every need according to His riches in glory by Christ Jesus." Do you need strength? (Isaiah 40:30-31). Do you need peace? (Isaiah 26:3). Do you need a friend? (John 15:14). Do you need joy or any of the other fruit of the Spirit? He will give it to you if you ask, seek and knock. (Luke 11:9-13). You are complete in Christ. (Colossians 2:9-10). You are sanctified wholly, through and through. (I Thessalonians 5:22-23). He will do more through you than you can imagine. (Ephesians 3:20-21).

This scat is a foretaste of what awaits us in the future. If we endure, we will reign with Him. (II Timothy 2:11). If we are victorious, He gives us authority over the nations. (Revelation 2:26). If we are trustworthy in small matters, we will have authority over many people. (Luke 16:10). "To the one who is victorious, I will give the right to sit with me on my throne, just as I was victorious and sat down with my Father on his throne" (Revelation 3:21). For an expansion of this theme see section VII. Our Amazing Future, the essay on, "Reigning with Christ."

Why did God raise us up to sit with Christ? (Ephesians 1:6). "In order that in the coming ages he might show the incomparable riches of his grace, expressed in his kindness to us in Christ Jesus. For by grace you are saved . . ." (vv. 7-8). To whom is He going to show the richest of His grace? He will display it to everyone: "God exalted him (Jesus) to the highest place and gave him the name that is above every name, that at the name of Jesus every knee will bow, in heaven and on earth and under the earth, and every tongue acknowledge that Jesus Christ is Lord, to the glory of God the Father" (Philippians 2:9-10).

We will observe and be awed by the riches of God's grace throughout the coming ages, i.e. throughout eternity. Every knee, both righteous and unrighteous will behold God's incomparable riches of His grace. All nations, rulers, authorities, dominions, powers, spiritual forces of evil in the heavenly realms, and every name that is named in heaven and on earth will be awed throughout eternity at the kindness of the riches of God's grace.

David through the inspiration of the Holy Spirit speaks of the kindness of God's grace for all future generations: "Let this be written for a future generation, that a people not yet created may praise the Lord: The Lord looked down from his sanctuary on high; from heaven he viewed the earth, to hear the groans of the prisoners, to release those condemned to death. So the name of the Lord will be proclaimed in Zion and his praise in Jerusalem when peoples and the kingdoms assemble to worship the Lord" (Psalm 102:18-22).

Ephesians 2:6 uses all plural pronouns. It says, "we," that means we are there with all God's people. How can we not get along with each other when we are sitting beside Jesus? "We . . . form one body, and each member belongs to all the others" (Romans 12:5).

Jesus, help me to remember where I am seated. Amen. Claim your seat!

A FRUITFUL LIFE
JOHN 15:1-16

An important aspect of a meaningful life is to know you are useful; you are making a contribution that will last for eternity. Jesus promised, "I am the vine; you are the branches. If you remain in me and I in you, you will bear much fruit, apart from me you can do nothing . . . This is to my Father's glory, that you bear much fruit, showing yourselves to be my disciples" (John 15:5 and 8). "You did not choose me, but I chose you and appointed you so that you bear fruit – fruit that will last" (v. 16).

Jesus said, "You will bear much fruit," not, you might be fruitful. The condition is, we remain or abide in Him for apart from Him you can do nothing. (v. 5). Nothing is less than zero. We are totally help-less – every heartbeat, every breath, every cell in our body is dependent upon Him. Isaiah reminds us that all our righteous efforts (good works) are as filthy rags. (Isaiah 64:6). On the other hand, Romans 12:3 reminds us, "Be honest in your estimate of yourselves, measuring your value by how much faith God has given you." In God's eyes we are more precious than gold. (I Peter 1:18-19). We are so important that God gave His Only Son to redeem us.

"If you do not remain in me you are like a branch that is thrown away and withers, such branches are picked up, thrown into the fire and burned" (John 15:6). True believers are fruitful branches who abide in Christ and bear much fruit. Those who grow cold in their walk with Jesus or who have made a superficial commitment will be separated from the vine and burned. Peter says some have turned their back on God's commands, it's better for them not to have known the way of righteousness than to have known it and turned their backs on God's way. (II Peter 2:21). Paul says: "Some people eager for money have wandered from the faith, pierced themselves with many griefs, and have departed from the faith" (I Timothy 6:10, 21).

Jesus tells us how to have a rich and fruitful harvest. "I assure you, most solemnly I tell you, unless a grain of wheat falls the earth and died, it remains [just one grain; never becomes more but lives] by itself alone. But if it dies, it produces many others and yields a rich harvest" (John 12:24 AMP). Just as Jesus had to die, we must die to self in order to have a productive life.

What is the fruit Jesus is referring to? It includes Christ-likeness as expressed in Galatians 5:22-23. "The fruit of the Spirit is love, joy peace, patience, kindness, goodness, faithfulness, gentleness and self-control." It also undoubtedly includes winning people for Jesus. Jesus begins and ends His ministry by stating the fruit He expects. When Jesus called His first disciples He said, "Come follow me, and I will send you out to fish for people" (Mark 1:17). Before He returns to heaven He said, "Go into all the world and make disciples" (Matthew 28:19-20).

Immediately after Paul lists the fruit of the Spirit he writes: "Against these things there is no law" (Galatians 5:23). There is no law against having too much patience, too much joy, too much self-control, too much kindness, etc. We never think to tell our spouse, you have too much patience or too much self-control. What a wonderful freedom we have in Christ!

The fruit receives all its life from the branches. As branches we receive our life from the vine and the vine receives its life from the roots. It all goes back to the root. Is your life rooted in Christ? Paul prays, "that you, being rooted and established in love, may have power … to grasp how wide and long and high and deep is the love of Christ"

(Ephesians 3:17-18). A fruitful life is one that has its roots in Christ and remains in Him.

Peter uses a different imagery for being fruitful or productive: "make every effort to add to your faith, goodness, knowledge, self-control, perseverance, godliness and love. For if you possess these qualities in increasing measure, they will keep you from being ineffective and unproductive" (II Peter 1:5-8). To add these, Peter says we must make every effort. There is no conflict between Peter's admonition of making every effort and John's abiding in the vine. We abide in the vine not by being idle but by giving active obedience to the Holy Spirit. Athletes go into strict training to receive a crown that will last forever. (I Corinthians 9:25). We train by exercising obedience in all things. God empowers and enables us, but he also gives us the responsibility to learn and to grow. (II Peter 3:18).

If you have a cluster of grapes and one grape is rotten the whole cluster is affected. If you practice all the characteristics on Peter's list but one is missing, the whole cluster is not appealing. For example, if we have knowledge but lack self-control, we will turn people off. We might persevere but lack goodness or godliness. We can have peace but not be patient, which means our testimony is unfruitful. We don't finish one and start on the next; we work on these qualities all together.

One of our basis problems is that we want instant fruit. Peter lists perseverance as one of the qualities necessary for being fruitful. We must have a will to work. Laziness and fruitfulness never go together. James says perseverance will make us complete, lacking in nothing. (1:2-3).

Jesus gave different abilities to each one of us. The one who received one talent buried it. Jesus called him worthless and had him thrown outside where there will be weeping and gnashing of teeth. (Matthew 25:30). We must put to work whatever talents Jesus gives us keeping in mind that the fruit is not always obvious immediately.

Oswald Chambers emphasizes the process of being fruitful being just as important as the fruit. "God does not give us an overcoming life – he gives us life as we overcome. The strain is the strength. If there is no strain, there is no strength. Are you asking God to give you life and liberty and joy? He cannot, unless you will accept the strain. Immediately you face the strain, you will get the strength . . .

"We are apt to imagine that if Jesus Christ constrains us, and we obey him, he will lead us to great success. We must never put our dreams of success as God's purpose for us; his purpose may be exactly the opposite. We have an idea that God is leading us to a particular end, a desired goal; he is not . . . What we call the process, God calls the end. His purpose is that I depend on him and on his power now. If I can stay in the middle of the turmoil calm and unperplexed, that is the end of the purpose of God. . . . God's end is to enable me to see that he can walk on the chaos of my life just now. If we have a further end in view, we do not pay sufficient attention to the immediate present; but if we realize that obedience is the end, then each moment as it comes is precious." (Jim Denison's blog, July 29, 2020).

Tom worked in a factory surrounded by men who could be quite vulgar. But when Tom showed up their language changed. He had won their respect and was able simply by his presence to change the atmosphere of the group. Jesus says we are to be salt. A little salt changed the atmosphere of Tom's group. Be a salty Christian.

Different times I hear, "Be faithful, and don't be concerned about being fruitful." If we are faithful in serving our Lord, we will be fruitful even though we may not see the fruit in our lifetime. The fruit of our labors carries into eternity. "Whatever you do, work at it with all your heart, as working for the Lord, not for human masters, since you know that you will receive an inheritance from the Lord as a reward. It is the Lord Christ you are serving" (Colossians 3:23-24).

A JOYFUL LIFE
JOHN 15:11

Surveys report that only 14% of Americans are happy. This is the lowest since 1972 when this survey began. Happiness is temporary but God's joy is eternal. Most of Hollywood's humor and the jokes people tell are artificial and shallow, leaving you empty while God's joy is satisfying and fulfilling.

Happiness, or better yet joy, should be one of the very first adjectives that come to our mind when we think of Christians. Do you describe your life as joyful? "The kingdom of God is not a matter of eating and drinking, but of righteousness, peace and joy in the Holy Spirit," or as the KJV says, "joy unspeakable and full of glory" (Romans 14:17). Joy is an essential expression of God's Kingdom. Our eternal home is a place of joy. (Luke 15:7).

Peter described the persecuted Christians to whom he was writing as being filled with "an inexpressible and glorious joy" (I Peter 1:8). The fruit of the Spirit is love expressed in eight ways the first of which is joy. The words joy, rejoicing and joyful appear about 450 times in the Bible while happy or happiness about 30 times.

There are degrees of joy. Jesus' joy is complete joy or fullness of joy. Jesus instructed the disciples concerning the need to abide in Him so that His joy would be in them and their joy would be complete. (John 15:11). The *Amplified Bible* reads: "I have told you these things that my joy and delight may be in you, and that your joy and gladness may be full measure, complete and overflowing." Again, he says, "Ask and you will receive, and your joy will be complete" (John 16:24). In praying to His Father for us, He explains that He is leaving earth so that His disciples will have the full measure of His joy within them. (John 17:13).

Take note of the source of joy. It is not our joy. Jesus says it is His joy alive in us. Joy comes from being intimate with Jesus. In Luke 10:20 the disciples were joyful because of their successful missionary journey when they healed and cast out demons, but Jesus said they were not to rejoice in their success, rather "Rejoice that your names are written in heaven." Jesus is teaching us this joy originates more from our intimacy with Him, truly knowing Him than it does with a successful mission outreach. There are times when our mission efforts do not yield immediate fruit and therefore our joy may be depleted, but while abiding in Jesus our joy is consistent.

When our lives are intertwined with His, He will help us walk through adversity without sinking into debilitating lows and manage prosperity without moving into deceptive highs. The joy of living with Jesus daily will keep us levelheaded, no matter how high or low our circumstances. Oswald Chambers reminds us, "Once we are intimate with Jesus, we are never lonely and we never lack for understanding or compassion . . . A true Christian doesn't know the joy of the Lord in spite of tribulation, but because of it."

We also experience joy as we fellowship with other Christians. Paul longed to see Timothy so that he could be filled with joy. (II Timothy 1:4). Other Christians who walk faithfully with the Lord bring us joy. Paul says to the church at Rome that he rejoices because of their faith. (Romans 16:19).

Psalm 16:11 underscores Jesus' teaching: "You made known to me the path of life, you will fill me with joy in your presence, with eternal pleasures at your right hand." "My heart leaps for joy, and with my song I praise him" (Psalm 28:7). Joy appears 53 times in the Psalms. That's one reason we enjoy reading the Psalms. Joy, music and praise are triplets that characterize the true Christian. Isaiah says, "You will find your joy in the Lord, and he will cause you to ride in triumph on the heights of the land" (Isaiah 58:14). Again, he says in speaking of the Lord's favor, "Everlasting joy will be yours" (Isaiah 6:7). "The joy of the Lord will overtake them" (Isaiah 35:10 & 55:11). Habakkuk says that no matter how bad things are, "I will rejoice in the Lord. I will be joyful in God my Savior" (3:18). "The joy of the Lord is your strength" (Nehemiah 8:10).

When you rejoice in the Lord during times of sadness, a marvelous thing happens; this sacrifice of praise and trust in the Lord will lift you above your circumstances. This puts you on an upward path of gratitude where your joy increases step by step. (Hebrews 13:15).

Often, we are reluctant and inhibited from expressing joy because we feel we will embarrass others and ourselves. David frequently shouted, which is a stretch for our well-structured worship services. When the Holy Spirit is moving in powerful ways it is often expressed with audible praise. "I remember how I used to go to the house of God with shouts of joy and praise among the festive throng" (Psalm 42:4). "Shout for joy to the Lord, all the earth. Worship the Lord with gladness; come before him with joyful songs" (Psalm 100:1-2). "Shout for joy to the Lord, all the earth, burst into jubilant song with music; make music to the Lord with the harp, . . . with the blast of the ram's horn – shout for joy before the Lord, the King" (Psalm 98:4-6).

John the Baptist says he is full of joy when he hears the bridegroom's voice. "That joy is mine and it is now complete" (John 3:29). I experience joy as I read God's Word and realize I am hearing His voice as He opens my mind to new truths. When you experience God's direction in everyday matters life is joyful. The first result of being filled with the Holy Spirit results in a joyful melody in our heart. (Ephesians 5:18).

If you were to visit Peter or Paul in prison would you come away hanging your head feeling depressed? Peter was flogged but rejoiced that he was counted worthy to suffer for Christ. (Acts 5:40-41). Joy is given by the Holy Spirit even in the midst of suffering. (I Thessalonians 1:6). Paul from his prison cell says, "Rejoice in the Lord always. I will say it again: Rejoice!" (Philippians 4:4). "Rejoice always," he writes to the Thessalonians. (5:16). Paul rejoices and then adds, "Yes, I will continue to rejoice," even though the Gospel is preached from false motives. (Philippians 1:15-18).

The Galatians lost their joy because of legalism. Legalism brings guilt rather than God's forgiving love. It produces self-hatred because we can never measure up to its standards. Bathe your soul in God's marvelous love and grace and claim His joy.

Jesus says, "Blessed . . . [with life-joy and satisfaction in God's favor and salvation, regardless of your outward conditions] – are you when people revile you and persecute you and say all kinds of evil things against you falsely on my account. Be glad and supremely joyful, for your reward is in heaven is great (strong and intense), for in this same way people persecuted the prophets who were before you" (Matthew 5:11-12 AMP). Jesus is informing us that we are to be supremely joyful in persecution because our eternal reward is great. Another version says, "leap for joy." Paul and Silas experienced this joy after being beaten and thrown in prison. They sang as all the prisoners listened. (Acts 16:25). Jesus would not be commanding us to be joyful if it would not possible to experience His joy even in suffering.

James says that we are to consider it pure joy when we encounter trials of any kind because they help us mature. (James 1:2). "In the midst of a very severe trial, the Macedonian churches overflowed with joy and their extreme poverty welled up in rich generosity" (II Corinthians 8:2). The worship services where poverty is real are often filled with passionate prayer and joyful celebration of God's blessing.

Give full allegiance to the Lord so you can move from the empty fun of the world to experiencing the real joy Jesus has for you. Jesus promised rivers of living water will flow from Him to us by means of His Holy Spirit. (John 7:37-39). If you are lacking joy, ask God to fill you with His Holy Spirit. The fruit or result of the Holy Spirit is joy. (Galatians 5:22). Can you describe your life as joyful?

Barney Elliott Warren's hymn: "I have found the pleasure I once craved, it is joy and peace within; What a wondrous blessing, I am saved from the awful gulf of sin. I have found the joy no tongue can tell, how its waves of glory roll; It is like a great o'erflowing well, springing up within my soul. [Refrain] It is joy unspeakable and full of glory, full of glory. It is joy unspeakable and full of glory, Oh, the half has never yet been told."

75 Scriptures That Will Amaze You

V.

OUR AMAZING WALK IN CHRIST

A. WALKING WITH JESUS

WHAT'S YOUR IMAGE OF JESUS?
MATTHEW 16:13-16

"Jesus asked his disciples, 'Who do people say the Son of Man is?' They replied, 'Some say John the Baptist, others say Elijah; and still others, Jeremiah or one of the prophets.' 'But what about you?' he asked. 'Who do you say I am?' Simon Peter answered, 'You are the Messiah, the Son of the living God'" (Matthew 16:13-16).

We see Jesus as gentle and mild, which is correct. To any who are weary and burdened He invites to come to Him. "I am gentle and humble in heart, and you will find rest for your souls. For my yoke is easy and my burden is light" (Matthew 11:28-29). The artist depicts Jesus with children surrounding Him. The people brought their babies to be blessed by Him as He placed His hands on them. (Mark 10:16). "Jesus called the children to him and said, 'Let the little children come to me, and do not hinder them, for the Kingdom of God belongs to such as these'" (Luke 18:15-16). Jesus is also frequently pictured surrounded by sheep as He carries a lamb in His arms. (Luke 10:1-16).

In spite of these tranquil representations of Jesus the people thought of Him quite differently. Those who walked and lived with Jesus thought of Jesus being like His older cousin, John the Baptist. John the Baptist lived in the desert, slept out, and ate whatever he could find: locust and honey. He wore an everyday outfit made of camel's hair with a leather belt around his waist. As a fiery preacher, John addressed his audience: "You brood of vipers!" and warned them of the coming wrath and being thrown into the fire unless they repent. (Matthew 3:4-10).

Others said that Jesus was like Elijah, the most dramatic of Israel's prophets, calling down fire and destroying 850 false prophets of Baal and Asherah. He caused it to rain following a three-year drought. Still others said Jesus was like Jeremiah, whose life was constantly in danger.

Mark writes, "Jesus was in the wilderness 40 days, being tempted by Satan. He was with the wild animals and angels attended him" (Mark 1:12-13). Can you picture Jesus, 40 days and nights without food or water, trying to sleep in the desert with the wild animals circling around him?

Jesus' closest disciple was John the Apostle whom he called a "Son of Thunder." (Mark 3:17).Apparently, John was rather macho. John pictures Jesus as a sword coming from his mouth and with eyes of blazing fire. (Revelation 1:14-16). He depicts some horrific scenes of God's judgment not only in his Gospel, but also especially in the book of Revelation. Luke reminds us John and his brother James wanted to call fire down from heaven to consume the Samaritans because they did not welcome Jesus and the disciples. Jesus had to rebuke them. (Luke 9:52-55).

Many times, as people looked on in amazement, Jesus did not hesitate to confront the demons, demanding they depart. Jesus stood up against the strongest world power, the Roman rulers as well as those in the Sanhedrin, the top government body of His Jewish people. He called Herod "a fox" which could easily have resulted in the death sentence. (Luke 13:32). He expresses His anger with the Pharisees by deliberately calling the man with a withered hand to the front of the synagogue and healing him on the Sabbath. They were so angry they wanted to kill Him. (Mark 3:1-6).

The most well known image of Jesus expressing anger is when He made a whip and drove the sheep and cattle out of the temple because the Pharisees had made it a house of profit when it was to be known as a house of prayer. (John 2:13-17). At no point did Jesus endanger or harm humans (see John 2:15). What a powerful statement Jesus made as He confronted the establishment. Malachi pictures Jesus coming as a refiner's fire. (Malachi 3:2).

As soon as Jesus was baptized, He began His ministry with a very countercultural message: "Repent, for the kingdom of heaven has come near." (Matthew 4:17). While His loving kindness is evident throughout His life, especially to the marginalized, He vehemently denounced the religious leaders calling them hypocrites at least seven times in His long fiery sermon recorded in Matthew 23:1-38. On several occasions He spoke pointedly about their hypocrisy endangering His life.

In half of Jesus' parables, He speaks of judgment. For example, He says: "those enemies who did not want me to be king – bring them here and kill them in front of me" (Luke 19:27). Six times in Matthew Jesus speaks of weeping and gnashing of teeth. The book of Revelation depicts God and Jesus expressing their wrath. "The people tried to hide from the wrath of the Lamb" (Revelation 6:16). Jesus' brother, Jude, caught some of Jesus' fire. He wrote that, "these incidents recorded in his book serve as an example of those who suffer the punishment of eternal fire" (v. 7). Some came to the love feasts but were promoting false doctrine: "They are . . . wandering stars, for whom blackest darkness has been reserved forever" (v. 13).

Have you ever questioned why more women than men are disciples of our Lord? Emphasizing the gentler side of Jesus tends to appeal to women more than men. God formed woman out of man. Satan uses that fact to give men an inflated ego making it difficult for them to come to humility and repentance. Understanding this is no excuse for men not to come to Jesus. I draw attention to these scriptures relating to Jesus' boldness to call for a more balanced view of Jesus so that men are drawn to our Lord and Savior just as much as women.

Names help us form images of people. Jesus' favorite designation of himself is, "Son of Man" a term used 88 times in the New Testament. "Son of Man" is a title referring to the humanity of Jesus Christ while "Son of God" refers to His deity. Both terms were used of Christ because He was fully man and He was God. "The Son is the image of the invisible God . . . In him all things were created . . . through him and for him. He is before all things, and in him all things hold together . . . For God was pleased to have all his fullness dwell in him and through him to reconcile all things to himself" (Colossians 1:15-20).

Jesus was man: "His very birth was questioned, and his mother's reputation was slandered. He was born in poverty. His race was ostracized and his hometown ridiculed. His father probably died when Jesus was young, and in his later years Jesus traveled the streets and cities homeless. He was misunderstood in his ministry, and abandoned in death. He did all this for you and me. He did it to identify with us in weakness: 'We have a high priest who is able to sympathize with our weakness, but one who in every respect has been tempted as we are, yet without sin. Let us then with confidence draw near to the throne of grace, that we may receive mercy and find grace to help in time of need'" (Hebrews 4:15-16). (Floyd McClung in *The Father Heart of God*, Harvest House, p. 29-30).

No other religion has such a superb Savior and Lord. He is God's gift too wonderful to be expressed in words. (II Corinthians 9:15).

YOU ARE A NEW CREATION
II CORINTHIANS 5:14-17

Have you ever wished you could start all over again with a clean sheet? Jesus gives you that opportunity. "If anyone is in Christ, he is a new creation; the old has gone, the new has come" (II Corinthians 5:17). "Those who become Christians become new persons. They are not the same anymore, for the old life is gone. The new life has begun!" (NLT). We are made new in the attitude of our minds; and to put on the new self, created to be like God in true righteousness and holiness. (Ephesians 4:23-24). We have the mind of Christ. (I Corinthians 2:16). Our spirits are one with Jesus. (I Corinthians 6:17). We are full of love, joy, peace, patience . . . (Galatians 5:22-23). We are complete in Christ. (Colossians 2:10). We can't be any more perfect than we are in God's sight. (Hebrews 10:14). Our challenge is to live out these astonishing facts.

Why do we need to be told 216 times that we are in Christ or Christ is in us? We forget. We are focused on ourselves. Our self-centered nature centers everything around us—it's our time, our money, our wants, desires and goals. Everything is me, me, me. When we come to Christ, we move from being me-centered, to living for Christ. The difference is so great Jesus calls it a new birth. (John 3:3). Some describe this transformation as moving from a caterpillar to a butterfly.

Conversion must include transformation or it is not genuine conversion. Today we talk more about justification than about transformation. We tend to avoid transformation because it places more responsibility on us to grow in obedience in our walk with Jesus. Paul says that when he came to Christ his values changed radically. "What I once thought was valuable is worthless. Nothing is as wonderful as knowing Christ Jesus my Lord. I have given up everything else and count it all as garbage. All I want is Christ and to know that I belong to him" (Philippians 3:7-9).

In our new creation the old things are gone. The "old" refers to everything that is part of our old selfish nature – pride, love of sin, reliance on works, and our former opinions, habits and passions. The supreme love of self with its self-righteousness, self-promotion, and self-justification must die. As John the Baptist says, "He must increase and I must decrease" (John 3:30). "He must become greater and greater and I must become less and less" (NLT).

The Christian looks outwardly toward Christ instead of inwardly toward self. The old things are nailed to the cross. We delight in the things of God while the things of the world become empty, meaningless and even eventually repulsive. The new creation does not destroy the old but re-creates it. The new life overcomes the old! The pin oak tree hangs onto its leaves all winter until spring when the new leaves push off the old leaves. It the same with us. (Ephesians 4:22-24).

When we are truly converted or born from above, we see the world from a new perspective. Things that meant so much to us before have lost their attraction. The change amazes us. When Isaiah saw the Lord, he said, "The whole earth is full of God's glory" (Isaiah 6:3). There is a new compassion for even our enemies. (Matthew 5:44). We have a hunger for God's word. (Psalm 119:20). We hate what is evil and cling to what is good. (Romans 12:9).

Christians are being made holy (sanctified), as they throw off their sinful practices. Sanctification involves strict training. (I Corinthians 9:25). We are not perfect. We unwillingly and frequently sin. Our new self hates the sin that still has a hold on us. "If we died with Christ, we believe that we will also live with him . . . Count yourselves or (consider yourselves) dead to sin but alive to God in Christ Jesus" (Romans 6:8-11). Sin no longer has power over us. When the old life raises its head, claim God's Holy Spirit power to overcome the old self-centered ways. What an amazing transformation is ours! We have no more claim to our old life than a dead man has.

If you claim to know Jesus and are not experiencing this new life, open yourself to God's searchlight. Ask Him to examine your life to see if there is anything that is not pleasing to Him. Confess it as sin and accept His forgiveness and promise with the help of His Holy Spirit to walk in obedience. Or if you know that there are things you are neglecting to do that you know you should be doing, confess them as sin and with God's help make every effort to move ahead in obedience even though you feel fearful or uncomfortable. Don't make excuses! We are infinitely creative at making excuses. Are you wasting your time on frivolous pursuits? Give Jesus your energy, your money, your talents, your goals. He is Lord. You will not experience the amazing supernatural life of Jesus living in you if you are not all-in for Him. If you are lukewarm, He will vomit you out of His mouth. (Revelation 3:16). Walk in victory. (John 10:10).

Hymn writer Annie Fisher wrote 100 years ago: "God has not promised skies always blue, flower strewn pathways all our lives through; God has not promised sun without rain, joys without sorrow, peace without pain. But God has promised strength for the day, rest for the labor, light for the way, grace for the trials, help from above, unfailing sympathy, undying love."

"You need to draw a line in the sand. You need to put Isaac on the altar like Abraham. You need to throw down your staff like Moses. You need to burn your plowing equipment like Elisha. You need to climb the cliff like Jonathan. You need to get out of the boat like Peter. There comes a moment when you throw caution to the wind. There comes a moment when you need to go all in. There comes a moment when you need to burn the ships. This is that moment. This is your moment. It's all or nothing. It's now or never." (Mark Batterson, *All In*, Zondervan, p. 32).

Let the supernatural become natural.

EVERYTHING WE NEED IS PROVIDED
II PETER 1, I CORINTHIANS 3:21-23

"God's divine power has given us everything we need for a godly life through our knowledge of him who called us by his own glory and goodness" (II Peter 1:3). "Seek first the kingdom of God and his righteousness, and all these things (food, clothing, the necessities of life), will be given to you" (Matthew 6:33). What amazing promises! Can there be any room for discouragement?

David and Paul agree with Peter. David says, "The Lord is my Shepherd, I lack nothing" (Psalm 23:1). Paul says, "My God will meet all your needs according to the riches of his glory in Christ Jesus" (Philippians 4:19). Jesus said, "I tell you do not worry about your life, what you will eat or drink; or about your body what you will wear. Is not life more than food, and the body more that clothes?" (Matthew 6:25). "If you who are evil, know how to give good gifts to your children, how much more will your Father who is in heaven give good gifts to those who ask him!" (Matthew 7:11). Our Father in heaven will give His Holy Spirit to all who ask Him. (Luke 11:13). We can't ask for anything more than His Spirit living in us. As long as we are obedient to Him, we walk in His blessing and power. As soon as we do anything that is not pleasing to Him or don't do what He desires us to do, we grief His spirit and His Resurrection power cannot operate freely in us.

Peter says our provision comes through our knowledge of Christ. (II Peter 1:3). Peter ends his first letter commanding us to grow in our knowledge of our Lord Jesus Christ. (3:18). The knowledge spoken of in these verses is experiential knowledge, not merely head knowledge. One can memorize the scripture and not experience the power of the resurrected Christ. How many seminary professors or Bible teachers can quote scripture but do not walk with Christ? The Pharisees knew the scriptures but were far from the Kingdom of God. (John 5:39-40). "In Christ are hidden all the treasures of wisdom and knowledge" (Colossians 2:3). They are hidden, which means we need to persistently search to find them. The longer we search the greater the joy when we find them and live in them. The searching is an indication of our sincerity to follow Jesus.

Are you growing in the knowledge of Christ? Are you hungry for God's Word? God's Word is alive and active. (Hebrews 4:12). "All scripture is God-breathed and is useful for teaching, rebuking, correcting and training in righteousness so that the servant of God may be thoroughly equipped for every good work" (II Timothy 3:16-17). "Whatever we do, do it all for the glory of God" (I Corinthians 10:31). "Our greatest fear should not be of failure, but of succeeding at things that don't really matter." (Francis Chan).

God's fullness or completeness lives in Christ. In Christ we are brought to fullness. (Colossians 2:8-9). Our goal is to know more of Christ. He is our focus, not His gifts – of joy, or peace, or blessings but to know Him. Knowing Him, we will have all we could possibly need for living a godly victorious life. Your Father wants you to receive His love and to know that you are special and unique in His eyes.

Since God has made available everything we need for a godly life we have no excuse for living in defeat. We are commanded to be filled with the Spirit. The result of His fullness is the fruit of the Spirit: love, joy, peace, patience, kindness, goodness, faithfulness, gentleness and self-control. (Galatians 5:22-23). John assures us that greater is he who is in us than he who is in the world. (I John 4:4). "God has said, I will not in any way fail you nor give you up nor leave you without support.

I [will] not, [I will] not, [I will] not in any degree leave you helpless, nor forsake nor let [you] down, [relax my hold on you], Assuredly not!" (Hebrews 13:5 AMP). "God is able to bless you abundantly, so that in all things at all times, having all that you need, you will abound in every good work" (II Corinthians 9:8).

To the Corinthians Paul writes in broad sweeping terms leaving us no room to question his provision: "God has already given you everything you need. He has given you Paul and Apollos and Peter as your helpers. He has given you the whole world, and life and even death are your servants. He has given you all of the present and all of the future. All are yours, and you belong to Christ and Christ is God's" (I Corinthians 3:21-23 TLB). "If we are children, then we are heirs, co-heirs of God and co-heirs with Christ, if indeed we share in his sufferings in order that we may also share in his glory" (Romans 8:17).

Apply these verses and God's joy will not only catch up with you it will overtake you. (Isaiah 35:10 and 61:3). How can we not live a joyful life? "No matter how many promises God has made, they are 'Yes' in Christ" (II Corinthians 1:20). "Though you have not seen Jesus, you love him; and even though you do not see him now, you believe in him and are filled with an inexpressible and glorious joy, for you are receiving the end of your faith, the salvation of your souls" (I Peter 1:8-9).

A chorus that has greatly blessed me is: "Jesus Christ is made to me, all I need, all I need; he alone is all my plea, he is all I need. Jesus is my all in all, All I need, all I need; while he keeps, I cannot fall, he is all I need. Chorus: Wisdom, righteousness and power, holiness forevermore, my redemption full and sure, he is all I need."

A puritan brother wrote of God's promises: "My grace is yours to pardon you, my power is yours to protect you, my wisdom is yours to direct you, my goodness is yours to relive you, my mercy is yours to supply you, and my glory is yours to crown you." Jesus is our all in all!

CONFIRM YOUR SALVATION
II PETER 1:5-11

"Make every effort to confirm your calling and election. For if you do these things, you will never stumble, and you will receive a rich welcome into the eternal kingdom of our Lord and Savior Jesus Christ" (II Peter 1:10-11). What things is Peter talking about?

"These things" are listed in verses 5-9: "Add to your faith goodness; and to goodness knowledge, and to knowledge, self-control; and to self-control, perseverance; and to perseverance, godliness; and to godliness, mutual affection; and to mutual affection love. For if you possess these qualities in increasing measure, they will keep you from being ineffective and unproductive in your knowledge of our Lord Jesus Christ. But whoever does not have them is nearsighted and blind, forgetting that they have been cleansed from their past sins."

How do we add these qualities? Paul explains it: "Continue to work out your salvation with fear and trembling, for it is God who works in you to will and to act in order to fulfill his good purpose" (Philippians 2:13). God is working in you making you willing and giving you the ability to obey. Good works are "produced by faith." Biblical faith is a verb; it demands action. (I Thessalonians 1:3). If you don't make efforts to bring the Good News and material needs to those who are in need of food, clothing, and shelter, then Jesus said we will be cast into eternal fire prepared for the devil and his angels. (Matthew 25:40-45).

Ask yourself, which one of these seven qualities Peter lists does God want you to add? Determine in yourself to do what Peter says, "make every effort to confirm your salvation." Be determined to do what you know God wants you to do. God loves desperate people, i.e. people who will love Him with all their heart. Burn your bridges behind you – say I will help this widow; I will write this email or send a text message. I will pay my debts. I will read my bible and pray. I will spend my money only on what I know Jesus would want me to purchase. I will visit this shut-in. I will speak to my co-worker about their faith. I will minister to those on the margins. Like David who was determined said numerous times, "I will . . . with all my heart." Get into the habit of listening and obey God. Don't be double-minded. (James 1:8).

Oswald Chambers says, "The greatest hindrance in our spiritual life is that we will only look for big things to do, yet, Jesus took a towel and washed the disciple's feet. (John 13:3-5). Realize that obedience even in the smallest detail of life has all of the omnipotent power of the grace of God behind it. If I will do my duty, because I believe God is engineering my circumstances, then at the very point all of the magnificent grace of God is mine through the glorious atonement by the Cross of Christ."

We are tempted to downplay these good qualities because Jesus paid the price for our sins and we are justified freely by His grace. But after we receive His salvation gift of grace, we are to confirm our salvation with these qualities. We are created in Christ Jesus to do good works, which God prepared in advance for us to do. (Ephesians 2:8-10). We are to let our light shine, so that others can see our good works and give glory to God. (Matthew 5:15-16). We are to be the aroma of Christ to the world. (II Corinthians 2:15-17).

No amount of good works can save us but we are to do good to all people. (Galatians 6:10). "God is not unjust; he will not forget your work and the love you have shown him as you have helped his people and continue to them" (Hebrews 6:10). "Behold, I am coming soon, and I shall bring my wages and rewards with me, to repay and render to each one just what his own actions and his own work merit" (Revelation 22:12 AMP).

Redeem the time. Be determined to not waste time. Life is but a breath. "Make use of every opportunity because the days are evil" (Ephesians 5:16). "Never be lacking in zeal, but keep your spiritual fervor, serving the Lord" (Romans 12:11). Paul worked night and day to preach the Gospel. (I Thessalonians 2:9). Run to win the prize. "Everyone who competes in the games goes into strict training. They do it to get a crown that will not last, but we do it to get a crown that will last forever. Therefore, I do not run like someone running aimlessly; I do not fight like a boxer beating the air. No, I strike a blow to my body and make it my slave so that after I have preached to others I myself will not be disqualified for the prize" (I Corinthians 9:25-27).

Some Christians apparently were stealing so Paul writes, "You must work, doing something useful with your own hands, that you may have something to share with those in need" (Ephesians 4:28). "Anyone who does not provide for their relatives and especially for their own household has denied the faith and is worse than an unbeliever" (I Timothy 5:8). The sins of lethargy and laziness are too often found in the church.

The Christian life is exciting because it is a life of growth. "We all . . . are being transformed into his image with ever-increasing glory, which comes from the Lord, who is the Spirit" (II Corinthians 3:18). In speaking of our earthly bodies Paul reminds us: "Though outwardly we are wasting away, yet inwardly we are being renewed day by day. For our light and momentary troubles are achieving for us an eternal glory that far outweighs them all" (II Corinthians 4:16-17).

Are you being renewed daily? One pastor said, "I would be happy if people in my congregation were renewed once a year." When we walk close to Jesus we can be renewed daily. "The righteous cry out, and the Lord hears them; he delivers them from all their trouble. The Lord is close to the brokenhearted and saves those who are crushed in spirit. The righteous person may have many troubles, but the Lord delivers him from them all" (Psalm 34:17-19). Some days troubles attack us at every turn but the Lord hears us and we get up again. Joseph was sold into slavery in a foreign land, away from family, accused falsely but each time with God's help he got up again. You can too. David ran from King Saul for ten years before he was raised to power.

"We are unlike the Christians of the New Testament. The thought of 'safety first' was not a drag on their enterprise as it is on ours. By being exuberant, unconventional and uninhibited in living by the gospel they turned their world upside down . . . Why are we so different? Whence comes the nervous, take-no-risks mood that mars so much of our discipleship? Why are we not free enough from fear and anxiety to allow ourselves to go full stretch in following Christ? . . . We are not persuaded of the adequacy of God to provide for all the needs of those who launch out wholeheartedly on the deep sea of unconventional living in obedience to the call of Christ . . . The name of the game we are playing is unbelief, and Paul's 'he will give us all things' stands as an everlasting rebuke to us." (J. I. Packer, *Knowing God*, p. 270).

At the final judgment Jesus says some will ask: "Lord when did we see you hungry or thirsty or a stranger or needing clothes or sick or in prison, and did not help you?" He replies, "Truly I tell you, whatever you did not do for one of the least of these you did not do for me. Then they will go away to eternal punishment but the righteous to eternal life" (Matthew 25:44-46). James reminds us "Do not merely listen to the word, and so deceive yourselves. Do what it says" (James 1:22).

"PROSPERITY GOSPEL?"
II CORINTHIANS 8:2, MATTHEW 6:33

The "prosperity gospel" with its focus on earthly possession has wormed its way into our minds and into many churches. This "feel-good gospel" overemphasizes God's promises of material blessings while neglecting Jesus' call to deny ourselves to serve Him. God wants us to prosper spiritually but not necessarily materially. There is a reason why Jesus speaks more about putting our trust in money and possessions than any other subject.

Most North Americans believe they're entitled to a happy life. We believe we can control our destiny. The renowned preacher John Wesley, leader of the Methodist movement in the 18th century, had a different perspective. He believed that God's blessing should result in us raising not our standard of living but our standard of giving. . . . He was afraid of storing up earthly treasure. He gave away millions and died with a few coins in his pocket but a storehouse of treasure in heaven. He prayed, "Lord, I am no longer my own but yours. Put me to what you will, rank me with whoever. Put me to doing, put me to suffering. Let me be employed for you or laid aside for you. Let me be full, let me to empty. Let me have all things, let me have nothing. I freely and heartily yield all things to your approval and disposal . . . Amen." Jesus and His disciples all died with few earthly possessions. Paul worked night and day so he would not be a financial burden to anyone. (Acts 20:31).

Jesus instructed us to pray for our Father's kingdom, not our kingdom. It's not about what I want but what He wants. (Matthew 6:10; Luke 22:42). God will supply all our needs, not our wants. (Philippians 4:19). Jesus taught us to deny ourselves, take up our cross and follow Him. "What good is it for someone to gain the whole world, and yet lose or forfeit their self?" (Luke 9:25).

"An Eastern Christian observed, 'You Western Christians often seem to consider material prosperity to be the only sign of God's blessing. On the other hand, you often seem to perceive poverty, discomfort and suffering as signs of God's disfavor. In some ways we in the East understand suffering from the opposite perspective. We believe that suffering may be a sign of God's favor and trust in the Christians to whom the trial is permitted to come'" (Philip Yancey, *Where Is God When It Hurts?*, p. 118).

This false "prosperity gospel" focuses on this world. John writes, "Don't love the world's ways. Don't love the world's goods. Love of the world squeezes out love for the Father. Practically everything that goes on in the world – wanting your own way, wanting everything for yourself, wanting to appear important – has nothing to do with the Father. It just isolates you from him. The world and all its wanting is on the way out – but whoever does what God wants is set for eternity" (I John 2:15-17 Msg.).

Jesus did not come to make us comfortable or rich, He came to make us righteous and holy, as He is holy. (I Peter 1:15-16). He came not primarily to make us "good" but to make us godly. One can be good but be very self-centered. Many people from most every religion are good people but there is a huge difference between being good to being godly.

The Macedonian churches experienced extreme poverty. "In the midst of a very severe trial, their overflowing joy and their extreme poverty welled up in rich generosity . . . You know the grace of our Lord Jesus Christ, that though he was rich, yet for your sake he became poor, so that you through his poverty might become rich" (II Corinthians 8:2, 9).

In many countries of the world where Christians live in poverty their worship services are filled with passionate prayer accompanied with joyful celebration of God's blessing. On the other hand, prosperity often gives us momentary happiness, which soon dissolves. We wonder why we feel empty, restless, lacking joy and peace.

Our human nature desires blessings, ease, comfort, and pleasure and all that makes for carefree living. We long for freedom from adversity, pain, suffering and poverty. The Bible has more to say concerning suffering and pain than it does about material blessing. Jesus said, "In this world you will have trouble (tribulation) but take heart I have overcome the world" (John 16:33). The Greek word for tribulation Jesus chose here is the same word used to describe a very heavy weight used for crushing grain. Jesus is saying that tribulation is a normal aspect of God's loving discipline.

The seven churches in Revelation 2 and 3 suffered hardship, affliction, poverty, persecution, along with God's rebuke and discipline. They were admonished to hold onto what they have until Jesus comes, to be faithful, to persevere.

Today, some pastors urge their people to tell God what they want, "name it and claim it." Paul knew little of health and wealth. Rather than "naming it and claiming it," he wrote: "Be content in every situation, whether well fed or hungry, whether living in plenty or in want." (Philippians 4:12). Paul explains to Timothy: "Godliness with contentment is great gain. For we brought nothing into the world, and we can take nothing out of it. But if we have food and clothing, we will be content with that . . . For the love of money is a root of all kinds of evil. Some people, eager for money, have wandered from the faith and pierce themselves with many griefs" (I Timothy 6:6-10).

"Prosperity Theology" tries to make God into a bellhop responding to our desires. Faith is trusting God for what He knows is best. It is throwing yourself with complete confidence upon God. As unworthy people we humble ourselves and ask, not demand. Like the prodigal we must move from "give me" to "make me." (Luke 15). We thank God for never leaving or forsaking us. We are His servants. With God's loving discipline we develop maturity so we can be trusted to ask for His will, even though His will may go against our natural desires.

George Muller said that it does not become the children of God to be ostentatious in style, dress, or manner of living. Expensiveness and luxury are not appropriate for professed disciples of the meek and lowly one who had no place to lay his head. A college president I know chooses to live frugally by driving an older used car and living in a modest house. What a powerful testimony to rich Christians and rich churches, not to mention to those in the world. He lives simply so others can simply live. Too often, more is given to the restaurant owner on Sunday than is given to God in the offering. Many people spend more on their pets than they give to the poor. Many moonlight just to fulfill their desire for more things that take time from our family and from their spiritual development. I watched as one man I knew who would call himself a Christian gave money to play the lottery even though his wife and children were not adequately fed and cared for.

We dare never shut our eyes to those who do not have the basic necessities of life. In our world 328 million children are living in extreme poverty. At least 17 million children suffer acute under-nutrition causing death for one million children every year. Every day 1,000 children, under the age of 5, die from illnesses caused by contaminated water and inadequate sanitation.

For Americans, how we use our money is perhaps the most tangible indicator of our faith. Maybe that's why Jesus talked more about money than any other subject. "If we give 2 percent of our income, can we say we are 100 percent committed to him? If we withhold the tithe, can we say, 'In God we trust'? If we give God our leftovers instead of the first fruits, can we say we're seeking first his kingdom?" (Mark Batterson, *All In*, pp. 68-69).

Parents have the responsibility to teach their children to be givers. When they receive a dollar help them to set aside 10 cents, or more, for others. If practiced consistently this will go a long way to teaching them to honor God in all of life and will bring great rewards for others. If they continue to give generously God will bless them both physically and spiritually.

Jesus said, "It's terribly hard for rich people to enter the kingdom of heaven!" Jesus died so we can love, honor and serve Him, not to make us rich. If we seek His Kingdom above everything, God will give us what is best. (Matthew 6:33). "If any of you wants to be my follower," Jesus said, "you must turn from your selfish ways, take up your cross, and follow me" (Mark 8:34-35).

David Pratt writes, "We look back on the slave-owning church-goers of 150 years ago and ask, 'How could they have treated their fellow human being that way?' Will followers of Christ 150 years from now look back at Christians today and ask, 'How could they live in such big houses? How could they drive such nice cars and wear such fine clothes? How could they live in such affluence while thousands of children were dying because they didn't have food and water? How could they go on with their life as though the billions of poor didn't even exist?" "If anyone has material possessions and sees a brother or sister in need but has no pity on them, how can the love of God be in that person?" (I John 3:17).

Abraham and Isaac were rich. Levi and Zacchaeus were wealthy tax collectors. Lydia was a wealthy businesswoman. Paul instructs Pastor Timothy, "Command those who are rich in this present world not to put their hope in wealth, but to put their hope in God. Command them to do good, to be rich in good deeds, and to be generous and willing to share. In this way they will lay up treasure for themselves in eternity" (I Timothy 6:17-19). When we honor God, He blesses us with spiritual blessings but often with material blessings as well. We are not to feel guilty with these blessings but be thankful and "be rich in good deeds, generous and willing to share."

It's helpful to remind ourselves that most of the rapidly-growing churches in the world today are in third-world countries where many of the church leaders are living in poverty and just learning to read and write. We are all created in God's image, whether rich or poor. God will use you to the extent that you give your allegiance to Him.

STOP STUMBLING AND START WALKING
I CORINTHIANS 10:32-33

"Whether you eat or drink or whatever you do, do it all for the glory of God. Do not cause anyone to stumble . . . – even as I try to please everyone in every way. For I am not seeking my own good but the good of many, so that they may be saved" (I Corinthians 9:31-33).

We are not perfect. At times we have been poor examples: We have been stumbling blocks. Paul writes, "though I am free, I have made myself a slave to everyone, . . . to the weak I became weak, to win the weak. I have become all things to all people so that by all possible means I might save some. I do all this for the sake of the gospel that I may share in its blessings" (I Corinthians 9:19-23). Paul was conscious of the unsaved people scrutinizing his life. He did not want anyone to stumble or be offended by his actions. There is no place for a proud independent spirit. We dare not have the attitude, "I don't care what others think or say, I'll do what I want to do." If you stumble, fall forward, i.e. learn from your mistakes.

"Don't cause problems for someone with a weak conscience, just because you have the right to eat anything. You know all this, and so it doesn't bother you to eat in the temple of an idol. But suppose a person with a weak conscience sees you and decides to eat food that has been offered to idols. Then what you know has destroyed someone for whom Christ died. When you sin by hurting a Christian with a weak conscience, you sin against Christ. So, if I hurt one of the Lord's followers by what I eat, I will never eat meat as long as I live" (I Corinthians 8:9-13).

Freedom has its limitations. "You say you have the right to do anything, but not everything is beneficial, not everything is constructive, not everything is helpful. No one should seek their own good but the good of others and what is best for them" (I Corinthians 10:23). "We who are strong ought to bear with the failing of the weak and not to please ourselves. Each of us should please our neighbors for their good, to build them up. For even Christ did not please himself . . ." (Romans 15:1-3).

We will be tempted to do what we feel is acceptable for us but we will choose not do it because of causing others to stumble. This will be difficult but God has promised, "No temptation has overtaken you except what is common to mankind. And God is faithful; he will not let you be tempted beyond what you can bear. But when you are tempted, he will also provide a way out so that you can endure it" (I Corinthians 10:13).

Our daily life needs to be above reproach as a witness to others. Paul writes, "Live your daily life in a way that will win the respect of outsiders" (I Thessalonians 4:12). David says: "God will make certain each step you take is sure. The Lord will hold your hand, and if you stumble, you won't fall" (Psalm 37:24 CEV). David also councils us: A love for God's Word will keep us from stumbling. (Psalm 119:165).

Being trustworthy servants will help others from stumbling. "Servants must obey their masters and do their best to please them. They must not talk back or steal, but they must show themselves to be entirely trustworthy and good. Why? Then, they will make the teaching about God our Savior attractive in every way . . ." (Titus 2:9-12). We are, "to carry each other's burdens, and in this way, you will fulfill the law of Christ" (Galatians 6:2).

Jude concludes: "God who is able to keep you from stumbling or falling and to present you before his glorious presence without fault and with great joy, to the only God our Savior be glory, majesty, power and authority, through Jesus Christ our Lord. Amen" (Jude 24-25). It gives God great joy to present you to His Father. Don't rob Jesus of this great joy by causing others to stumble.

A few years ago, it was popular for Christians to wear a bracelet with WWJD, which stood for "What would Jesus do?" Let's form the habit of continually asking, "What would Jesus do?" then we will keep people from stumbling.

Prayer: Lord, help me to be a good example and become all things to all people that I might by all means save some. Amen.

BOAST IN YOUR WEAKNESS
II CORINTHIANS 12:1-10

Braggarts and boasters are obnoxious. "Let not the wise boast in their wisdom or the strong boast of their strength or the rich boast of their riches, but let the one who boast, boast about this: that they have the understanding to know me, that I am the Lord, who exercises kindness, justice and righteousness on earth for in these I delight" (Jeremiah 9:23-24). However, it's ok to boast if: "We boast in Christ

Jesus" (Philippians 3:3). "God chose the lowly things of this world and the despised things . . . so that no one may boast before him. It is because of him that you are in Christ Jesus, who has become for us wisdom from God – that is, our righteousness, holiness and redemption. Therefore, as it is written, 'Let the one who boast, boast in the Lord'" (I Corinthians 1:28-31).

When it came to spreading the Gospel throughout the Roman World, the Apostle Paul's accomplishments were a cut above all the New Testament apostles. His education was far superior to theirs having been trained by the prestigious Rabbi and scholar, Gamaliel. Before his conversion he was a member of the Sanhedrin, the Jewish ruling counsel. After his dramatic conversion he could have boasted how God met him on the Damascus Road and dramatically changed his life. He learned to boast only in the Lord. He said, "We boast in the hope (boast in the certainty) of the glory of God" (Romans 5:2). "We boast in God though our Lord Jesus Christ, through whom we have now received reconciliation (or friendship)" (Romans 5:11).

Paul was caught up into the third heaven. No one else could make that claim. The thief on the cross received the promise from Jesus that he would be with Jesus in Paradise but he did not return to earth as Paul did. (Luke 23:43). When Paul was in Paradise he was shown "surpassing great revelations," and things he was forbidden to tell. He writes, "Therefore, in order to keep me from becoming conceited, I was given a thorn in my flesh, a messenger of Satan, to torment me. Three times I pleaded with the Lord to take it away but he said to me, 'My grace is sufficient for you, for my power is made perfect in weakness.' Therefore, I will boast all the more gladly about my weakness, in insults, in hardships, in persecutions, in difficulties. For when I am weak, then I am strong'" (II Corinthians 12:1-10). Paul was not boasting about his weakness in the sense that he was bragging. The Corinthian Church was questioning his apostleship. He writes this to establish his authority as an apostle to this church.

While it is counterintuitive, I'm sure Paul thanked God often for the thorn that Satan put on him because it kept him humble. Paul referred to himself many times as a slave or servant of Jesus. Paul recognized any accomplishments were only through Christ: "I can do all things through Christ who gives me strength" (Philippians 4:13).

He expresses his humility: "For I am the least of the apostles, and do not even deserve to be called an apostle, because I persecuted the church of God" (I Corinthians 15:9). Five years later he writes, "I am less than the least of all the Lord's people, (but) his grace was given, that I should preach among the Gentiles the unsearchable riches of Christ" (Ephesians 3:8). Then four years later before he died, he writes, "This is a trustworthy saying, . . . that Christ Jesus came into the world to save sinners of whom I am the worst" (I Timothy 1:15). "I have made myself a slave to everyone, to win as many as possible" (I Corinthians 9:19). Paul kept growing in humility and grace. The more we see ourselves as unworthy servants the more grace we receive and the more fruit we bear for our Lord.

Perhaps Paul learned from Peter whom the Lord rebuked, when Jesus called Peter, Satan. (Luke 16:23). Peter wrote: "Humble yourselves under God's mighty hand and he will lift you up in due time" (I Peter 5:6). James, as the leader of the church in Jerusalem was also a model for Paul. James could have referred to himself as the brother of Jesus but instead he referred to himself as a servant or slave of Jesus. He writes, "God resists the proud but gives grace to the humble" (James 4:6). James also says that the ones who are in a humble position should take pride (or boast) in their high position and those who are rich should take pride in their humiliation because they will pass away like a wild flower. (James 1:9-10).

Of course, our best model is Jesus: "Who being in very nature God, did not consider equality with God something to be used to his own advantage; rather, he made himself nothing by taking the very nature of a servant (slave) being made in human likeness. And being found in appearance as a man, he humbled himself by becoming obedient to death, even death on a cross!" (Philippians 2:6-8). He came not to be served but to serve. (Matthew 20:28).

The scriptures are full of examples that teach us to be humble. In Judges 7 God tried to teach Israel to not trust in their army of 35,000 men to destroy the Midianites. They were to trust in the Lord to fight their battles. The Lord told Gideon that if he left these men fight, Israel would boast, "My own strength has saved me." Tell your men if they are afraid, to go home. Twenty-two thousand went home. But there were still too many. The Lord instructed Gideon to take the men to the river and have them drink. Gideon was to take only those who lap water like a dog with their tongues. This left only 300 men who God used to defeat the Midianite army. (Judges 7:1-8). There was no room for boasting since everyone knew it was God who gave the victory over the huge army of Midian.

David writes, "Some trust in chariots and some in horses, but we trust in the name of the Lord our God" (Psalm 20:7, 33:7). When David realized his people, including his family and his possessions, were taken by the Amalekites, he wept. His men were considering stoning him but he humbled himself and received strength from the Lord. (I Samuel 30:6). When David was victorious, he gave credit to God: "With your help I can advance against a troop; with my God I can scale a wall" (II Samuel 22:30; Psalm 18:29).

When Samuel wanted to anoint Saul as King, Saul resisted saying that he was from the small or lesser tribe of Benjamin, implying he was not worthy. He was asking, why do you want me to be king? When they wanted to make him king he hid. However, it wasn't long before Saul became proud. He disobeyed God by marrying foreign women who led him and the nation astray. (I Samuel 10).

God scattered the people of Israel in the desert because they were proud. "These things happened as examples and were written down as warnings for us. So, if you think you are standing firm, be careful that you don't fall!" (I Corinthians 10:11-12). God spoke to Israel: "He has shown you, O mortal what is good and what does the Lord require of you? To act justly and to love mercy and to walk humbly with your God" (Micah 6:8).

Jesus said that a proud Pharisee and a tax collector went to the temple to pray. The Pharisee thanked God that he was not like evildoers or adulterers but rather he fasted and gave a tithe. The tax collector prayed for God's mercy and God heard him rather than the proud Pharisee. (Luke 18:9-14).

God does not shield us from trials and troubles but He allows them to overwhelm us with a sense of our own inadequacy, and to drive us to cling to Him more closely. He is trying to teach us to "wait on the Lord" and to "cast our cares on Him." To the Romans Paul says, "We boast in God through our Lord Jesus Christ, through whom we have now received reconciliation" (5:11).

Apart from Christ we are nothing and can do nothing. When God blesses us, we can develop an over-inflated opinion of ourselves. We "glory" in our accomplishment. God is the one who deserves the glory, not us! God says, "I will not yield my glory to another" (Isaiah 42:8). A humble person is one who is aware that they are unworthy. "We are all unworthy servants" (Luke 17:10).

Have you come to the place where you can accept your weakness, your humble position and sincerely thank God for this position? Can you like Paul "boast" about insults, hardships, persecutions and difficulties? It's when we learn we are weak Jesus makes us strong. (II Corinthians 12:1-10). Choose the path of humility. Lean on Him, He has broad shoulders.

LIVE IN GOD'S WORD
JOHN 15:7, 17:17

I commend to you one book that contains 66 books, written by 40 or more authors, covering 16 centuries. Rulers and governments have outlawed the Bible but it will never be destroyed. It has been translated in more than 3,000 languages. People are giving their life for the Bible so others can read its message. Some have given their life because they had one page in their possession. Today Orthodox Jews lock the Torah, the first five books of scripture, in a secure cabinet to preserve and set it apart from all other books.

The early Christians devoted themselves to the scriptures every day. (Acts 2:41, 46-47). To devote means to diligently listen, and focus exclusively and passionately upon the word. The scriptures were read each Sabbath in the synagogue. Jesus likely memorized the complete Torah or Books of Moses. I'm sure He also memorized such scriptures as: "Your word is a lamp to my feet and a light for my path" (Psalm 119:105). "I have treasured the words of his mouth more than my daily bread" (Job 23:12).

When Jesus was tempted, He said repeatedly, "It is written" (Matthew 4:4-10). When He was challenged by the Pharisees, Sadducees, and Greeks, Jesus regularly quoted the Old Testament scriptures. Jesus and the Word are so closely identified that He says, "If you remain in me and my words remain in you, ask whatever you wish, and it will be given you" (John 15:7).

Christians are people who submit without reserve to the Word of God. The Word of God both convicts us of sin and assures us of forgiveness. We aspire like David, to have our whole lives brought into line with God's Word. "Oh, that my ways were steadfast in obeying your decrees!" Its promises are before them as they pray, and the precepts are before them as they go about their daily tasks.

Read and reread God's Word. Study the Word. There is a huge difference between reading and studying. To mature as a Christian, you must study the Word. Saturate your mind; absorb the Word. Keep learning. "Let the word of Christ dwell in you richly, (let if have the run of the house) as you teach and admonish one another with all wisdom, and as you sing psalms, hymns and spiritual songs with gratitude in your hearts to God" (Colossians 3:16). The Bible is more than a book of knowledge; it is life changing.

Picture your thumb and four fingers. Let the fingers stand for listening, reading, studying and memorizing. The thumb stands for meditation and application. Fingers alone cannot do much but close them to the thumb and it makes all the difference. Meditation and application are the keys.

I like to read long passages, memorize and meditate on the Word. The Holy Spirit can't bring God's Word to your mind unless you first learn the Word. Apply it to your daily living. I have found memorizing word for word can become a legalistic and frustrating exercise. Memorization need not intimidate you. It's helpful to know that when Jesus and the New Testament writers quoted the Old Testament, they often gave the essence of the passage rather than a word-by-word translation. Memorize and study from a version that you find easy to understand.

"You no more need a holiday from spiritual concentration than your heart needs a holiday from beating. You cannot have a moral holiday and remain moral, nor can you have a spiritual holiday and remain spiritual. God wants you to be entirely his, and this means that you have to watch to keep yourself fit." (Oswald Chambers).

Peter instructs us to grow in the knowledge of God. (II Peter 3:18). Knowledge spoken of here is experiential knowledge, not simply head knowledge. The devil as well as Simon the sorcerer believed with head knowledge only. (James 2:19, Acts 8:13).

Love God's Word, study God's Word, and share God's Word. It is alive and active like no other book. God's Word is truth. (John 17:17). It's the truth that sets us free! (John 1:25; 8:36). Don't water down God's Word to the level of your experience. Let it mean what it says and ask God's Spirit to help you live just as it reads.

Mark your Bibles; make notes in the margins to help you remember what was meaningful to you. Use a Bible that has references, which lead you to other scriptures expressing the same truths using different wording. Your best commentary is to compare scripture with scripture.

In Acts 2:37 following 10 days of prayer and through the power of the Holy Spirit the people were cut to the heart as they listened to God's Word. Too often we have a form of godliness but no power because God's words are not undergirded with prayer and the Holy Spirit's anointing. (II Timothy 3:5). Pray before you read: "Lord open my eyes to see what I need to learn from this passage." If you sincerely pray, He will open your eyes to new truths.

Peter says, "If anyone speaks, they should do so as one who speaks the very words of God" (I Peter 4:10-11). God's Word is just as powerful as if He were here speaking them in person. Since God's Word is truth realize you are speaking the truth. Paul writes: "Jesus is the divine Yes – God's affirmation. For all of God's promises have been fulfilled in him. That is why we say 'Amen' when we give glory to God through Christ" (II Corinthians 1:19-20).

God's Word is the anchor for your life. Passion and love of God's Word will be the strength of your soul's conviction. Paul writes, "The gospel came to you not simply with words but also with power, with the Holy Spirit and deep conviction" (I Thessalonians 1:5). Many have a casual attitude as they read and then wonder why God's Word is meaningless. "The Word of God is living and powerful, and sharper than any two-edged sword, piercing even to the division of soul and spirit. It's a discerner of the thoughts and intents of the heart" (Hebrews 4:12). The Word is alive! This is a metaphor but the Word becomes alive to you as you "feel" or "sense" God speaking through it.

Acts 17:11 records, "The Bereans were of more noble character than those in Thessalonica, they received the message with great eagerness and examined the scriptures every day to see if what Paul said was true." If you simply read the Word because you feel you must it will often be meaningless. Ask God to give you a love for His Word. Study and meditate on it day and night. (Psalm 119:97, 103). David was so intrigued with God's Word that he wrote the longest chapter in the Bible, Psalm 119, with 176 verses, explaining the importance God's Word had for his life. When you love God's Word there will be times when you will get so absorbed in it that you will forget to eat. (Psalm 119:103).

When was the last time you read the Bible and your life was changed? When is the last time you shared what God's Word meant to you? When we share the Good News with our friends, especially those who don't know Jesus, we are motivated to study the scripture in order to explain it to those we are discipling and mentoring. Paul instructs Timothy to be diligent to study the Word so he could interpret it accurately. (II Timothy 2:15). He reminds the Romans: "Everything that was written in the past was written to teach us, so that through endurance and the encouragement of the scriptures we might have hope" (Romans 15:4).

Don't say you don't have time to read and study God's Word! You have time for what is important. For many people, reading God's Word means reading a daily verse off a calendar or listening to a biblical sermon once a week. A couple minutes a day will not offset a couple hours of TV each evening.

My friend Brian, a truck driver, hands out hundreds of New Testaments. Many tell him they don't have time to read. Brian says, "I don't have time either." They respond, "What do you mean you don't have time, you're always quoting scripture." Brian carries a New Testament in his pocket. He has several in his truck. Testaments can be found all over the house marked and bent out of shape. You can tell Brian loves God's Word.

We are to: "Consider how we may spur one another on toward love and good deeds, not giving up meeting together as some are in the habit of doing, but encouraging one another . . ." (Hebrews 10:24-25). Meeting together around God's Word builds us up. Be sure you are part of a church in which God's Word is central. If going to church is not a highlight of the week you need to find out why. We need each other to keep us strong in the faith. We are members one of another. (Romans 12:5). There are seventy-six one-other admonitions in the New Testament. God designed His children to live in community. Living in a healthy church community you will never be lonely as you grow in your faith.

Too often we read a scripture with no understanding of its original purpose and context then wonder why it is not making sense with other scriptures or why it does not seem relevant. The *Life Application Study Bible* helps as it introduces each book stating the purpose, author, original audience, date written, setting, key verses, key people and key places.

Pray for a love of God's Word. Linger in His presence with an open Bible. It is powerful! Pray for the more than two billion people who do not have God's Word. Pray for the Wycliffe Bible translators and all translators as they translate the Bible into many more languages. Jesus said when the "Gospel of the kingdom is preached to the whole world then the end will come" (Matthew 24:14). Don't let another day pass without living in God's Word.

BIBLE: A BOOK OF JOY AND MUSIC
PSALM 96:1-3

Many people who don't read the Bible view it as a heartless, joyless collection of dry rules and regulations. However, there are more than 500 references to joy, rejoicing, delighting, and celebrating, while there are less than 200 references to sadness, tears, and mourning. The Bible is a joyful book. Our human nature pulls us towards the negative verses.

Many think of God as a stern judge who wants to make life miserable. Ask people "Does God smile?" Many can't perceive of God smiling. The majority of pictures of Jesus don't picture Him with a smile. There are exceptions as when Jesus is pictured blessing the little children or carrying a lamb. Most pictures depict Jesus suffering for our sins. Isaiah 53 describes Him as a man of sorrows, grief and suffering. But even in His horrendous suffering Hebrews 12:2 says, "Who for the joy set before him, endured the cross, scorning its shame, and sat down at the right hand of the throne of God."

All is well that ends well. Read the last page and burst forth with Hallelujah! The last chapter in our Bible, Revelation 22, describes the River of Life as crystal bright, flowing from God's throne. On either side of this river was the Tree of Life producing fruit every month. The leaves of the tree are for the healing of the nations. There will be no more night in heaven. God is the light and we will reign with Him forever and ever. There will be no more death or mourning, or crying. God will wipe away all tears and there will be no more pain, for the old order of things has passed away. Jesus invites everyone who is thirsty to take the free gift of the water of life. Can anything be better than that?

All animosity will be gone; love will flow freely. People from every nation will sing together joining our voices in praise to God. Our love for one another deepens. All walls will be torn down.

David reminds us that the Lord inhabits the praises of Israel. (Psalm 118:3). Forty-two of the 150 Psalms encourage us to sing. "Sing praises to God, sing praises; sing praises to our King, sing praise.

For God is the King of all the earth; sing to him a psalm of praise" (Psalm 47:6-7)."Sing God a brand new song! Earth and everyone in it, sing! Sing to God – worship God! Shout the news of his victory from sea to sea. Take the news of his glory to the lost, news of his wonders to one and all!" (Psalm 96:1-3 Msg.).

Zephaniah reminds us that God sings over us: "He will take great delight in you, he will quiet you with his love, he will rejoice over you with singing" (Zephaniah 3:17).

We know there are celebrations in heaven whenever a sinner comes home. (Luke 15:7, 10). The twenty-four elders each had a harp and they sang a new song. (Revelation 5:9). The elders in a loud voice sang: "Worthy is the Lamb, who was slain, to receive power and wealth and wisdom and strength and honor and glory and praise" (v. 12). "To him who sits on the throne and to the Lamb be praise and honor and glory and power, for ever and ever!" (v. 13). The Bible is a book of joy, rejoicing and singing. Let's join those around the throne crying: Holy, Holy, Holy.

Paul and Silas were severely flogged and thrown in prison, (Acts 16:25), "About midnight Paul and Silas were praying and singing hymns to God." Many of the martyrs in the sixteenth century sang as they were being burned at the stake. (See *Martyrs Mirror* by Thieleman van Braght.) The authorities put screws in their tongue so they could not sing or give praise to God as they were being burned to death. The persecutors did this so the people looking on could not hear them praising God. The authorities finally put them to death in basements so the public would not hear them sing and quote scripture. It is estimated that for every martyr there were thirty persons who came to Christ. Since they were singing as they were dying, we can be sure they will be singing with greater joy in heaven.

Jesus and the disciples sang. After instituting the Lord's Supper, Jesus and His disciples sang a hymn and then went out to the Mount of Olives. (Matthew 26:30). Scholars agree, they sang the *Hallel*, "hymns of praise," Psalms 113 through 118, which were sung during the evening prayers on the first night of Passover remembering God's deliverance of His people from 430 years of slavery in Egypt.

When we know Jesus and are filled with His Holy Spirit, Ephesians 5:18 says that we have a melody (or a harmony) in our heart. Out of us will flow rivers of living water. (John 7:39). I encourage you to pray each morning asking God to fill you with His Holy Spirit. It's great to wake up morning after morning with God's melody reverberating from your innermost being.

Most people in our culture believe everyone is going to heaven. If you question this just go to a funeral and no matter the lifestyle of the deceased everyone talks about how much better they are now. Jesus said, "Not everyone who says to me, 'Lord, Lord,' will enter the kingdom of heaven, but only the one who does the will of my father who is in heaven" (Matthew 7:21). Jesus continues in vv. 13-14: "Enter through the narrow gate, for wide is the gate and broad is the road that leads to destruction, and many enter through it. But small is the gate and narrow the road that leads to life and only a few find it." "Only a remnant will be saved" (Romans 9:27). There will be no singing if they are separated from our Savior.

Father, may the joy of the Lord be our strength and our song. We look forward to heaven when we will be singing with the millions from every nation giving vibrant praises to You forever. Amen. (For more on the theme of joy see the essay, "A Joyful Life" in Part IV.)

B. WALKING IN INTIMACY

AMAZING – A HOME FOR JESUS
JOHN 14:2, 23

You can prepare a home for Jesus and welcome Him into your home. Incredible! Hours before Jesus went to the cross, He informed the disciples they are not to worry or be troubled even though He had told them several times that He will be leaving them. He knew they didn't understand. He says: "Do not let your hearts be troubled. You believe in God, believe also in me. There are many rooms (abodes, dwellings, homes) in my Father's house; . . . If (since) I go and prepare a place for you, I will come back and take you to be with me that you also may be where I am" (John 14:1-3).

Jesus uses the same Greek word in verses 2 and 23, which translates rooms, homes or dwellings, when He speaks of preparing a place (rooms or dwellings) for His disciples as He does in verse 23 when He speaks of making His home in us. "Anyone who loves me will obey my teaching. My Father will love them and we will come to them and make our home with them." We can make a home or a place for God and for Jesus in our hearts even as He is making a home for us. (v. 2).

How can that be? Pentecost made all the difference. "I'm telling you the truth. It's for your advantage that I'm going away, because if I don't go away, the Helper won't come to you. But if I go, I will send him to you" (John 16:7). "If you love me keep my commands. And I will ask the Father and he will give you another advocate to help you and be with you forever . . . You know him for he lives with you and will be in you" (John 14:15-17). Jesus is living in us in the person of His Holy Spirit even as we are living in Him.

God's word is simple but so profound: Christ living in us. That truth will revolutionize your life. Take time to digest the impact of Jesus' words. To make our heart His home we must obey His teaching. (John 14:15). Are we loving, trusting and obeying Jesus with all our heart, soul, mind and strength? You can be as close to God as you want to be. "You will seek me and find me when you search for me with all your heart" (Jeremiah 29:13). "Come near to God and he will come near to you" (James 4:8).

Jesus said and did only what the Father told Him to say and do. We are His children. Our Father will do the same for us as He did for Jesus. We learn to hear His voice. Learning is a process. It takes time and effort. We are His sheep. He goes ahead of His sheep. His sheep follow Him because they know His voice. (John 10:1-10). Jesus speaks primarily through His word. David knew the shepherd's voice. He said, "The Lord is my shepherd, I lack nothing . . . my cup (of joy) runs over. Surely goodness and love will follow me all the days of my life" (Psalm 23:1-6). Develop this intimate relationship with Jesus. Our steps our ordered by Him. (Psalm 37:23). He knows our thoughts. (Psalm 139:23). We have the mind of Christ. (I Corinthians 2:16).

Ask for wisdom. You have not because you do not ask. (James 4:2). Paul sought the Lord with all his heart even being willing to identify with Christ's suffering and death. He writes, "I want to know Christ – yes the power of his resurrection and participate in his sufferings, becoming like him in his death" (Philippians 3:10). He is speaking here of experiential knowing, not mere head knowledge.

When we were born again, we received the life of our risen Lord. "What his resurrection means for us is that we were raised to his risen life, not to our old life . . . We can know here and now the power and effectiveness of his resurrection and can walk in this new life" (Romans 6:4) Paul's determined purpose was to know Him and the power of

His Resurrection. (Philippians 3:10). "His Spirit can work the very nature of Jesus into us, if we will only obey him." (Oswald Chambers). When we come to Christ, he gives us a new nature. (II Peter 1:3-4).

St. Patrick's prayer speaks of intimacy with Jesus: "I arise today through God's strength to pilot me: God's might to uphold me, God's wisdom to guide me, God's eye to look before me, God's ear to hear me, God's word to speak for me, God's hand to guard me. Christ with me, Christ before me, Christ behind me, Christ in me, Christ beneath me, Christ above me, Christ on my right, Christ on my left, Christ when I lie down, Christ when I sit down, Christ when I arise." (Jim Denison, April 3, 2020, blog).

Lord, I thank you that my heart is Your home and Your home is where my heart is.

CHRIST IN YOU
GALATIANS 2:20

After my first visit with Jim I went away pondering, *I'm not sure I want Jim to come to church.* In my many years of ministry I don't think I ever felt that way about another person. His anger was deep, very deep, boarding on rage. Some neighbors were accusing him of sexual improprieties. I was afraid he might harm anyone who crossed his path. Jim was so angry with his neighbors, so focused on revenge, that he was contemplating their murder. *Should I call the police?* I would not have been surprised if I opened tomorrow's newspaper and read that Jim was in jail for alleged murder.

Amazingly, Jim came to church week after week. For Jim the change was gradual but quite obvious to me. He became a new creation in Christ. His hatred was turned to love. I was surprised with his gift of mercy and care in reaching out to persons who were in need of a loving touch. Thank you, Jesus!

"If anyone is in Christ, the new creation has come. The old has gone, the new is here!" (II Corinthians 5:17). To be "in Christ" determines the Christian's position, privileges and possessions. Closer than Christ, with you, above you, upon you is Christ in you. Paul prays that Christ may live in your hearts by faith. (Ephesians 3:17). Not until this time has God "chosen to make known among the Gentiles the glorious riches of this mystery, which is Christ in you the hope of glory" (Colossians 1:27). "In Christ" is the key to the whole New Testament.

"To be in Christ is to share what Christ has. All that Christ possesses we possess. Every spiritual blessing in him – joy, peace, victory, power, holiness – is ours here and now. If we are children of God, then we are his heirs and joint-heirs with Christ, so that all the Father has given to his Son, the Son shares with us . . . Do you believe you are a spiritual multi-millionaire?" (Ruth Paxton in *Rivers of Living Waters*, p. 64-65). We are engraved in the palm of His hand. (Isaiah 49:16).

Not only is Jesus with you all the time, but He gives you His undivided attention: "Let him have all your worries and cares, for he is always thinking about you and watching everything that concerns you" (I Peter 5:7 TLB). Jesus says that He numbers the hairs of our head. (Luke 12:7). He is painting a picture of how well He knows us and how much He cares about us.

"I have been crucified and with Christ and I no longer live, but Christ lives in me. The life I now live in the body, I live by faith in the Son of God, who loved me and gave himself for me" (Galatians 2:20). There are seven personal pronouns in this verse. Read, or better yet, memorize this verse and place your name where the pronouns appear. This will raise your faith level.

Without a Crucifixion there can be no Resurrection. So many don't realize they must be crucified with Christ. The thought is repulsive. We must die to self. "We know (whenever we read those two words, 'we know,' ask yourself, 'Do I really know?') – we know that our old self was crucified with him so that the body ruled by sin might be done away with, that we should no longer be slaves to sin – because anyone who has died has been set free from sin" (Romans 6:6-7).

Notice the word, "in" in the following verses: "There is no condemnation for those who are IN Christ Jesus" (Romans 8:1). "To God's holy people IN Christ Jesus at Philippi" (Philippians 1:1). "To God's holy people in Colossae, the faithful brothers and sisters IN Christ" (Colossians 1:2). "To God's holy people in Ephesus, the faithful IN Christ Jesus" (Ephesians 1:1). "IN Christ we live and move and have our being (our existence)" (Acts 17:28). Peter concludes his first letter: "Peace to all of you who are IN Christ" (I Peter 5:14). "For you have died, and your life is hidden with Christ IN God" (Colossians 3:3). According to this verse, as I have said before, not only are we in Christ but Christ is in God, therefore we are in both Christ and in God. How secure! By faith live in that security today.

To be "in Christ" means we have accepted His sacrifice as payment for our sin. He knows every sinful thought, attitude or actions we have ever committed. As Romans 3:10-12 reminds us, we all have sinned. We are enemies of God. (Romans 5:10). When we accept IIis sacrifice on our behalf, He switches accounts with us. He exchanges our list of sins for His perfect account that is totally pleasing to God. (II Corinthians 5:21). "Christ suffered for sins, the righteous for the unrighteous, to bring us to God" (I Peter 3:18). Only "in Christ" is our sin debt cancelled, our relationship with God restored, and our eternity secured. (John 3:16-18). When we are in Christ we are rescued from the present evil world. (Galatians 1:4).

We must be in Christ to be right with God. (I Corinthians 1:30). In Christ, God no longer sees our imperfections; He sees the righteousness of His Son. "We are arrayed in a robe of his righteousness" (Isaiah 61:10). "Whoever believes in Jesus is not condemned, but whoever does not believe stands condemned already because they have not believed in the name of God's one and only Son"... "Whoever believes in the Son has eternal life, but whoever rejects the Son will not see life, for God's wrath remains on them" (John 3:18, 36).

Paul expresses what it meant for him to be "in" Christ. "I consider my life worth nothing to me; my only aim is to finish the race and complete the task the Lord Jesus has given me – the task of testifying to the good news of God's grace" (Acts 20:24).

When we are living in intimate friendship with Jesus you will know His will. Oswald Chambers writes, "When you have a right standing with God, you have a life of freedom, liberty and delight; you are in God's will. And all of your commonsense decisions are actually his will for you, unless you sense a feeling of restraint brought on by a check in your spirit. You are free to make decisions in light of a perfect and delightful friendship with God; know that if your decisions are wrong, he will lovingly produce that sense of restraint. Once he does, you must stop immediately." (March 20 devotional).

Daniel W. Whittle expresses our relationship with Jesus so graphically in the hymn "Christ Liveth In Me": "As lives the flower within the seed, as in the cone the tree, so, praise the God of truth and grace, his Spirit dwelleth in me." Stay in God's presence and you will have fullness of joy. (Psalm 16:11).

GROWING IN GOD'S LOVE
JOHN 3:16, EPHESIANS 3:17-18

If you were raised under Christian influence, perhaps the first verse of the Bible you heard was, "God so loved the world that he gave his one and only Son, that whoever believes in him shall not perish but have eternal life" (John 3:16). If you were raised in church you likely are familiar with the hymn, "The Love of God," by Frederick Martin Lehman, 1868-1953: "The love of God is greater far than tongue or pen can ever tell; It goes beyond the highest star, and reaches to the lowest hell. The guilty pair, bowed down with care, God gave his Son to win; His erring child He reconciled, and pardoned from his sin. . . .

"When hoary time shall pass away, and earthly thrones and king-doms fall, when men, who hear refuse to pray, on rocks and hills and mountain call, God's love so sure, shall still endure, all measureless and strong; Redeeming grace to Adam's race the saints' and angels' song. . . .

"Could we with ink the ocean fill, and were the skies of parchment made. Were every stalk on earth a quill, and every man a scribe by trade, to write the love of God above would drain the ocean dry. Nor could the scroll contain the whole, though stretched from sky to sky. . . .

"(Chorus) O love of God, how rich and pure! How measure-less and strong! It shall forever more endure, the saints' and angels' song."

God is love. Our human nature tends to focus on God's love often overlooking His many other attributes. While the Bible clearly states, "God is love," it gives us many direct statements, images, and metaphors to help us understand His love. There is no one-word adjective or superlative in the English language that can completely describe God's love. Some use secular terms such as extravagant, outlandish, and outrageous, but these words sound nearly sacrilegious in comparison to words like holy, pure, righteous, just, and perfect, which are used in the Bible to describe God.

Life is exciting when we grow in God's love. "In this is my prayer that your love may abound more and more in knowledge and depth of insight, so that you may be able to discern what is best and may be pure and blameless for the day of Christ, filled with the fruit of righteousness that comes through Jesus Christ – to the glory and praise of God" (Philippians 1:9-11). "We grow from one degree of glory to another" (II Corinthians 3:18).

No one can fully grasp God's love but we can grow in our appreciation of His love. "God's greatness no one can fathom" (Psalm 145:3). Paul was called to preach the unsearchable riches of Christ. (Ephesians 3:8 KJV). "Now we see only a reflection as in a mirror; then we shall see face to face. Now I know in part; then I shall know fully, even as I am fully known" (I Corinthians 13:12). John the Baptist says, "I am of the earth and my understanding is limited to the things of the earth, but Jesus has come from heaven. He tells what he has seen and heard" (John 3:31-32 NLT). Grow in your love for Jesus and your love for others will grow.

We want microwave Christianity but slow cooker Christianity is the reality. Are we afraid to grow because we will need to change? Change can be initially frightening but eventually refreshing. Perseverance is the way godly character is formed making us mature and complete. (James 1:4). "You do love all of God's family throughout Macedonia. Yet we urge you to do so more and more" (I Thessalonians 4:10). Paul thanks God that the Thessalonians are growing in love. (I Thessalonians 1:3). He prays, "May your roots go down deep into the soil of God's marvelous love. And may you have the power to understand . . . how wide, how long, how high and even how deep his love really is. May you experience the love of Christ; though it is so great you will never fully understand it. Then you will be filled with the fullness of life and power that comes from God" (Ephesians 3:17-19 NLT).

God's love is total, reaching every corner of our experience. "God's love is wider – it covers all of our life's experiences, and it reaches out to the whole world. It's long – continuing the length of our lives. It is high – it rises to the heights of our joy and delight. His love is deep – it reaches to the depths of discouragement, despair, and even death. When you feel shut out or isolated, his love is there!" (From the *Life Application Bible* notes). "God's love comes from a pure heart, a good conscience and a sincere faith" (I Thessalonians 1:5). Therefore, the best way to grow in God's love is to see that our heart is pure, our conscience innocent and our faith serious.

God's loving presence is one of our greatest comforts. God knows when I sit or get up. He knows my thoughts and my words even before I speak them. If I go up to the heavens or descend to the depth, He is there. He saw me as I was being formed in my mother's womb. (Psalm 139:8, 15-16). "Keep yourselves in God's love as you wait for the mercy of our Lord Jesus Christ to bring you to eternal life" (Jude 21).

Jesus commands us to love with a mature or perfect love. (Matthew 5:48). Jesus raised the bar to new heights: "A new commandment

I give you: Love one another, as I have loved you, so you must love one another. By this everyone will know that you are my disciples" (John 13:34-35).

God showed His love by giving His very best – His Only Son. "God demonstrated (proved) his love for us in this: While we were sinners, Christ died for us" (Romans 5:8). Jesus modeled love as He stooped to wash the disciple's feet. "I have set you an example that you should do as I have done for you ... No servant is greater than his master ... Now that you know these things, you will be blessed if you put them into practice" (John 13:15-17). We grow in love as we practice love. Human love has limitations. Only God's love given through the Holy Spirit will enable you to love everyone, including your enemies and those who slight you and overlook your efforts.

If you are not experiencing His promised overflowing life of love, discover why. Adam and Eve had an overflowing life of love. Their relationship was broken as they chose to disobey. Is there any area in your life where you have chosen to disobey?

Pay attention to your conscience. The conscience has been compared to the human nervous system. When we are wounded, we know something is wrong. When we sin the warning light in our mind sounds an alarm. If we ignore the alarm we ultimately wear away our conscience, sear our conscience. How often do we know what we should be doing but we put it off until we forget about it, or how often are we doing things we should not be doing but we make excuses for not being obedient? The result is our conscience no longer speaks. I received a greeting from a friend in another state. I thought, *Now I must send them my love and prayers.* While I prayed for them, I did not do what I should have done. I received a report that he committed suicide. I thank God for His forgiveness and mercy but I need to learn from that experience.

Jesus promised an overflowing life of love. "At the feast Jesus stood up and cried in a loud voice, 'If anyone is thirsty, let them come to me and drink! He who believe in me – cleaves, trusts and relies on me – as the scripture has said, out from his innermost being springs and rivers of living water flow continuously'" (John 7:37-38). Jesus was speaking of the Holy Spirit in us. (v. 39).

Many walls separate families. Thank God that His love is able to break down every wall of resentment that Satan would erect in our minds. Peter reminds us "Love covers a multitude of sins" (I Peter 4:8). Let God's love heal every hurt in every corner of your life.

Our friends, John and Sandy, model this life of love. John and Sandy teach their children to love God's Word by reading and discussing it with their four school-age children. The children are models to other children in our church. They are constantly helping others—they deliver food from the community food bank, their family helps people move, they take people to church every Sunday usually arriving early for service, and they participate in a small group. They lead by giving sacrificial service. They are helping others to grow in God's love.

THE OVERFLOWING LIFE – TAKE UP YOUR CROSS
LUKE 9:23

Jesus said, "Whoever wants to be my disciple must deny themselves and take up their cross daily and follow me" (Luke 9:23). Even though it sounds counterintuitive, taking up our cross leads to an overflowing life.

Margie was married to a stern, rigid, career military officer. He seemed to be sincere in his commitment to Jesus but lived a double life. He was active in church, even assisting with many church activities. Finally, his double life caught up with him. His infatuation with another woman, and nights spent on the town, broke the hearts of his wife and children. After a long and painful divorce, the loving care of several sisters in the congregation and the prayers of God's people helped Margie heal. She is now ministering to other divorced women. Her former pain, prayers and tears now bring healing to others.

"God comforts us in all our troubles so that we can comfort others. When others are troubled, we will be able to give them the same comfort God has given us. You can be sure that the more we suffer for Christ, the more God will shower us with his comfort through Christ" (II Corinthians 1:4-5 NLT).

Margie has found what so few Christians have found—the overflowing life in Jesus. Jesus has come that we may have life abundant. (John 10:10). The abundant life is readily available for all who will pay the price to walk daily in Jesus' presence.

"Before we become Christians, we each take as our starting point our ordinary self with its various desires and interests. When we become followers of Christ, we know that we will need to give up some of these desires and interests and add others in their place. We will have to go to church, read our bibles, pray, give, serve, and so on. But we are hoping that when all the demands of our religion have been met, we will still have the chance to get on with our own lives and do, as we like. We are like an honest man who pays his taxes but hopes there will be money left over for him to spend as he wishes. . . .

"Christ says, 'Give me all. I don't want so much of your time and so much of your money and so much of your work: I want You. I have not come to torment your natural self, but to kill it. No half-measures are any good. I don't want to cut off a branch here and a branch there, I want to have the whole tree down. Hand over the whole natural self, all the desires, which you think innocent, as well as the ones you think wicked – the whole outfit. I will give you a new self instead. In fact, I will give you myself; my own will shall become yours. . . .

"It is so hard to hand over our entire lives to Jesus – all our time, our money, our abilities, our ambitions. Not just part of them so we can live as we like – all of them. The almost impossible thing is to hand over your whole self to Jesus. But it is far easier than trying to remain what we call 'ourselves,' to keep our personal happiness, yet at the same time be good Christians. As Jesus said, a thorn bush cannot produce figs. Grass cannot make wheat. If I want to produce wheat, the change must go deeper. I must be plowed up and re-sown. My whole life must belong to God. . . .

"At the moment we wake up in the morning. All our wishes and hopes for the day rush at us like wild animals. And the first job consists simply in shoving them back – in listening to that other voice, letting the other larger, stronger, quieter life of Jesus come flowing in. Standing back from all our natural hopes and desires – coming in and out of the wind – listening to Jesus. We can only do it for moments at first. But from these moments a new life begins to spread through our system. Now we are letting Jesus work at our souls. It is the difference between paint, which is merely laid on the surface and a dye or stain, which soaks right through. . . .

"Jesus never talked in vague, idealistic terms. When He said, 'Be perfect,' He meant it. He meant that we must go in for the full treatment. It is hard; but the sort of compromise we are trying to make is harder – in fact, it is impossible. It may be hard for an egg to turn into a bird; it would be even harder for it to learn to fly while remaining an egg. We are like eggs at present. And you cannot go on indefinitely being just an ordinary, decent egg. You must be hatched or go bad.

'This is the whole of Christianity. There is nothing else.'" (Jim Denison quotes C. S. Lewis).

The overflowing life is a life of habitual victory. "Thanks be to God! He gives us the victory through our Lord Jesus Christ" (I Corinthians 15:57). Victory comes the same way salvation came to us. "As you received Christ Jesus as Lord, continue to live your life in him, rooted and built up in him . . . overflowing with thankfulness" (Colossians 2:6-7). You accepted Christ by faith, now exercise your faith daily growing, overcoming sin and walking in obedience with Him.

The victory Paul is referring to is a result of Christ's Resurrection. The victory includes victory over all sin. Paul writes in Romans 8:37, "In all these things (trials) we are more than conquerors through him who loved us." Notice he says, "more than conquerors" not just squeaking by. Again, he writes, "Thanks be to God who always leads us as captives in Christ's triumphal procession and uses us to spread the aroma of the knowledge of him everywhere" (II Corinthians 2:14). Note the word "always." Always includes every situation no matter if you feel the situation you are in is impossible. Believe that God can enable you to live the overflowing life continuously. "Since we have these promises let us purify ourselves from everything that contaminates body and spirit, perfecting holiness out of reverence for God" (II Corinthians 7:1). This does not mean we are never sinful. (I John 1:8-10).

Give everything to Christ. You can't know Christ until all you have is Christ. Oswald Chambers wrote, "One life totally devoted to God is of more value to Him than one hundred lives which have been simply awakened by His Spirit." When you are totally devoted to Christ there are some things that are acceptable for others that are unacceptable to you. But they are easy to give up because our love for Jesus transcends whatever He asks of us. Take up your cross daily and follow Christ. His overflowing life in you will amaze you. (Luke 9:23). Is your life totally devoted to Christ?

NEVER HUNGER OR THIRST
JOHN 8:35

"Jesus declared, 'I am the bread of life. Whoever comes to me will never go hungry, and whoever believes in me will never be thirsty'" (John 6:35). To the woman at the well He said, "Everyone who drinks this water will be thirsty again, but whoever drinks the water I give them will never thirst. Indeed, the water I give them will become in them a spring of water, welling up to eternal life" (John 4:13-14).

Much of Jesus' teaching is in parables or figures of speech. When He says He is the vine and we are the branches we don't take that literally. Or when He says He is the door, or He is the shepherd and we are the sheep we know He is speaking figuratively. What does Jesus mean when He says we will never hunger or thirst again? We all know we need to eat and drink therefore it's obvious this is not to be taken literally. Jesus helps us understand when He says: "The Spirit gives life; the flesh counts for nothing. The words I have spoken to you – they are full of the Spirit and life" (John 6:63).

Eating and drinking of Jesus quenches our deepest thirst and meets the deepest longings of our life. When you feel lonely, He is your companion who will never leave you or forsake you. "I will ask the Father, and he will give you another advocate (comforter) to help and be with you forever" (John 14:17, Hebrews 13:5). When you are anxious, He is your peace. "Peace I leave with you . . . Do not let your hearts be troubled and do not be afraid" (John 14:27). When you worry, He says, "Do not worry about your life, what you will eat or drink; or about your body, what you will wear" (Matthew 6:25). See how God takes care of the birds and the flowers; how much more will He care for you. (Matthew 6:25-34). When your thoughts are not in line with God's will, know that you can bring every thought captive and make it obedient to Christ. (II Corinthians 10:5).

From prison Paul writes: "Do not be anxious about anything, but in every situation, by prayer and petition, with thanksgiving, present your requests to God. And the peace of God, which transcends all understanding, will guard your hearts and your minds in Christ Jesus" (Philippians 4:6-7). When you are concerned about your future, Jesus promises He will never leave us. (Matthew 28:20). "He will wipe every tear from their eyes. There will be no more death, or mourning or crying or pain, for the old order of things has passed away" (Revelation 21:4).

When we are suffering, we want to know our suffering is fulfilling a meaningful purpose. "The Lord disciplines the one he loves, and he chastens everyone he accepts as his son. Endure hardship as discipline; God is treating you as his children" (Hebrews 12:6-7). We cannot mature without discipline. We can't mature if there are no obstacles to overcome.

Is it possible to eat and drink of Jesus so we never thirst again? Would He command us to do something that is impossible for us to attain? Let me share a few incidents of those who are drinking of the living water and eating the living bread. As pastor I received a phone call informing me that Katie Kurtz, age 92 and blind, had a stroke. I went to the nursing home. As I walked down the hall to her room, I heard her softly humming hymns, as was her holy habit. I entered her room and said, "This is Pastor Dave, I am sorry to hear you had a stroke." Her immediate response, "Oh, I'm so glad it was on my left side, I can still feed myself." That is victory!

Ken, age 63, was a picture of health. He was diagnosed with stage-four cancer of the pancreas. We prayed and for months his pancreas seemed to function as normal but then he got weak and lived in pain. All this time he claimed his life verses which carried him through victorious until the Lord called him home. Those verses were from Habakkuk 3:17-19, "Though the fig tree does not bud and there are no grapes on the vines, though the olive crop fails and the fields produce no food, though there are no sheep in the pen and no cattle in the stalls, yet I will rejoice in the Lord, I will be joyful in God my Savior. The Sovereign Lord is my strength; he makes my feet like the feet of a deer; he enables me to tread on the heights."

Horatio Spafford's son died. He lost his possessions in the Chicago fire of 1871, which ruined him financially. He had planned to travel to Europe with his family. In a late change of plans, he sent the family ahead while he was delayed on business. While crossing the Atlantic Ocean, the ship sank rapidly after a collision with a sea vessel and all four of Spafford's daughters died. His wife Anna survived and sent him the telegram, "Saved alone . . ." Shortly afterwards, as Spafford traveled to meet his grieving wife, he was inspired to write these words as his ship passed near where his daughters had died: "When peace like a river, attendeth my way, When sorrows like sea billows roll; Whatever my lot, Thou hast taught me to say, It is well, it is well, with my soul. Refrain. It is well, (it is well), with my soul, (with my soul), It is well, it is well, with my soul. Though Satan should buffet, though trials should come, Let this blest assurance control, That Christ has regarded my helpless estate, And hath shed His own blood for my soul. My sin, oh, the bliss of this glorious thought! My sin, not in part but the whole, Is nailed to the cross, and I bear it no more, Praise the Lord, praise the Lord, O my soul."

"If you are thirsty, come and drink water! If you don't have any money, come, eat what you want! Drink wine and milk without paying a cent. Why waste your money on what really isn't food? Why work hard for something that doesn't satisfy? Listen carefully to me, and you will enjoy the very best foods. Pay close attention! Come to me and live" (Isaiah 55:1-3 CEV).

Madame Guyon suffering in a dungeon in France would say, "I ask no more, in good or ill, but union with your holy will." Paul writes: "I have learned to be content whatever the circumstance. I know what it is to be in need; I know what it is to have plenty. I have learned the secret of being content in any and every situation, whether well fed or hungry, whether living in plenty or in want. I can do all this through him who gives me strength" (Philippians 4:9).

Was Paul perfect? "Not that I have already obtained all this, or have already arrived at my goal, but I press on to take hold of that for which Christ Jesus took hold of me. I do not consider myself yet to have taken hold of it, but one thing I do: forgetting what is behind and straining toward what is ahead. I press on toward the goal to win the prize which God has called me heavenward in Christ Jesus" (Philippians 3:12-14).

When he comes to the end of his life, he shares this testimony: "I have fought a good fight, I have finished the race, I have kept the faith. Now there is in store for me the crown of righteousness, which the Lord, the righteous judge will award to me on that day and not only to me, but also to all who have longed for his appearing" (II Timothy 4:7).

Jesus said, "Blessed are those who hunger and thirst for righteousness; for they will be filled" (Matthew 5:6). Claim Jesus' promise, (to hunger and thirst for Him), and you will be completely satisfied. (AMP).

MORE THAN YOU CAN IMAGINE
EPHESIANS 3:20-21

"God is able to do immeasurably more than all we ask or imagine according to his power that is at work within us, to him be glory in the church and in Christ Jesus throughout all generations, for ever and ever!" (Ephesians 3:20-21).

In my fifty years of pastoral ministry I have seen God's power at work in redeeming many lives and reviving churches. After moving from our church plant in Florida we relocated to pastor a sixty-year-old declining church just outside of Washington, D.C. I gave the congregation of forty-five attendees, including children, three choices: stay here and die, stay here and become indigenous to the community, i.e. make some radical changes so we can identify with the people in the community, or third, relocate. After four months of prayer we voted unanimously, 23 to 0, to move to a new location not having any idea where we would go. After an intensive search the Lord miraculously opened the door for us to rent the Capital College auditorium ten miles away in Laurel, Maryland.

The congregation grew steadily to a couple hundred. After an intensive three-year search God provided land to build our own facility. People from twenty-some nationalities came together as one family. It was like heaven on earth. God had moved beyond my imagination. God is willing and able to give us exceedingly more than we ask or imagine! Hallelujah!

Audrey, as a little girl, was terrified of her alcoholic father. Whenever he came home, she would hide in the closet. As an adult she gave her life to Christ, and her emotionally crippled life began to be healed. It was not an easy road for Audrey, but she is reaching her family, including her father and friends for her Lord. "Those who become Christians become new persons. They are not the same anymore, for the old life is gone. A new life has begun!" (II Corinthians 5:1 NLT).

Because God is almighty (omnipotent) or all powerful, all knowing (omniscience), everywhere present (omnipresent) it is no stretch of faith to believe God can do more than we imagine but it is a stretch of faith to believe He can do "all things" through you and me. Do you believe He wants to express Himself through you and your church, even things beyond your imagination? If only we could exercise our faith to believe this verse, we would see God's transforming power expressed in people like Audrey who are all around us.

God has equipped you with many gifts. "You have different gifts according to the grace given to you" (Romans 12:6). "The Spirit has given each of us a special way of serving others" (I Corinthians 12:7 CEV). Don't look at other people who can do things you can't do. You are special, one of a kind. Thank God for you. You are so valuable to Him that He gave His Son to die for you. There are things God has equipped you to do that no one else can do. Do what God created you to do and it will surprise you and surpass your imagination. We waste so much time and energy looking at how God is using other people wishing we could do what they do. Claim your God-given gifts; use them for His glory. You will be overtaken by His joy.

"We are God's [own] handiwork (his workmanship), recreated in Christ Jesus, [born anew] that we may do those good works which God prepared beforehand for us, (taking paths which he prepared ahead of time) that we should walk in them – living the good life which he prearranged and made ready for us to live"(Ephesians 2:10 AMP).

The best way to discover God's plan for you is to look at how He made you. "Do not think of yourself more highly than you ought, but rather think of yourself with sober judgment, in accordance with the faith God has distributed to each of you" (Romans 12:3). God did not miss you when He distributed His gift of faith.

Take inventory of your strengths and weaknesses. Opportunities to do good are all around you. Pray for God to guide you, then move ahead trying different things. You will discover what brings you peace, satisfaction and the joy in serving your Lord. There are more than thirty spiritual gifts mentioned in the Bible. In one sense there are thousands of spiritual gifts because we are all different and God equips us or gifts us uniquely for our given personality and situation. You have been blessed with several gifts. Discover what they are, move ahead in faith, God will supply the strength you need. "Never be lacking in zeal, but keep your spiritual fervor, serving the Lord" (Romans 12:11).

Every Christian should have a passion. If you are lacking passion pray for the Holy Spirit to open your eyes to the reality of eternity. Life is but a breath and eternity is forever. Don't waste your time. (Psalm 90:12). Make use of every opportunity because the days are evil. (Ephesians 5:14-16). God wants to do more than you can imagine and He wants to do it through you! That is amazing!

Just before Paul informs us that God can do through us even more than we can imagine he prays that we can grasp the love of God and be filled with the measure of the fullness of God. We have all the fullness of God available to us. (Ephesians 3:17-19). "In Christ all the fullness of the Deity lives in bodily form, and in Christ you have been brought to fullness" (Colossians 2:9).

Meditate on the phrase: "fullness of God in you." What does this mean for where you are today? Use your God-given gift of imagination. Oh, if only we would grasp the fullness of life that God has for us!

OVERWHELMING VICTORY
ROMANS 8:35-39 (AMP)

In the throes of pain and tremendous physical and emotional persecution Paul says: "Who shall ever separate us from Christ's love? Shall suffering and affliction and tribulation? Or calamity and distress? Or persecution, or hunger, or destitution, or peril or sword? . . . Yet, amid all these things we are more than conquerors and gain a surpassing victory (super-victors) through him who loved us. For I am persuaded beyond doubt – I'm sure – that neither death, nor life, not angels, not principalities, nor things impeding, nor things to come, nor powers, no heights, nor depth, nor anything else in all creation will be able to separate us from the love of God which is in Christ Jesus our Lord" (Romans 8:35-39 AMP).

Has anyone suffered more than Paul: imprisoned, flogged, five times he received thirty-nine stripes, three times beaten with rods, stoned, three times shipwrecked, lived with hunger, was cold, naked and despaired of life itself? (II Corinthians 11:23-29; 1:8). Paul was a super-victor in the midst of all of tests because Jesus Christ was with him.

Oswald Chambers writes, "I feel sorry for the Christian who doesn't have something in the circumstances of his life that he wishes was not there. A true Christian doesn't know the joy of the Lord in spite of tribulation, but because of it. Paul said, 'I am exceedingly joyful; in all our tribulation' (II Corinthians 7:4 KJV). It is a shameful thing for a Christian to talk about getting the victory. We should belong so completely to the Victor that it is always his victory, and 'we are more than conquerors through him . . .' (Romans 8:37)."

Sufferings and trials are given to us to make us grow up. "I am well pleased and take pleasure in infirmities, insults, hardships, persecutions, perplexities and distresses; for when I am weak (in human strength), then am I [truly] strong – able, powerful in divine strength" (II Corinthians 12:10 AMP). James says that we are to be glad when our faith is tested because it teaches us perseverance, which makes us mature. (James 1:2-4).

Sometimes we feel like David: "Lord, do not rebuke me in your anger or discipline me in your wrath . . . There is no health in my body, no soundness in my bones because of my sins. My guilt has overwhelmed me like a burden too heavy to bear. My wounds fester and are loathsome because of my sinful folly. All day long I go about mourning. My back is filled with searing pain; there is no health in my body. I am feeble and utterly crushed. I groan in anguish of heart. . . . my strength fails me; Lord, I wait for you; you will answer, Lord my God. I confess my iniquity; I am troubled by my sin . . . Do not forsake me. Come quickly to help me my Lord and my Savior" (Psalm 38:1-22).

David did not have the advantage we have since Pentecost. We have the continual abiding presence of God's Holy Spirit. Move from living under the Old Covenant with David and live in the New Testament covenant of Christ who continually lives and dwells in us. He is our life. (Colossians 3:4). "In him we live and move and have our being (our existence)" (Acts 17:28).

As our society becomes more pagan, American Christians are being forced to move to "higher ground." Jim Denison reports in his December 11, 2018, blog, "Peter Vlaming teaches French at West Point High School in West Point, Virginia. He was fired by the school board Dec. 6, 2018 for refusing to use a transgender student's preferred pronoun. (The student was born as a biological female but wishes to use the pronouns 'he' and 'him.')"

Open Doors reports that "245 million Christians around the world—1 in 8 globally—are suffering from persecution. On average, 11 believers are killed every day for their faith. Chinese pastors and believers who will not submit to the control of the government are being imprisoned and their churches closed. North Korea is ranked #1 as the most dangerous country for Christians. During the World Watch List 2018 reporting period: 3,066 Christians were killed; 1,252 were abducted; 1,020 were raped or sexually harassed; and 793 churches were attacked."

Pray daily for the millions who are being persecuted for their faith in countries like North Korea, Nigeria, India, Iran, Saudi Arabia, etc. There are 60 million refugees because of war and persecution. Paul claimed overwhelming victory amidst all his sufferings. "Through glory and dishonor, bad report and good report; genuine, yet regarded as impostors; known yet regarded as unknown; dying, and yet we live on; beaten and yet not killed; sorrowful, yet always rejoicing; poor, yet make many rich; having nothing, and yet possessing everything" (II Corinthians 6:8-10).

Embrace Paul's view of sufferings: "I consider that the sufferings of this present time (this present life) are not worth being compared

with the glory that is about to be reveled to us and in us and for us and
conferred on us!" (Romans 8:18 AMP). "For our light, momentary affliction (this slight distress of the passing hour) is ever more and more
abundantly preparing and producing and achieving for us an everlasting weight of glory – beyond all measure, excessively surpassing all
comparisons and all calculations, a vast and transcendent glory and
blessedness never to cease!" (II Corinthians 4:17 AMP).

Paul experienced overwhelming victory because Jesus is greater
than all opposition, even Satanic or demonic opposition. He writes:
"Jesus created; all things in heaven and on earth, visible and invisible,
whether thrones or powers or rulers or authorities; all things were created by him and for him. He is before all things, and in him all things
hold together" (Colossians 1:16-17). Since the creator, Jesus, is above
His creation we can rest in His provision and protection.

Bishop Johnson Oatman was an overcomer. He expresses it with
this hymn: "I pressing on the upward way, new heights I'm gaining
every day; Still praying as I'm on-ward bound, Lord, plant my feet on
higher ground.

"My heart has no desire to stay where doubts arise and fears
dismay; Tho' some may dwell where these abound, my prayer, my aim
is higher ground.

"I want to live above the world, though Satan's darts at me are
hurried; For faith has caught the joyful sound, the song of saints on
higher ground.

"(Chorus) Lord, lift me up and let me stand, by faith, on heaven's
tableland, a higher plane than I have found; Lord, plant my feet on
higher ground."

Why are so many living on the lower ground of worry, complaining, frustration, and without joy? Confess these expressions as sin since
they are a lack of trust in the promises of God's Word. Nothing can
separate you from His presence, not even the fear of death. Jesus said,
"Do not be afraid of those who kill the body but cannot kill the soul.
Rather, be afraid of the One who can destroy both soul and body in
hell" (Matthew 10:28). Jesus is greater than any disappointment or any
evil that Satan may try to bring upon you.

If you could have visited John on the "prison" island of Patmos
before he died, would you find him discouraged? John's spirit would be
triumphant even though he wrote about the terrible suffering coming
upon humanity. His book of Revelation is a book of victory: Satan is
defeated, there will be no more sin, tears or sorrow, the curse is re-

moved, Paradise is regained, death is defeated and believers are forever with God. He wrote of the multitude shouting "Hallelujah" again and again for "our Lord God Almighty reigns. Let us rejoice and be glad and give him glory! For the wedding of the Lamb has come, and his bride has made herself ready" (Revelation 19:1-7). John was joyful amidst his physical and emotional pain.

How exceedingly blessed we are to live where suffering is very minimal. Pray daily for the persecuted. God hears your prayers. You are making a difference in their suffering. Paradoxically you will be rewarded with joy.

LEAPING WALLS
PSALM 18:19-33

"With my God I can leap a wall (or run through a barricade). God's way is perfect. The Lord's word is flawless; he shields all who take refuge in him. For who is God besides the Lord? And who is the Rock except our God? It is God who arms me with strength and keeps my way secure. He makes my feet like the feet of a deer; he causes me to stand on the heights" (Psalm 18:29-33 or II Samuel 22:30).

What wall or barricade are you facing today? God promises He will help you either overcome it by going over it or through it. The Lord says, "When you pass through the waters, I will be with you, and when you pass through the rivers, they will not sweep over you. When you walk through the fire, you will not be burned; the flames will not set you ablaze. For I am the Lord your God the Holy One of Israel, your Savior" (Isaiah 43:1-3).

"You will find your joy in the Lord, and he will cause you to ride in triumph on the heights of the land and to feast on the inheritance of your father Jacob. For the mouth of the Lord has spoken it" (Isaiah 58:14).

David says, "Even though I walk through the darkest valley, I will fear no evil, for you are with me, your rod and your staff, they comfort me" (Psalm 23:4). As the Israelites walked through the Red Sea with a wall of water by their side God will take you through with victory. God's rod is an instrument of authority used by the shepherds for guiding, rescuing and protecting his sheep. The staff is like a hiking stick to help stable you as you walk over rocky ground. When sheep wander off and need correction the shepherd uses his staff to pull them in line. Thank God for His rod and staff.

Live in these promises otherwise we will be discouraged when we read commands like Philippians 2:14-15: "Do everything without grumbling (complaining) or arguing, so that you may become blameless and pure, children of God without fault in a warped and crooked generation." If you are honest you will say, "This is impossible. I find it so natural to complain." Paul gives us the secret for accomplishing this "impossible" command in verses 12-13: "Continue to work out your salvation with fear and trembling, for it is God who works in you to will and to act in order to fulfill his good purpose."

Imagine what our homes and churches would be like if we put aside all complaining, grumbling and arguing? When we cry out to God for determination and the power to not grumble or complain He will surprise you! He can guide your tongue. David writes, "Set a guard over my mouth, Lord; keep watch over the door of my lips" (Psalm 141:3). James says, "No human being came tame the tongue" (3:7). Trust the Lord to guide your heart and your tongue. The Lord will amaze you with His victory.

Many Christians battle with discouragement. "Whenever trouble comes our way, let it be an opportunity for joy. For when your faith is tested, your endurance has a chance to grow. So let it grow, for when your endurance is fully developed, you will be strong in character and ready for anything" (James 1:2-4 NLT). The NIV says that we are to count our trials as pure joy. This is the only time in the Bible the adjective pure is used to describe joy. Pure is defined as vibrant, rich, deep, clear. That should give us incentive to leap over our walls today. The Christian life with its pure joy is truly amazing.

"God will bless you when people insult you, mistreat you and tell all kinds of evil lies about you because of me. Be happy and excited! You will have a great reward in heaven" (Matthew 5:11-12 CEV). In all our trials Peter says: "you greatly rejoice though now for a little while you may have had to suffer grief in all kinds of trials" (I Peter 1:6).

When Paul prays for the church in Ephesis, which many believe was a circle letter to several churches, he prayed: "that God . . . may give you the Spirit of wisdom and revelation, so that you may know him better. I pray that the eyes of your heart may be enlightened in order that you may know the hope to which he has called you, the riches of his glorious inheritance in his holy people, and his incomparable great power for us who believe. That power is the same as the mighty strength he exerted when he raised Christ from the dead" (Ephesians 1:17-20).

Claim God's amazing Resurrection power and joy, leap walls and go through barricades.

ARE YOU ENTHUSIASTIC?
ROMANS 12:11

An old Russian proverb said: "He who has this disease called Jesus will never be cured." I like to be around people who are enthusiastic. Have you lost your gusto or enthusiasm, your passion? Paul writes: "Never be lacking in zeal, but keep your spiritual fervor, serving the Lord" (Romans 12:11). Other translations read: "Never be lazy in your work, but serve the Lord enthusiastic." "Don't burn out; keep yourselves fueled and aflame. Be alert servants of the master." To the Ephesians Paul wrote, "Work with enthusiasm, as though you were working for the Lord rather than for people. Remember that the Lord will reward each one of us for the good we do whether we are slaves or free" (Ephesians 6:7-8). Solomon wrote, "One who is slack in work is brother to one who destroys" (Proverbs 18:9).

Paul oozed enthusiasm. He says that even though he is free he makes himself a slave to everyone, to win as many as possible. He enters into strict training to receive an eternal crown. (I Corinthians 9:19-27). He reminds the Ephesians: "Remember that for three years I never stopped warning each of you night and day with tears" (Acts 10:31). In coaching over 70 churches in church consultation work I discovered several small groups seldom, if ever, opened their Bible or prayed together. They were simply a social club. Contrast this with the early church that met together daily for Bible study, fellowship, the Lord's Supper and prayer. (Acts 2:42). One doesn't need to think twice as to why the church has lost its witness to the world. How can we call ourselves Christian and not mention what God is doing in our life?

Jesus' primary characteristic was compassion. Compassion is made from two words: "con" means "with" and "passion" which equals com-passion. Jesus lived with passion, zeal and focus. Jesus stood up and shouted on the last day of the Feast of Tabernacles: "If anyone thirsts, let him come to me and drink. Rivers (or fountains) of living water will brim and spill out (or overflow) of the depths of anyone who believes in me this way" (John 7:37-38 Msg.). When we drink this water Jesus offers, we will be enthusiastic.

Why is it so easy to lose our enthusiasm? Jesus said, "Because of the increase of wickedness, the love of most will grow cold" (Matthew 24:12). On another occasion Jesus asked, will there be any faith when I return. (Luke 18:8). It's obvious an enthusiastic life is a fight to the finish. God never promised us a comfortable and easy life here on earth in the midst of a "sinful and perverse generation" (Matthew 16:4). However, His love can heal all the pain of our unjust past. His grace is always more than sufficient to continue the fight of faith. (I Timothy 6:12).

It is easy to lose enthusiasm when we feel we are alone. But we are surrounded by a great cloud of witnesses who have been faithful. Hebrews 12:1-2 continues with, "throw off the burdens, and your past sins that can so easily entangle and cause you to lose your zeal. Instead run with patient endurance, steady and active persistence in the course set before you. Keep your eyes on Jesus, look away from the worldly things that will distract you. For the joy of obtaining the prize that was set before him, Jesus endured the cross, despising and ignoring the shame, and is now seated at the right hand of the throne of God."

Time seems to sap our enthusiasm. Thirty years after Jesus ascended to heaven most of the seven churches in Revelation 2 and 3 had grown cold or indifferent. To the church at Ephesis Jesus says, "You don't love me or each other as you did at first. Look how far you have fallen from your first love! Turn back to me and work as you did at first. If you don't, I will remove your lamp stand from its place among the churches" (Revelation 2:4-5).

The longer we are Christians, surveys indicate we witness less. We lose our first love. It's exciting working with those who come to faith for the first time. New Christians bring joy and enthusiasm to any congregation. Their enthusiasm encourages the church. Our nation has lost its way because the church has lost its fire.

Lethargy will rob our enthusiasm. Jesus says to the Church in Laodicea, "You are neither hot nor cold . . . since you are lukewarm, I will spit you out of my mouth! . . . You don't realize that you are wretched and miserable, poor, blind and naked" (Revelation 3:15-17 NLT). There is no room in the Christian life for laziness. Run with perseverance, fight the good fight of faith, make every effort, forget what is behind and strain forward to what lies ahead. (Philippians

3:14). "The Lord enables me to tread on the heights" (Habakkuk 3:19).

Grieving the Holy Spirit will cause us to lose our enthusiasm. "Do not grieve or offend the Holy Spirit. . . . Get rid of all bitterness, resentment, quarrelling, contention, anger, complaining, faultfinding, grumbling and slander along with every form of malice or ill will" (Ephesians 4:30-31). If there is anything you know God wants you to do that you are not doing or if there are things you are doing that you know God is not pleased with you, you are grieving the Holy Spirit. Your zeal and enthusiasm will drain away quickly.

Promised rewards encourage enthusiasm. "Be strong and steady, always be enthusiastic about the Lord's work, for you know that nothing you do for the Lord is ever useless" (I Corinthians 15:58). "God is not unjust; he will not forget your work and the love you have shown him as you have helped his people and continue to help them. We want each of you to show this same diligence (enthusiasm) to the very end, so that what you hope for may be fully realized. We do not want you to become lazy, but to imitate those who through faith and patience inherit what has been promised" (Hebrews 6:10-12).

Enthusiasm is to last until God calls us home. Just before his death Paul writes: "I have fought the good fight; I have finished the race. I have kept the faith. Now there is in store for me the crown of righteousness, which the Lord, the righteous Judge, will award to me on that day – and not only to me, but also to all who have longed for his appearing" (II Timothy 4:7-8).

Persistence will result in enthusiasm. "Don't get discouraged and give up, for we will reap a harvest of blessing at the appropriate time. Whenever you have the opportunity, do good to everyone" (Galatians 6:9-10).

Enthusiasm and zeal will infuse us with energy overcoming weariness and fatigue. When Jesus heard that John the Baptist was killed, He tried to get alone but the crowds continued to follow Him. He healed their sick and fed the multitude. Finally, Jesus gets alone but what does He do? He prays and then teaches the disciples a dramatic lesson at three A.M. when He comes walking on the water. Across the lake, a crowd was already gathering. Jesus was tired but He did not turn them away. He healed their sick. Jesus laid aside His need for rest to teach the disciples and to serve people. (Matthew 14:13-25). What passion!

Jesus' time with God in prayer enabled Him to be enthusiastic even when He was exhausted. (Matthew 14:23). "Those who wait on the Lord, (those who pray), will find new strength. They will fly high on wings like eagles. They will run and not grow weary. They will walk and not faint" (Isaiah 40:31). Always go back to the source of springs of living water and you will be rejuvenated. (John 7:38).

Loving God's Word builds enthusiasm and zeal. "How sweet are your words to my taste, sweeter than honey to my mouth" (Psalm 119:103). "Your statues are my heritage forever; they are the joy of my heart. My heart is set on keeping your decrees to the very end" (Psalm 119:11-12). His Word equips us for every good work. (II Timothy 3:17).

Thanksgiving and praise encourage enthusiasm. "Let those who favor my righteous cause and have pleasure in my uprightness shout for joy and be glad, and say continually, Let the Lord be magnified" (Psalm 35:27 AMP). "Give thanks to the Lord; his love endures forever" (Psalm 118:29).

Lord, forgive us for our lethargy. Wake us up from our compliancy. Help us to mount up with wings like eagles, to run and not be weary but enthusiastically serve you today. Amen.

C. PRAYER

THE AMAZING GOOD FIGHT OF FAITH
I TIMOTHY 6:12

Many American Christians believe the Christian life should be a cakewalk. The Bible teaches quite the opposite; we are to "Fight the good fight of faith . . ." (I Timothy 6:12). The church in China speaks of "open face warfare." This fight is a struggle to the finish. Taking up our cross as Jesus instructed us is not an easy life. Jesus promised the disciples they will experience tribulation. (John 16:33). Jesus didn't die to make us comfortable. He died to make us like Himself, i.e. we are to be holy as He is holy. (I Peter 1:16). He took up His cross and we must take ours. "People are born for trouble as predictably as sparks fly upward from a fire" (Job 5:7 NLT). "How short is life and how full of trouble" (Job 14:1 NLT). "Our days of labor are filled with pain and grief" (Ecclesiastes 2:23).

Since life is a battle we are to pray continually. (1 Thessalonians

5:17). Prayer is an effort of the will. Prayer is the main business of our life. Apart from Jesus we can do nothing. "Our Father knows what you need before you ask him" (Matthew 6:8), therefore, prayer is not to inform Him of our needs. Rather we pray to bring our hearts in line with the Father's heart.

Praying opens our heart to receive God's grace. When we pray, we enable God to mold us into the character of Christ. (Romans 8:29). We draw close to Him to hear His Spirit's voice, to seek an intimate, personal, passionate relationship with our Father. We pray to our Father but do we know Him? (Philippians 3:10). Are we more concerned about getting or receiving things from our Father than we are to know Him? Does your child simply want your gifts or does he or she love you? Loving you will make a huge difference in what they ask of you. Are we concerned about how our prayer affects the heart of our Father?

We have one main battle in life, the battle of faith: Do I believe God? Faith is mentioned more than 300 times in the New Testament. We must meet two qualifications to come to God: believe that He exists and second, that He rewards those who earnestly seek Him. (Hebrews 11:6).

How do we know God exists? "What may be known about God is plain to everyone, because God has made it plain to them. For since the creation of the world God's invisible qualities – his eternal power and divine nature – have been clearly seen, being understood from what has been made, so that people are without excuse" (Romans 1:19-20).

God makes it hard for people to go to hell but our self-centered nature blinds us and makes it difficult for us to recognize Him. If you wear a watch, do you say the watch came into existence on its own? Of course not. Someone had to design the watch. We see God's creation, which is far more complex, and say it just happened. Man designed the watch. God designed His creation. The devil blinds us so we simply take His creation for granted or worst yet, attribute it to chance.

People suppress the truth by denying the obvious, which is wickedness. (Romans 1:18). The truth is everywhere: in every blade of grass, every leaf, every fruit-bearing tree, and every birth of a baby. "The heavens declare the glory of God" (Psalm 19:1). How can anyone not see a beautiful sunset, the formation of the clouds, the blessing of rain upon dry land and not recognize God? God makes it hard for people to deny Him. Compared to the greatness of God we in all our learning know very little. Science can't explain existence or the purpose of our existence. We are thankful for what science can do but science can't heal all our diseases, give us a life's purpose or keep us from death.

The other qualification for faith according to Hebrews 11:6 is that God rewards those who earnestly seek Him. He pleads and begs for us to believe He hears our prayers. "Call to me and I will answer you and tell you great and unsearchable things you do not know" (Jeremiah 33:3). "The Lord is near to all who call on him, to all who call on him in truth" (Psalm 145:18). Jesus promised: "Ask and it will be given you; seek and you will find; knock and the door will be opened to you. For everyone who asks receives; the one who seeks finds; and to the one who knocks, the door will be opened" (Matthew 7:7-8).

Jesus did only what the Father told Him to do and said only what the Father told Him to say. (John 5:19; 12:49-50). As we walk with Jesus, we too will learn to put our faith into action so we can do and say what Jesus would have us say and do.

Jesus said, "If you remain in me and my words remain in you, ask whatever you wish (exercise your faith), and it will be done for you" (John 15:7). The key to this seemingly unconditional promise is for His Word to remains in us. When our life lines up with His Word and His will we never ask Him for anything except only what is His will and therefore our prayers are always answered. God answers every prayer, "yes," "no" or "wait." However, many times God's timing is different than ours.

To fight the good fight of faith we stand firmly on God's word, considering ourselves dead to our feelings and our human reasoning, not letting sin rule in our mortal body by obeying its self-centered desires. We live by the Spirit and put to death the misdeeds of the body. (Romans 8:13). This is a fight because our ego does not die easily.

To fight the fight of faith we must wear the full armor of God to battle with Satan. "Stand firm with the belt of truth buckled around your waist, (you saturate your being with God's truth), with the breastplate of righteousness in place, and with your feet fitted with the readiness that comes from the gospel of peace. In addition take up the shield of faith, (you deliberately hold it up), with which you can extinguish all the flaming arrows of the evil one. Take the helmet of salvation and the sword of the Spirit, which is the word of God. And pray in the Spirit" (Ephesians 6:13-18).

There is a mystery here. We can't always see things as God sees them. Why do the babies die or planes fall out of the sky? Why all the suffering? Why all the natural disasters: hurricanes, tsunamis, floods, fires, earthquakes and famines? Why all the hatred, violence and wars? God can see the beginning and the end. He allows these things to show people and nations their own sinfulness, and to show them by bitter experience and suffering the true alternative to rejecting Jesus and going their own way. He knows how every action, both good and evil, plays out in the end and overrules so that all things work together for good to those who love Him. (Romans 8:28). He will never cause us a needless tear. What an amazing God!

I am writing this during the pandemic of the coronavirus. At the same time racial inequality and prejudice are causing consternation around the world. God is using these to bring many people to Himself. The coronavirus hopefully helps us to remember that God is the only one who has the cure for our bodies. The racial conflicts should open our eyes to see the evil of prejudice we all find in our heart. May we seek forgiveness and receive His healing thus making our world a bit more like heaven on earth.

THE MYSTERY AND POWER OF PRAYER
LUKE 5:15-16

"Pray continually" (I Thessalonians 5:17). How is that possible? Prayer must never turn into a legalistic ritual like a routine exercise. Prayer is our life. Special times of prayer are also necessary for a close walk with Jesus. Henri Nouwen's perspective is helpful: "To pray, I think, does not mean to think about God in contrast to thinking about other things, nor does it mean spending time with God instead of spending time with other people. As soon as we begin to divide our thoughts into thoughts about God and thoughts about other things, like people and events, we separate God from our daily life . . .

"At that point, God is allocated to a pious little niche in some corner of our lives where we only think pious thoughts and experience pious feelings. Although it is important and even indispensable for our spiritual lives to set apart time for God and God alone, our prayer can only become unceasing when all our thoughts – beautiful or ugly, high or low, proud or shameful, sorrowful or joyful – can be thought in the presence of the One who dwells in us and surrounds us . . .

"By trying to do this, our unceasing thinking is converted into unceasing prayer, moving us from a self-centered monologue to a God-centered dialogue. To do this, we want to try to convert our thoughts into conversation. The main question, therefore, is not so much what we think, but to whom we present our thoughts." (Henri Nouwen, from Jim Denison's blog, April 24, 2020).

We are to pray continually as well as to rejoice and give thanks continually. (I Thessalonians 5:17). To pray continually we develop a walking and talking relationship with Jesus. The exercise of spiritual breathing will help us. Just as we exhale and inhale, we can exhale or confess our sins to Jesus and inhale His grace, forgiveness and blessing. God knows our thoughts: "You perceive my thought from afar" (Psalm 139:2). Sharing your thoughts with God will help you pray continually.

Many are too busy—watching TV, moonlighting, following sports or playing games—they crowd out prayer unless they come against a wall. A life of carnality blocks the power of prayer. Prayer becomes no more than religious ritual. Isaiah 1:14-17 *Message Bible*, describes it: "When you put on your prayer performance, I'll be looking the other way. No matter how long or loud or often you pray, I'll not be listening . . . Clean up your act. Sweep your lives clean of your evildoings . . . Say no to wrong . . . Work for justice. Help the down-and-out. Stand up for the homeless. Go to bat for the defenseless."

Jesus set aside times for prayer. Crowds of people came to Jesus for healing. Jesus left the crowds and withdrew to a lonely place to pray. (Luke 5:15-16). In fact, Luke says, "He often went to lonely places and prayed" (Luke 5:16). Mark writes, "Very early in the morning, while it was still dark; Jesus got up, left the house and went off to a solitary place, where he prayed" (Mark 1:35, Luke 4:42).

For what did Jesus pray? He prayed to know the Father's heart, His Father's will and for courage to obey His Father. Jesus was intimate with His Father. Prayer was Jesus' communication line so that He said only what the Father told Him to say and did only what the Father told Him to do. He did only what pleased the Father. (John 5:19; 8:28-29; 12:49-50). We have the same privilege Jesus had.

Jesus said, "Remain in me, as I also remain in you" (John 15:4). Obeying this command results in the same intimacy Jesus had with the Father. Jesus promised if we abide in Him and in His Word, we can ask whatever we wish, and it will be done for us. (John 15:7). That promise should give us great incentive to cultivate intimacy with Jesus. Living on that level the supernatural becomes natural.

Prayer is where the action is. Prayer is the weapon God gave us to defeat our sinful desires, to overcome the way of the world as well as overcoming satanic forces. "Our struggle is not against flesh and blood, but against the rulers, authorities, powers of this dark world and against the spiritual forces of evil" (Ephesians 6:12). "In this world we will have trouble," said Jesus, "but take heart! I have overcome the world" (John 16:33).

Jesus gave us the keys of the kingdom, "whatever you bind on earth will be bound in heaven, and whatever you lose on earth will be loosed in heaven" (Matthew 16:19, 18:18). After He arose, He said, "'As the Father has sent me, I am sending you.' And with that he breathed on them and said, 'Receive the Holy Spirit. If you forgive anyone's sins their sins are forgiven; if you do not forgive them, they are not forgiven'" (John 20:21-23). Too often we fail to act upon the sweeping authority God has delegated to us. Jesus gives us His authority to be His faithful witness and to make disciples. He promised to be with us every day until He returns. As the Father sent Jesus, He sends us to rescue a fallen world. Prayer grows our faith. Prayer allows God to use us in ways that are utterly beyond who we are in our humaneness.

Before Jesus returned to heaven, He told His disciples to wait in Jerusalem for the gift of the Holy Spirit. One hundred twenty disciples of Jesus prayed in the upper room for ten days – Pentecost came. The early church devoted themselves to the scriptures, to fellowship, and to prayer. (Acts 2:42). Jesus said, "My house shall be called a house of prayer" (Mk. 11:17). What will it take for our churches to be known as "Houses of Prayer?" Since Pentecost we don't need to pray for ten days for the Holy Spirit to come but we do need to pray daily for the fullness of the Holy Spirit and for times of refreshing and empowerment. (Ephesians 5:18, Acts 3:19).

I help to lead a weekly prayer group that focuses on world needs. After every meeting I experience joy and a renewed faith to believe God is answering these prayers both at home and around the world. Prayer changes our world.

Jesus instructed us to pray for workers to reach our world. He said, "The harvest is plentiful but the workers are few. Ask the Lord of the harvest . . . to send out workers into his harvest fields" (Matthew 9:36-38). Do we believe that the number of the labors and the measure of the harvest actually depends upon our prayers? Without our prayers, fields ready for reaping will be left to perish.

Pastor Brother Yun from China says that he corrects Western

Christians who say they pray for the government in China to collapse so Christians can live in freedom. He says, "Don't pray for the persecution to stop! We shouldn't pray for a lighter load to carry, but a stronger back to endure! Then the world will see that God is with us, empowering us to live in a way that reflects his love and power. This is true freedom!" (Paul Hattaway, *Back to Jerusalem*, pp. 57-58).

How sincere are our prayers? In the garden before His Crucifixion, Jesus "agonized" in prayer, (Luke 22:44). Peter was in prison and the church was "earnestly" praying for him and he was delivered. (Acts 12:5). Paul writes, "I want you to know how much I am 'struggling' for you and for those in Laodicea, and for all who have not met me personally" (Colossians 2:1). Paul agonized for those he never met. What love! "Epaphras . . . is always 'wrestling' in prayer for those in Colossi, that they may stand firm in all the will of God, mature, and fully assured" (Colossians 4:12).

Jesus' brother, James, was nicknamed, James "camel knees" because his knees were calloused from kneeling in prayer. He writes, "The effectual fervent prayer of a righteous man availeth much" (James 5:16). "You will seek me and find me when you seek me with all your heart" (Jeremiah 29:13). The phrase *with all your heart* means "with extra energy." It means giving it everything you've got – 100 percent. It means doing something like your life depended on it. Oh, that we would have a passion like Jesus who got up before sun up and prayed. (Mark 1:35).

Missionary statesman Don Jacobs writes: "We Christians discover that our most powerful weapon against Satan is fervent prayer. When I asked some Ethiopians why their church grew so much during their 10 years of severe persecution (1982-1992), they responded: 'We learned to pray out of our desperation.' . . . Persecution drives saints to give themselves to imploring prayer, because they can simply do nothing about the situation. Churches around the world are rediscovering the mighty power of prayer. Entire congregations are praying aloud; all at once for a long time, praying fervently, begging in fact. They are experiencing the truth of Jesus' invitation to ask . . . to seek . . . and to knock. . . (Matthew 7:7)."

My Ethiopian roommate in seminary knew what it was to give extensive time to prayer. His holy habit had a life-changing effect on me.

Hear God's voice. Jesus said, "Father, I thank you that you have heard me. I knew that you always hear me, but I said this for the benefit of the people standing here, that they may believe that you sent me" (John 11:41-42). "I know my sheep and my sheep know me . . . They will listen to my voice" (John 10:4). In order to hear God's voice, we need to take time to quiet ourselves and listen and walk in the Spirit. Seldom does the Spirit speak with a shout. It's usually the small voice deep within us. It's so easy to let our rational minds overpower it.

The most frequent way God speak to us is when we read and study His Word. I try to breathe a prayer every time I read His Word: "Lord open my eyes and my heart to learn what you want to teach me today." I assure you He will answer that prayer.

The Moravian Community of Herrnhut in Saxony, in 1727, commenced a round-the-clock "prayer watch" that continued nonstop for over a hundred years. By 1791, 65 years after commencement of that prayer vigil, the small Moravian community had sent 300 missionaries to the ends of the earth. This was the beginning of the modern missionary movement. Every spiritual awakening in America began with prayer. Jim Denison's blog, April 1, 2020, reports: "The First Great Awakening began with the prayer meetings of Theodore Frelingheusen. The second was sparked by Isaac Backus' call to prayer. The third was birthed in Jeremiah Lamphier's prayer meeting at Old North Dutch Church in New York City on September 23, 1857. The Fourth Great Awakening began in 1904 in a prayer meeting led by Evan Roberts."

Fasting is seldom mentioned today. Fasting is an indication that we are serious with God. We say "no" to our worldly desires so that our spirits can gain strength. It's only in a life of moderation, temperance and self-denial that we have the heart and strength to pray.

Jesus said, "When you fast," not "if you fast" (Matthew 6:16). Jesus fasted. (Matthew 4). The apostles, prophets and teachers in Antioch fasted. (Acts 13:2-3). Jesus said, "when the bridegroom is taken from you then you will fast" (Luke 5:35). With tears Paul told the Philippians, "many live as enemies of the cross, their god is their stomach, all they think about is their appetites, their mind is on things of this world" (Philippians 3:18-19). I think Paul would say the same thing to the church today. In John 4 the disciples urged Jesus to eat but He said His food was to do God's will and to finish His work. (John 4:32). Do we have a passion for lost people so we forget to eat? This is true fasting.

BEING THANKFUL
BRINGS AMAZING RESULTS
PSALM 30:12, LUKE 17:11-19

Thankfulness is the key to a meaningful and productive life. Psalms is filled with thanksgiving. "O Lord my God, I will give you thanks forever" (Psalm 30:12). "Give thanks to the Lord, for he is good; his love endures forever" (Psalm 107:1). "Let them give thanks to the Lord for his unfailing love and his wonderful deeds. He satisfies the thirsty and fills the hungry with good things" (Psalm 107:8-9). "Oh come, let us sing to the Lord; . . . Let us come into his presence with thanksgiving; let us make a joyful noise to him with songs of praise! For the Lord is a great God, and a great King above all gods" (Psalm 95:1-3).

"Make a joyful noise unto the Lord all ye lands. Serve the Lord with gladness – come before his presence with singing . . . Enter into his gates with thanksgiving and into his courts with praise. Be thankful unto him and bless his name. For the Lord is good: his mercy is everlasting: and his truth endures to all generations" (Psalm 100).

From prison Paul writes, "Give thanks always to God the Father for everything, in the name of our Lord Jesus Christ" (Ephesians 5:20). "In every situation, by prayer and petition with thanksgiving, present your request to God" (Philippians 4:6). We are to sing with thanksgiving to the Lord with "psalm, hymns and songs from the Spirit, singing to God with gratitude in your hearts. And whatever you do, . . . do it all in the name of the Lord Jesus, giving thanks" (Colossians 3:15-17).

When we are filled with God's Spirit the first evidence is that we have a song or melody in our heart. (Ephesians 5:18-19). I wake up at night and in the morning with a hymn or Gospel song I learned as a youth. I thank God often for this song—it's usually with me 24/7. The second result of being filled with the Holy Spirit is to "always give thanks to God the Father for everything in the name of our Lord Jesus Christ."

How can we give thanks for everything including the tragedies of life—a baby dying, car accidents, cancer that robs us of our health, storms that destroy crops, or forest fires? We live in a fallen world controlled by Satan the prince and power of the air, the present ruler of this evil age. (Ephesians 2:2). Therefore, terrible things happen every day. We give thanks not for difficulties or disasters but for the fact that God is in control. He will overrule in all these tragic situations. He will use them for good—often as a wake-up call—for us to walk closer to Him.

"Give thanks in all circumstances for this is God's will for you in Christ Jesus" (I Thessalonians 5:18). "Since we are receiving a kingdom that cannot be shaken, let us be thankful, and so worship God with reverence and awe, for our God is a consuming fire" (Hebrew 12:28-29). Generosity causes others to offer thanksgiving to God. (II Corinthians 9:11-12). Accompany your prayers of petition with thanksgiving. I try to begin my day thanking God for the night's rest and the dawn of a new day as well as to thank and praise Him throughout the day.

Learn to thank God for the difficult times. David writes: "Before I was afflicted, I went astray" (Psalm 119:67). "It was good for me to be afflicted so that I might learn your decrees" (v. 71). We rejoice in our trials because they refine us. (James 1:2-3). Oswald Chambers says, "No matter how difficult something may be. I must say, 'Lord, I am delighted to obey you in this.' Instantly, the Son of God will move to the forefront of my life, and will manifest in my body that which glorified him."

Thankfulness brings amazing results. "It's reported that neuroscientists have discovered that thankful thoughts produce pleasure in the brain. Thankfulness stimulates areas of the brain regulating stress. A multiple of studies have connected gratitude with resilience. The more grateful you are, the more likely you are to exhibit patience and self-control . . . Grateful people sleep better. Couples who exhibit thankfulness tend to be more committed to each other and are more likely to remain in their relationships. The spiritual benefits are even more impressive." (Jim Denison's blog).

Thankfulness builds faith and promotes love. Praise and thanksgiving drive out depression, discouragement, doubt, and reduces mental illness, and promotes health, fulfilling marriages and healthy home life.

We often focus on things we don't have and fail to appreciate and thank God for what He has given us. Jesus and His disciples entered a village. Ten lepers stood at a distance and called out; "Jesus have pity on us." Jesus told them, go show yourselves to the priest. As they went, they were healed and made clean. However, only one returned to thank Jesus. (Luke 17:11-19). Do we find ourselves with the ungrateful nine?

Lord, we confess that we are too often among the nine that forget to thank You. Forgive us. All that we are and have You have given us. Thank You for Your forgiveness and Your mercies. With Your help we vow to be people with a spirit of thanksgiving and to bless Your name forever. Amen.

AMAZING POWER OF PRAISE
PSALM 34:1

Praise is mentioned nearly 450 times in the Bible. "I will praise the Lord at all times; his praise will always be on my lips, I will glory in the Lord, let the afflicted hear and rejoice. Glorify the Lord with me; let us exalt his name together" (Psalm 34:1). "Praise be to the God and Father of our Lord Jesus Christ who has blessed us . . . with every spiritual blessing in Christ" (Ephesians 1:3). Every day the church in Acts 2 met and praised God. "And the Lord added to their number daily those who were being saved" (Acts 2:46-47).

Praise starts with a holy reverence for God based on God's own word. "Whatever you don't turn into praise turns into pride." Corrie ten Boom said, "Take compliments and offer them as a bouquet in thanksgiving to God."

We need to have such a close relationship with God and Jesus that we naturally overflow with praise 24/7. When God delivered the Children of Israel from slavery in Egypt, Miriam led God's people in this song of praise. "I will sing to the Lord, for he is highly exalted. Both horse and driver he has hurled into the sea. The Lord is my strength and my defense, he has become my salvation. He is my God and I will praise him; my father's God and I will exalt him" (Exodus 15:1-2).

Paul Billheimer writes, "The missing element that is necessary to energize prevailing prayer that binds and casts out Satan is triumphant faith. And the missing element that is necessary to energize triumphant faith is praise – perpetual, purposeful, aggressive praise. Praise is the highest form of prayer because it combines petition with faith. Praise is the spark plug of faith. It is the one thing needed to get faith airborne, enabling it to soar above the deadly fog of doubt . . .

"Praise is the detergent which purifies faith and purges doubt from the heart. The secret of answered prayer is faith without doubt. (Mark 11:23). The secret of faith without doubt is praise, triumphant praise, continuous praise, praise that is a way of life. This is the solution to the problem of a living faith and successful prayer. We need a massive program of praise." (*Destined for the Throne*, p. 18). Praise lifts our spirits. That's one reason we enjoy the Psalms:

Praise the Lord from the heavens; praise him in the heights above.
Praise him, all his angels; praise him, all his heavenly hosts.
Praise him, sun and moon; praise him, all you shining stars.
Praise him, you highest heavens and you water above the skies.
Let them praise the name of the Lord, for at his command they were created, and he established them forever and ever – he issued a decree that will never pass away.
Praise the Lord from the earth, you great sea creatures and all ocean depths; lightning and hail, snow and clouds, stormy winds that do his bidding, you mountains and all hills, fruit trees and all cedars, wild animals and all cattle, small creatures and flying birds, kings of the earth and all nations, you princes and all rulers on earth, young men and women, old men and children.
Let them praise the name of the Lord, for his name alone is exalted; his splendor is above the earth and the heavens. He has raised up for his people a horn, the praise of all his faithful servants of Israel, the people close to his heart.
Praise the Lord" (Psalm 148).

Peter reminds us who we are and why God blessed us. "You are a chosen generation, a royal priesthood, a holy nation, his own special people, (why) – that you may proclaim the praise of him who called you out of darkness into his marvelous light" (I Peter 2:9). David writes, "sing to the Lord, sing praise to him; tell of all his wonderful acts" (Psalm 105:2). Were you ever in a meeting when the leaders invited you to share praise or thanks and everything was quiet? May the Lord embolden us to share His praise and blessing with others.

Craig Courtney expresses it so well: "I'll praise my Maker while I've breath; and when my voice is lost in death, praise shall employ my nobler powers. My days of praise shall ne'er be past, while life, and thought, and being last, or immortality endures. (2). Happy are they whose hopes rely on Israel's God, who made the sky and earth and seas, with all their train; whose truth forever stands secure, who saves the oppressed and feeds the poor, and none shall find God's promise vain. (3) The Lord pours eyesight on the blind; the Lord supports the fainting mind and sends the laboring conscience peace. God helps the stranger in distress and widow and the fatherless; and grants the prisoner sweet release." (Repeat stanza #1)

There are times in our walk with Jesus that we are bombarded with troubles. We find it hard to praise God. I thank God for the book of Job. When word came to Job that his servants and possession were destroyed and that a storm destroyed the house where his children were gathered and only the one who brought the report was spared, he says, "Naked I came from my mother's womb, and naked I will depart. The Lord gave and the Lord has taken away, may the name of the Lord be praised" (Job 1:20-21). Job offered a "sacrifice of praise." He made a deliberate choice to praise God. We must learn from Job. We are to love God not for His gifts; they were all removed from Job. Job loved God for who He was, not for His blessings. We don't need to wonder why he is described as a blameless, upright and God-fearing man.

Sarah Young in her book *Jesus Today* writes, "You used to walk in spiritual darkness before you trusted me as Savior. I personally brought you out of that darkness into my light – so that you might proclaim my praises. This is a delightful privilege and responsibility. I have entrusted you with the task of telling others about my awesome qualities. To carry out this assignment effectively, you need to delve into the riches of who I am by studying my word. You also need to delight yourself in me. Then the joy of my presence will shine from your face as you tell others about me." "God inhabits the praises of his people" (Psalm 22:3 KJV).

While in prison Paul begins his letter to the Ephesians with praise. Once he starts, he can't get stopped for 14 verses. He praises the God and Father of our Lord Jesus Christ, who blessed us in the heavenly realms with every spiritual blessing in Christ. Then he lists several blessings of the Father, Son and the Holy Spirit: God chose us before the creation of the world to be holy and blameless in His sight. He predestined us for adoption to His sonship. We are forgiven and redeemed. He lavished His grace on us. We are given hope, all to the praise of His glory. The Holy Spirit is given as a deposit guaranteeing our inheritance—all to the praise of God's glory.

"Praise the Lord. Praise God in his sanctuary; praise him in his mighty heavens. Praise him for his acts of power; praise him for his surpassing greatness. Praise him with the sounding of the trumpet;

praise him with the harp and lyre. Praise him with timbrel and dancing, praise him with strings and pipe, praise him with the clash of cymbals, praise him with resounding cymbals. Let everything that has breath praise the Lord. Praise the Lord!" (Psalm 150). Praise lifts our spirits and opens the door for joy to fill our souls.

Are you a person of praise? Apparently, the Christians in Philippi needed to improve their praise level. Paul instructs them, "Do everything without grumbling or arguing, so that you may become blameless and pure, 'children of God without fault in a warped and crocked generation'" (Philippians 2:14-15). "Do not let any unwholesome talk come out of your mouth, but only what is helpful for building others up . . . that it may benefit those who listen" (Ephesians 4:29). Practicing continual praise will overcome the grumbling spirit found too often among God's people.

"Let us give thanks (praise) to the Lord for his unfailing love and for his wonderful deeds to mankind, for he satisfies the thirst and fills the hungry with good things" (Psalm 107:8-9). How often have you praised or thanked the Lord today? May we overflow with praise and thanksgiving. (Colossians 2:6).

AMAZING POWER OF ASKING ANYTHING IN JESUS' NAME
JOHN 14:13-14

From childhood Jesus' sweeping promises have amazed me. Jesus said, "I will do whatever you ask in my name, so that the Father may be glorified in the Son. You may ask me for anything in my name, and I will do it" (John 14:13-14). "Whatever you ask in my name the Father will give you. This is my command: Love each other" (John 15:16-17). "My Father will give you whatever you ask in my name. Until now you have not asked for anything in my name. Ask and you will receive and you joy will be complete" (John 16:23-24). Jesus repeated this promise three times in His final instructions to His disciples, just hours before going to the cross. In addition, John 15:7 is nearly the same: "If you remain in me and my words remain in you, ask whatever you wish, and it will be done for you" (John 15:7).

"Have faith in God. Truly I tell you, if anyone says to this mountain, 'Go, throw yourself into the sea,' and does not doubt in their heart but believes that what they say will happen, it will be done for them. Therefore, I tell you, whatever you ask for in prayer, believe that you have received it, and it will be yours. And when you stand praying, if you hold anything against anyone, forgive them, so that your Father in heaven may forgive you your sins" (Mark 11:22-25). "If you have faith as small as a mustard seed, you can say to this mountain, 'Move from here to there; and it will move.' Nothing will be impossible for you" (Matthew 17:20).

Jesus' beloved disciple John adds this in his first letter: "This is the confidence we have in approaching God: that if we ask anything according to his will, he hears us. And if we know that he hears us – whatever we ask – we know that we have what we asked of him" (I John 5:14-15).

There are seven conditions attached to these sweeping promises: (1) We must remain or dwell in Jesus and His words must remain in us. To remain or abide in Jesus, we will do only what Jesus would do. We will love His Word and meditate on it day and night. (John 15:7). (2) We must love each other. (John 15:16-17). (3) We must not doubt but believe what we ask, and then it will be done. (Mark 11:23). (4) We must forgive each other. (Mark 11:23-24). (5) We must ask according to His will. It is not my will, my desires, my goals, and my vision. It is His will for my life. (I John 5:14-15). (6) We must keep His commandments. (I John 3:21-23). And (7) We must ask in His name. (John 16:24).

A person's name represents his or her character. To do something in a person's name means to do only what is in line with that person's character and with his or her authority. When we do something in the name of someone else, we do it on his or her behalf and with their blessing. We express the person's will and rely on their authority. For instance, when an assistant calls "in the name of his or her boss," the assistant is carrying out the boss's will with the boss's authority, the assistant has the right to make arrangements because of who the boss is. When we pray in Jesus' name, we do the same thing. We are praying with His authority.

We pray in accordance to His will based upon the fact that we are in Christ and He is in us. (John 15:7). Praying in Jesus' name we also pray with His blessing. Because we can claim Jesus' work on the cross for our salvation, we can approach God in prayer. Jesus is the sacrificial lamb that purifies us. (John 1:29). He is our high priest who represents us so we can approach God with confidence. (Hebrews 4:14-5:10).

When we approach God in Jesus' name, we are claiming His redemption and therefore our worthiness to communicate with God.

Asking in Jesus' name is no magic formula. God is not Santa Claus. Praying in Jesus' name is an expression of our position in Christ. "If our hearts do not condemn us, we have confidence before God and receive from him anything we ask because we keep his commands and do whatever pleases him" (I John 3:21-22).

At times our prayers are not answered because of lack of faith, (Matthew 17:20), and because we do not obey His commands. Often His timing is different than ours. Some of our prayers will not be answered until after we die. James also adds: "You ask and do not receive, because you ask wrongly, to spend it on your passions" (James 4:3). "You do not have because you do not ask God. When you ask, you do not receive because you ask with wrong motives that you may spend what you get on your pleasures" (James 4:2-4). If we treasure or value sin the Lord will not hear our prayers. (Psalm 66:18). "If anyone turns a deaf ear to my instruction even their prayers are detestable" (Proverbs 28:9).

Jesus reminds us we need to be persistence in our prayers. Persistence is an indication of our faith. When the man went to his friend for bread in the middle of the night his friend said, "No." Jesus continues: "Even though he will not get up and give you the bread because of friendship, yet because of your shameless audacity he will surely get up and give you as much as you need" (Luke 11:8-9).

Corrie Ten Boom said, "Prayer is not the spare tire but the steering wheel." John Wesley said, "God will do nothing but in answer to prayer." S. D. Gordon said, "The greatest thing anyone can do for God and for man is to pray. You can do more than pray after you have prayed, but you cannot do more than pray until you have prayed." E. M. Bounds said, "God shapes the world by prayer." Let's make prayer our main business.

As we pray, we pray according to His will, we pray with a pure heart, in faith, based upon our position as God's child, upon His authority and it will be done for us in His time and way.

It is absolutely amazing that the God who created the cosmos inclines His ear, or turns His ear to hear His children. (Psalm 116:2). Let's honor Him with our prayers of faith.

AMAZING SOLITUDE
PSALM 46:10

"Be still, and know that I am God" (Psalm 46:10). "In quietness and trust is your salvation" (Isaiah 30:15). "The fruit of righteousness will be peace; its effect will be quietness and confidence forever" (Isaiah 32:17).

After a hectic day in Jesus' ministry, "Very early in the morning, while it was still dark; Jesus got up, left the house and went off to a solitary place, where he prayed" (Mark 1:35). On another occasion Jesus went to the mountainside to pray, and spent the whole night praying to God. (Luke 6:12). In fact, "Jesus often withdrew to lonely places and prayed" (Luke 5:16). Solitude was important in the life of our Lord.

One of the major problems in our American culture is loneliness. David said, "You fill me with joy in your presence, with eternal pleasures at your right hand" (Psalm 16:11). When we abide in Jesus as the branch abides in the vine Jesus call us His friends. (John 15:15). Being Jesus' friend will go a long way to take care of our loneliness problem. Being intimate with Jesus, i.e. knowing Him, not just knowing about Him is necessary to relieve loneliness. We hear Him best when alone with Him.

There is a major difference between knowing about Jesus and knowing Jesus. We can read our Bible, pray, go to church, give in the offering, help in the church's program, and even be a leader in your church and still not know Jesus. You must spend time in His presence to really know Him. Paul says that his goal in life is to know Christ. (Philippians 3:10). Ask yourself, do I know Jesus? If you really know Him your loneliness problem will vanish.

While we need to be careful not to take God's friendship lightly or approach Him flippantly, He wants to be intimate with us. The song by Austris Whithol, "My God and I Go in the Field Together" has meant much to me. "My God and I go in the field together. We walk and talk as good friends should and do. We clasp our hands, our voices ring with laughter. My God and I walk through the meadow's hue ... He tells me of the years that went before me. When heavenly plans were made for me to be. When all was but a dream of dim reflection, to come to life, earth's verdant glory sees ... My God and I will go for aye together. We'll walk and talk just as good friends do. This earth will pass, and with it common trifles. But God and I will go unendingly."

He invites us to come to Him: "Come to me, all you who are weary and burdened, and I will give you rest . . . I am gentle and humble in heart and you will find rest for your souls" (Matthew 11:28-29). Fannie Crosby expresses being in solitude in these words: "He hideth my soul in the cleft of the rock that shadows a dry, thirsty land; He hideth my life in the depth of His love, And covers me there with His hand."

After Jesus' Crucifixion the disciples were devastated. Two of them decided to return home to Emmaus. Jesus appeared to them on this seven-mile walk and asked them what they were discussing. They couldn't believe He hadn't heard about Jesus of Nazareth being crucified. They believed Jesus was the Messiah and now He is dead. Jesus explained to them what was said about Him in all the scriptures concerning Him. (Luke 24:13-35). How often, like these disciples, does Jesus walk beside us and we are unaware of His presence. Ask God to open your eyes to recognize Jesus in our daily walk of life. Can we be any closer to Jesus than if He were here in bodily form?

Must we have human friendship to be completely fulfilled? God designed for us to be in a family and to have many brothers and sisters but when because of various circumstances we are forced to be alone, such as some missionaries working in fields where no one has taken the Gospel, Jesus is a friend that is closer than our earthly family or relationships of our friends.

Loneliness is one of the top complaints of Americans. A healthy church will go a long way to overcoming this need. The house church model is much better equipped to meet this need than the large gatherings that characterize most churches today. It is difficult to have in-depth relationships with more than 25 or so in a group. If you have attended church regularly for years and do not have a friend who you feel comfortable to call when in need—either you are attending an unhealthy church or you are not building deep relationships. "We belong to one another" (Romans 12:5). There are 76 "one another" admonitions in the New Testament that our often overlooked in our individualistic culture.

The New Testament house churches consisted of being members of one another. They cared for one another, loved each other, served each other, prayed for each other, etc. Paul says that he will be refreshed by the company of the church family in Rome. (Romans 15:32). "I was glad when Stephanas, Fortunatus and Achaicus arrived, because . . . they refreshed my spirit and yours also" (I Corinthians 16:17-18). Healthy churches meet the needs of those who are lonely.

Learn to abide in that solitary place with Jesus. The Psalmist writes, "Whoever dwells in the shelter of the Most High will rest in the shadow of the Almighty. I will say of the Lord, 'He is my refuge and my fortress, my God, in him I trust. . . .' 'He will cover you with his feathers, and under his wings you will find refuge'" (Psalm 91:1-4). A persecuted Christian said, "We don't call 9-1-1, we call Psalm 91:1: We dwell in the shelter of the Most High and rest in the shadow of the Almighty."

Jesus says, "My sheep know my voice" (John 10:3-4). How do we hear His voice? Elisha was alone when he heard the "gentle whisper" of God. (I Kings 19:12). Jacob was transformed by his solitary encounter with God (Genesis 32:22-32). Moses met God when he was alone in the desert (Exodus 3:1-2). When Peter was alone, he received a vision that transformed his thinking so that from then on, he invited the Gentiles into God's family. (Acts 10:15). John was alone "in the Spirit on the Lord's day" when he met the risen Christ on Patmos. (Revelation 1:9).

Parents use isolation to discipline their children: "Go to your room until you can learn to play without fighting with your siblings." Prisoners are often placed in solitary confinement. For those who don't know Jesus as their friend, being alone for extended periods can be serious punishment. But for those who know Jesus, they know He promised to never leave us or forsake us. (Hebrews 13:5).

Paul was often alone in prison. He filled his mind with positive thoughts: "Whatever is true, whatever is noble, whatever is right, whatever is pure, whatever is lovely, whatever is admirable – if anything is excellent or praise-worthy – think about such things" (Philippians 4:8). Isaiah reminds us: "Thou will keep him in perfect peace whose mind is stayed on thee" (26:3 KJV).

David spent many nights alone meditating as he tended the sheep. For example, the word "meditation" appears six times in Psalm 119. Worry is basically the same as meditation except one is positive, and the other, worry is negative. Worry leads to frustration and depression. Meditation on God's Word and works leads to joy and peace.

"Writing for the *New York Times*, Tim Herrera praises the value of solitude. He notes that it helps regulate our emotions, conveying a calming effect that prepares us to better engage with other people. Solitude also replenishes us in vital ways: it helps us discover new ideas and interests, improves empathy, and boosts productivity. An online survey asked 18,000 people in 134 countries if they would like more rest. Unsurprisingly, 68.4% said yes. When asked which activities were most restful for them, their top responses (in order) were:

"reading"
"being in the natural environment"
"spending time alone"
"listening to music"

"The first activity that clearly involved other people, was 'seeing friends and family,' which came in twelfth on the list. In other words, to find the peace and rest we need we spend time away from other people." (Jim Denison's blog 1/1/20).

Are you too busy with the cares of this world and satisfying your own pleasures to take time to be alone with God? Can you get up before dawn like Jesus and enjoy God's presence? Get alone with Jesus, tune out the world, and you will have a new conception of God. Your life will be refreshed.

AMAZING MIRACLES
JOHN 20:30

I received a call early one morning that a six-year-old boy in our congregation had fallen on his neck and was rushed to the hospital. Reports were that his neck was broken. The phone lines were busy as the church prayed for him. The surgeons were about to begin surgery but decided to take another X-ray. They were dumbfounded to discover his neck was normal. God had performed a miracle. We were exceedingly thankful.

To me, life is a miracle. My very existence is a miracle. With all our advances in science we still can't explain the meaning of existence or the purpose for existence. God explains existence in the opening words of the Bible: "In the beginning God created the heavens and the earth. The earth was formless and empty, darkness was over the surface of the deep and the spirit of God was hovering over the waters" (Genesis 1:1-2). As a believer in Jehovah God Almighty I accept the Bible as God-breathed, i.e. God inspired.

"In the beginning was the Word, and the Word was with God,

and the Word was God. He was with God in the beginning. Through him all things were made; without him nothing was made that has been made. In him was life, and the life was the light of all mankind. The light shines in the darkness, and the darkness has not overcome it" (John 1:1-5).

"The Word was a term used by theologians and philosophers in many different ways. In Hebrew scripture, the word was an agent of creation, the source of God's message to his people through the prophets, and God's law, has standards of holiness. In Greek philosophy, the word was the principle of reason that governed the world, or the thought still in the mind, while in Hebrew thought, the Word was another expression for God." (*Life Application Study Bible* notes).

The Apostle John speaks of Jesus in John 1:14: "The Word became flesh and made his dwelling among us. We have seen his glory, the glory of the one and only Son, who came from the Father, full of grace and truth." John is speaking of Jesus, a human being he knew and loved, but at the same time the Creator of the universe, the ultimate revelation of God, the living picture of God's holiness, the one in whom "all things hold together" (Colossians 1:17). To the Greeks this was unthinkable. To John, the Word was the Good News of Jesus Christ.

There is no better explanation of existence than Genesis 1:1-2 and John 1:1-5. All other explanations are theories or suppositions. If Jesus is God then of course He can create by simply speaking. He can feed the multitudes, He can heal the sick, He can curse the mulberry tree, He can raise the dead and He Himself can rise from the dead and ascend into heaven as His disciples watch Him go.

In that sense Christmas is the greatest miracle: God coming as a human being is the foundation of all miracles and the first step to faith. God created everything so naturally and can alter His creation with what we call miracles anytime He so desires. "Anyone who comes to God must believe that he exists and that he rewards those who earnestly seek him" (Hebrews 11:6).

This is why I say all of life is a miracle. How can anyone see a beautiful sunrise or sunset, a flower, a newborn baby and realize there is not a creator who is God? God is involved in our daily life. We are not deists who believe God created the world like a clockmaker and then leaves it to run on its own. A deist believes that God exists and created the world, but does not interfere with His creation. God is involved in every detail of our lives: every cell, every heartbeat, every breath, every step, every motive, and every thought. Everything we have ever said and done is recorded in our brain and God created our brain, so naturally He knows us intimately.

The steps of a good person are ordered by the Lord. (Psalm 37:23 KJV). For the believer there is no such thing as luck, coincidence, fate, chance or accidents. How often do you hear the expression, "It was an accident" or "It's just my luck?" For those who are conscious of Jesus living in them and they in Jesus there are no such things as accidents, misfortunes, interruptions or luck. For Jesus' followers it's proper to think of "common sense" as wisdom given by God. God is in control of our life, which includes our time, our circumstances—everything that comes across our path.

Every person we meet, God has permitted to come into our life for a purpose. Often, we do not understand His purpose but frequently it is to encourage others. When you experience God's direction in everyday matters life is exciting. You sense His presence, experience His joy and continually thank Him for His leading. The supernatural becomes natural. Life is one continuous miracle. That doesn't mean everything will be smooth and easy. C. K. Chesterton said, "Jesus promised three things to his disciples – they would be completely fearless, absurdly happy and in constant trouble."

Ask God to open the door for you to extend His love to people. He will amaze you. Be pro-active, assertive, not aggressive or passive. There are too many shy, apologetic Christians who hide behind the excuse, "I don't want to interfere with the private life of others." You have the map to eternal life, don't be shy; it's a matter of eternal life and death.

The book of Acts talks about extraordinary miracles. "God did extraordinary miracles through Paul, so that even handkerchiefs and aprons that had touched him were taken to the sick, and their illnesses were cured and the evil spirits left them" (Acts 19:11-12). "People brought their sick into the streets and laid them on beds and mats so that at least Peter's shadow might fall on some of them as he passed by. Crowds gathered from the towns around Jerusalem, bringing their sick and those tormented by impure spirits, and all of them were healed" (Acts 5:15-16).

God gives many spiritual gifts such as faith, wisdom, knowledge, and gifts of healings and miraculous powers. (I Corinthians 12:8-10). Jesus had all the gifts. The Spirit was given to Him without limit. (John 3:34). No other person in the scripture is described as one on whom the Spirit is given without limit. As we grow in Jesus, becoming more and more like Him, I believe we can develop in all areas of our life and become more effective in our prayer life and in our service with Him.

I frequently read accounts of amazing miracles from various mission agencies. The following is an example taken from the *Global Disciples* newsletter, February 17, 2020. "Tet started a discipleship-mission training in Myanmar three years ago. He didn't expect that some hard-to-reach people would show up for the training! The first was a Buddhist monk and leader of the local monastery, curious to see if this training was a threat, instead he heard about Jesus. He asked many questions about God as Spirit, as Creator, and this Jesus who can save people from sin. He went to Tet's home at night for long conversations . . .

"'Now that I have heard about Jesus, I cannot sleep,' he told Tet. Then he disappeared. Other monks asked Tet what he had done with their leader. Boldly sharing the Gospel, he explained, 'I think he received Jesus Christ; that's why he left. Jesus died for your sins, and you should receive Him too . . .

"Several monks showed up at the next training. They came to stop us but after hearing about Jesus, they had many questions, Tet reported. He talked about God's love and how Jesus died for sinners. But these men wanted proof . . .

"'If your God is real,' they challenged, 'tell him to send food and rain when you pray. Then we will believe!' It was the hot, dry season but in faith, Tet agreed. They met in a forest clearing the next morning as agreed. Like Elijah before the prophets of Baal, Tet began to pray. Around noon, a stranger stumbled into the clearing, lost but carrying food – which he eagerly shared. God had answer one prayer, but still no rain. Late in the day, the monks said, 'No more, your God is not as you say.' And they went home . . .

"Then the rain came – heavy, flooding rain! In the morning, Tet heard a knock and there stood the monks: 'Yes, we believe your Jesus.' They returned to the forest clearing and in prayer gave their lives to Jesus, discarding their robes and their identity as followers of Buddha."

Jesus said, "Whoever believe in me will do the works I have been doing, and they will do even greater things than these, because I am going to the Father" (John 14:12). According to the Internet, between 70,000 and 100,000 people are accepting Christ each day around the world. Can there be any greater miracle than people being born again? Since God is moving so mightily this is the greatest time to be alive.

"Jesus performed many other signs in the presence of his disciples, which are not recorded in this book. But these are written that you may believe that Jesus is the Messiah, the Son of God, and that by believing you may have life in his name" (John 20:30-31). (See the next two essays for more on miracles and healing.)

D. PAIN, SUFFERING AND TRIALS

WHERE IS GOD WHEN IT HURTS?
ROMANS 5:3-5

"We glory in our sufferings, because we know that suffering produces perseverance, perseverance, character; and character, hope. And hope does not put us to shame, because God's love has been poured out into our hearts through the Holy Spirit, who has been given to us" (Romans 5:3-5). Comfort and prosperity have never enriched the world as much as adversity has. No pain, no gain is a slogan for athletes but the concept applies to our faith walk.

God's love has no limits. A leper came to Jesus begging for healing. Jesus touched this untouchable man and healed him. He told him to show his healing to the priests as a testimony to them. (Matthew 8:2-4). The Jews hated Roman centurions since they were part of the Roman army that forced them to pay exorbitant taxes. A centurion's servant was about to die. Jesus performed a miracle and the centurion's servant was healed. (Luke 7:2-10).

What are we to do when it seems that God has not answered our prayers, when leprosy is not healed or the centurion's son dies? Jesus healed many people, often healing all who came to him. Other times, as in John 5, where a great number of disabled people used to lie by the pool—the blind, the lame, and the paralyzed—they were not healed. An invalid for thirty-eight years was there. Jesus healed him but did not heal the others. (For additional accounts when people were not healed in the New Testament see the opening paragraph in the next essay: "Illness and Healing."

If Adam had never sinned there would be no pain, sickness or suffering. When we receive our resurrected bodies all pain and illness will be eliminated forever. (Revelation 22:4). Hallelujah! God uses pain for His purposes. "I gave you empty stomachs in every city and lack of bread in every town, yet you have not returned to me" (Amos 4:6). On nearly every page the prophets of God warned Israel that they would face calamity (pain) if they continued to disobey His laws.

Many today believe, especially many prominent preachers, that it is always God's will to heal everyone. Isaiah 53:5 has become a "proof text" for them. This verse includes physical healing but its primary emphasis is on the healing and forgiveness of our sins. Peter cites this scripture: "He himself bore our sins in his body on the tree, so that we might die to sins and live for righteousness; by His wounds you have been healed." It's obvious that Peter is speaking primarily of spiritual healing. Isaiah 53 foretells of Jesus' life on earth. It speaks of His torture and death: "He was pierced for our transgressions, he was crushed for our iniquities; the punishment that brought us peace was upon Him, and by his wounds (stripes) we are healed" (Isaiah 53:5; 1 Peter 2:24). This text can include physical healing but it does not have to. Certainly, God frequently heals physically but to demand that He must always heal is a misapplication of this text.

I had more than a hundred funerals, including some for infants and younger persons. My neighbor boy was killed in an auto accident. Tragedies happen every day. God loves us. He gave His Son to die for us. He has healed all of us many times. His Son endured Crucifixion, a form of execution so horrific it is outlawed all over the world today, but He died that horrific death just for you. He knows every sin you've committed or will commit. Think of all the ways He has already blessed you. Does your family love you? So many are trapped in loveless, abusive homes. Has He provided for your material needs through physical abilities and vocational opportunities? So many are trapped in endless poverty. Has He given you the privilege of life in America's freedom? Who of us earned the right to be born in this country?

Remember God's grace in your life. Understand that His ways are higher than ours. The leper has it right: "If you will, you can make me clean." Joseph didn't understand why he was enslaved in Egypt. Moses didn't understand why he had to spend forty years in the desert. Joshua didn't understand the flooded Jordan River and fortified city of Jericho. Daniel didn't understand the lion's den, or Paul his thorn in the flesh, or John his Isle of Patmos prison. It was all part of God's larger plan. Too often we pray for God to remove us from our trial when He wants to improve us through the trial. Sometime God stills the storm; sometime He stills the storm in us.

When we pray for something God does not grant, we can know

that it is best that He acted as He did, even when we do not understand why. The person did not get well. The house burned down; the divorce became final; the car wreck happened. We do not understand why God did not grant us our prayer. "My thoughts are not your thoughts, neither are your ways my ways. For as the heavens are higher than the earth, so are my ways higher than your ways and my thoughts than your thoughts" (Isaiah 55:8-9). Several times, God healed a dear friend of cancer. Then he died in the prime of life. His contribution to God's Kingdom on earth must have been completed. Trust God to give you what you ask or something better.

Not until I became a father, did I understand some of the things my father said and did. Not until we are in glory will we understand completely our Father's will and ways—we see through a glass darkly. (I Corinthians 13:12). When we cannot see His hand, we can trust His heart. That's the faith assumption we must make when God does not grant what we ask: He is doing something even better. Though our finite, fallen mind cannot begin to imagine how that could be so, we must trust His love and compassion enough to accept it by faith.

Sometimes Jesus heals us physically, but a greater miracle is spiritual healing. One is temporal the other is eternal. Sometimes He removes the pain, and sometimes He does an even greater work of giving us the strength to endure the pain with joy. God gives strength and courage to bear up under life's sufferings. We know the sufferings of this life are not worth comparing to the joy that awaits us in heaven. (Romans 8:17). He can heal our bodies, and our souls. Which do you need Him to do for you today?

Prayer: Lord, like Job who said, "Though he slay me I will serve him," give us faith to trust You even when we don't understand.

ILLNESS AND HEALING
GALATIANS 4:13-14

"Before I was afflicted, I went astray, but now I obey your word . . . It was good for me to be afflicted so that I might learn your decrees" (Psalm 119:67, 71). When Paul came to Galicia he was ill. The Galatians treated him as if he were an angel because of his illness. (Galatians 4:13-14). Paul left Trophimus ill at Miletus. (II Timothy 4:19). Timothy was frequently sick. (I Timothy 5:23). Jesus said we are to visit the sick. (Matthew 25). Other times He said we are to heal the sick. (Luke 10:8).

Tim Hansel was brutally hurt in a rock-climbing accident that crushed much of his upper body. The doctor told him he had to learn to live with intense pain, which he would experience for a lifetime. Years later he writes in his book, *You Gotta Keep Dancin'*, p. 123, for years people asked me, "Haven't you prayed to the Lord for healing?" My obvious answer: "Of course." "Why do you think he hasn't healed you?" "He has." "But I thought you were still in pain." "I am." "I don't understand." "I have prayed hundreds, if not thousands, of times for the Lord to heal me – and he finally healed me of the need to be healed. I had discovered a peace inside the pain. I finally came to the realization that if the Lord could use this body better the way it is, than that's the way it should be."

Learn to thank God for the difficult times in your life. The Lord needs to purify us in the furnace of discipline to burn away the dross (trash) as He molds us into His likeness. He is making us like Himself so the light of Christ shines more clearly through us. David says, "In faithfulness you have afflicted me" (Psalm 119:75). "If you would not have been my delight I would have perished in my affliction" (Psalm 119:92). A few verses later he says, Loving God's word enables us to triumph in affliction. (Psalm 119:97). Mark Batterson has said, "You can be saved without suffering, but you cannot be sanctified without suffering." Someone else said, "If God can accomplish his purpose through a broken heart then why not thank him for breaking yours."

When I was 15 in high school, I had a heart condition that caused me to miss five months of school. During those five months I read missionary biographies. It was a major time of spiritual growth in my life and had an impact on my call to the ministry. Whom the Lord loves, He disciplines. (Hebrews 12:6). Illness and suffering affects our life and those around us. It opens our eyes to look beyond ourselves to God who understands because Jesus suffered far more than we can imagine.

Nights can seem long when you have trouble sleeping. My wife, Helen, lie awake tossing and turning to find a comfortable position to ease pain. Nothing helped. Getting up, she reached for Sarah Young's devotional book, *Jesus Today*. "I am calling you to live joyfully in the midst of your struggles. You yearn for a freer most independent way of life than you're currently experiencing. You pray fervently – then wish hopefully for the changes you desire. When I don't answer your prayers according to your will, you sometimes get discouraged. It's easy for you to feel as if you're doing something wrong – as if you're missing out on what is best for you. When you think that way, you are forgetting a most important truth: that I am Sovereign, I am in control, and I am taking care of you . . .

"I want you to accept your dependent way of living as a gift from me. Moreover, I want you to receive this gift joyfully – with a glad and thankful heart: – actually, nothing will lift you out of the doldrums faster than thanking and praising me. And nothing will help you enjoy my presence more delightfully!"

We can't achieve patience without tribulation. Hebrews informs us: "For the moment all discipline seems painful rather than pleasant, but later it yields the peaceful fruit of righteousness to those who have been trained by it" (Hebrews 12:11). Training is both time-consuming and painful. James wrote, "Consider it pure joy, my brothers and sisters, whenever you face trials of many kinds, because you know that the testing of your faith produces perseverance" (James. 1:2-3). Even if our suffering is lifelong, Paul reminds us that, "this slight momentary affliction is preparing for us an eternal weight of glory beyond all comparison" (II Corinthians 4:17).

God calls us to, "Be holy, as he is holy" (I Peter 1:16). God is more interested in our character than our comfort. He will remove our comfort so He can refine our character. It's always appropriate to pray with David, "Search me, God and know my heart, test me and know my anxious thoughts. See if there is any offensive way in me, and lead me in the way everlasting" (Psalm 139:23-24).

Our culture teaches us to be independent. Jeremiah prays (10:23), "Lord, I know that people's lives are not their own; it is not for them to direct their steps." We must learn to depend on Him. "In him we live and have our existence" (Acts 17:28). We need to be like clay in the hand of the potter. (Jeremiah 18:6). "Does the clay say to the potter what are you making?" (Isaiah 45:9). "Who are you to reply against God? Will the thing formed say to him who formed it, 'Why have you made me like this?'" (Romans 9:20).

When we accept the sovereignty of God things go better! "The Sovereign Lord comes with power, and his arm rules for him. See, his reward is with him, and his recompense (or payment) accompanies him" (Isaiah 40:10). There is no growth without accepting the discipline of the Lord.

For years I have tried to pray every morning and often throughout the day for God's will to be done, "not my will Lord but your will Lord Jesus." When I was younger, I believed God's will was finding my way through a maze where only one path is right. I thought following that path would always feel safe and secure. When I am in God's will, I feel comfortable and at peace, but at other times I feel anxious and unsettled, for He often leads me into unfamiliar waters. I must not allow these feelings to guide me.

I am learning to fix my eyes on Jesus who knows what is best for me. He has blazed the trail He chose for me. I attempt to throw off everything that hinders me—the doubts, the worry, and the cares that so easily entangle my feet and mind—and run with perseverance the race He has marked out for me. I fix my eyes on Jesus who endured the cross, scorning its shame, and has sat down at the right hand of God. (Hebrews 12:1-3). Reflect, ponder, contemplate Him and throw all your worries and cares on Him. Jesus said, "Come to me and rest."

TRAGEDIES CAN BE BLESSINGS
JOHN 11:4

Sue started to come to church. I inquired concerning her husband. She said to me several times, "He will never come to church." However, he was involved in a car accident. Following the accident, he has come every Sunday. Painful experiences are often ignored, but for Sue's husband the accident opened his eyes.

Because of the coronavirus pandemic some persons are interested in exploring faith in God. Every day we hear of disastrous situations: car, train, airplane, or motorcycle accidents. Why are there tornados, hurricanes, famines, wars, or fires? Is it fair that people suffer for years while others seem to have it easy?

Jesus answers: "There were some present at that time who told Jesus about the Galileans whose blood Pilate had mixed with their sacrifice. Do you think that these Galileans were worse sinners than all the other Galileans because they suffered this way? I tell you, no! But unless you repent, you too will all perish. Or those eighteen who died when the tower of Siloam fell on them – do you think they were guiltier than all the others living in Jerusalem? I tell you, no! But unless you repent, you too will all perish" (Luke 13:1-5).

People in Jesus' day assumed that all calamities came because of sin. Jesus says these tragedies come to remind us that unless we repent, we too will perish. God speaks loudly and clear every day. Our response should be, "Jesus that could just as well have been me."

In another occasion the disciples when they saw a man who was blind from birth asked Jesus: "Who sinned, this man or his parents that he was born blind?" (John 9:1-2). Jesus said, "Neither this man nor his parents sinned, but this happened so that the works of God might be displayed in him" (v. 3).

In John 11, Mary and Martha sent word to Jesus that their brother, Lazarus, was very sick. Jesus did not go immediately and Lazarus died. "When Jesus heard about his death he said, 'Lazarus's sickness will not end in death. No, it happened for the glory of God so that the Son of God will receive glory from this'" (John 11:4, NLT). Even in death Jesus can receive glory. We say with Paul: "I am persuaded that neither death nor life, nor angels, nor principalities, or powers, nor things present nor things to come, nor height nor depth, nor any other created thing, shall be able to separate us from the love of God which is in Christ Jesus our Lord" (Romans 8:38-39).

Today many who are healed give glory to God and many who are not healed bring glory to God as they rejoice in the grace of God who enables them to triumph in their pain. It's clear much suffering is brought on to help us see our need to repent. Other times suffering occurs to bring glory to God as we are healed either physically or spiritually. When we are joyful in our suffering people will hopefully see the Lord's love in a new light.

Sometimes God brings suffering for sins, as for example, an alcoholic who develops liver disease, but often this fails to wake them up. "The rest of mankind who were not killed by these plagues still did not repent of the work of their hands; they did not stop worshiping demons, and idols of gold, silver, bronze stone and wood. Nor did they repent of their murders, their magic arts, their sexual immorality and their thefts" (Revelation 9:20-21).

In Moses' time God sent the ten plagues, "that you might see my power and that my fame might spread throughout the earth" (Exodus 9:16, 29). A few days after the last plague the Israelites had a meltdown of their faith. When they came to the Red Sea the Egyptian army caught up with them and the Israelites "cried out to the Lord. They said to Moses, 'Was it because there were no graves in Egypt that you brought us to the desert to die?'" (Exodus 14:10-11). Shortly after the miracle of deliverance from Pharaoh's army they completely forgot God's miracles, grumbling because of lack of water and lack of meat. (vv. 15 and 16). Worst yet in chapter 32 Aaron built a golden calf for them to worship, which resulted in total depravity. Because of their wickedness God had the Levites destroy 3,000 of them, which was also followed by a plague. Moses interceded for his people or God would have destroyed them. When we deliberately forget God's blessings, we pay a high price.

No matter what happens we must learn to trust our amazing God. He is working things out for our best. (Romans 8:28). Habakkuk could not understand why God would punish Judah for their sins while employing the fiercely wicked nation of Babylon to punish Judah. Even though he does not understand he says to the effect that no matter what happens I will rejoice in the Lord. (Habakkuk 3:17-19). When accidents happen, we try to find the cause to be sure it does not happen again. But there are many things that are out of our control that no doctor can cure or weather forecast can foresee.

Hurricanes and acts of God are a result of our fallen sinful world. Jesus said when we hear of wars we should not be alarmed. These things must take place; they are part of our sinful culture. They often happen to remind us to repent, that is, turn from our evil ways and follow Him. God is in control. We need not fear. Jesus said, "Don't be afraid of those who can kill the body but cannot kill the soul. Rather, be afraid of the one who can destroy both body and soul in hell" (Matthew 10:28). No matter how or when tragedies occur, death is not the end. Jesus promises that, "those who believe, that is trust in, cling to and rely on him will not perish but have eternal life" (John 3:16 AMP).

On the other hand, Romans 2:4 reminds us that the goodness of God is also meant to lead us to repentance. Frequently we don't recognize His goodness. Our spiritual eyes and heart are dull. Prosperity, instead of bringing us closer to God so often does the opposite. Material things cause us to focus on the earthly "blessings." They take our time, our energy, and our money, even our heart! Be on your guard concerning God's blessings. Make special effort to not take them for granted, always remembering to thank Him. Ask God for grace to thank Him both for the adversity and the blessings we experience. This balance will help us mature in our walk with Jesus. "Give thanks in all circumstances; for this is God's will for you in Christ Jesus" (I Thessalonians 5:18).

Christians sometimes glibly quote Romans 8:28, "In all things God works for the good of those who love him, who have been called according to his purpose." We can't always see His purpose. This verse is given in the context of Paul's horrendous sufferings. (vv. 31-39). In all these things (trials and sufferings) we are more than conquerors. Even death and demonic activity will not separate us from God. Even though most people say they do not believe in demons the sadistic activity is certainly present in the many sins in our culture, such as murders, human trafficking, etc.

The news reported that a teenager walking home from church is now missing. Reports are she was a well-adjusted girl in every way. Hundreds are searching for her. We don't understand. We do know that hundreds, even thousands, are affected by her sudden disappearance. I'm sure many, especially teens that seldom think of the brevity of life are made conscious of the fact it could have been them, and hopefully are more God conscious. People are praying. We search and ask why? We will never understand fully but since we know God loves her, we must place her in His hand and cast our pain on Him. (Matthew 11:28-30). When we get to heaven, we may understand but I doubt if we will need an explanation since the former things are passed away.

We can only see in part and know or understand in part. (I Corinthians 13:12). Job questioned God for 30-some chapters but God did not answer Job with an explanation, rather God pointed out His greatness, His surpassing knowledge. (Job 38-39). "His greatness no one can fathom" (Psalm 145:3). I suspect it's like a University mathematician trying to explain a long equation to his six-year-old son. The son becomes exasperated. The father says, "You will just have to trust me." Some things we will never fully understand but what alternative do we have? To rebel and be lost or to trust a God that we know loves us even though we don't understand all things.

GOD'S DISCIPLINE—
A NECESSARY BLESSING
HEBREWS 12:4-11

Can you remember a time when you desperately wanted to pass

a test? The teacher stated in no uncertain terms that you would have to discipline yourself to master the material. You stayed up late, you prayed, you made every effort to master the material. You were greatly rewarded and rejoiced with the results.

How desperate are you to please God? We struggle to love Him with all our heart. Hebrews explains how we can win this good fight of faith. "In your struggle against sin, you have not yet resisted to the point of shedding your blood. And have you completely forgotten this word of encouragement that addresses you as a father addresses his son? It says, 'My son, do not make light of the Lord's discipline, and do not lose heart when he rebukes you, because the Lord disciplines the one, he loves, and he chastens everyone he accepts as his son.'

"Endure hardship as discipline; God is treating you as his children. For what children are not disciplined by their father? If you are not disciplined – and everyone undergoes discipline – then you are not legitimate, not true sons and daughters at all. Moreover, we have all had human fathers who disciplined us and we respect them for it. How much more should we submit to the Father of spirits and live! They disciplined us for a little while as they thought best; but God disciplines us for our good, in order that we may share in his holiness. No discipline seems pleasant at the time but painful. Later on, however, it produces a harvest of righteousness and peace for those who have been trained by it" (Hebrews 12:4-11).

David understood this: "It is good for me that I was afflicted, that I might learn your statutes. The law of your mouth is better to me than thousands of gold and silver pieces" (Psalm 119:71-72). How determined are you to know the joy God has for you? How eager are you to be free from the empty, meaningless life—free from the additions of worry, free from your impure heart and mind, free from the sin that so easily entangles you? (Hebrews 12:1). Beg for God to discipline you; to bring into your life whatever it takes to make you more like Him. He will answer that prayer. He will give you a passion and love that satisfies your inner most being that will flood your heart with unspeakable joy and peace beyond anything you can put into words.

James understood discipline, "Consider it pure joy, my brothers and sisters, whenever you face trials of many kinds, because you know that the testing of your faith produces perseverance. Let perseverance finish its work so that you may be mature and complete, not lacking anything" (James 1:2-4). Even if our suffering is life-long, Paul reminds us "this slight momentary affliction is preparing for us an eternal weight of glory beyond all comparison" (II Corinthians 4:17).

God wants us to be holy. We are never promised ease or happiness but we are commanded to be holy, as He is holy. (I Peter 1:16). God is more interested in our character than in our comfort. We must learn to forgo our comfort to achieve His holiness. We cannot "pursue, righteousness, godliness, faith, love, endurance and gentleness" without discipline. (I Timothy 6:11).

When you feel God's discipline, when you are convicted as you read the Bible or convicted from hearing a sermon then thank God for this conviction. Don't feel "Oh, I'm so terrible, won't I ever learn, don't feel guilty. Thank God that He loves you enough to help you grow. Thanking Him for facilitating the healing of our sins helps you move on to greater things.

God has had to discipline me many times. I would not exchange any of my discipline-afflictions for anything. In fact, I have made it a habit to keep asking God to discipline me. This isn't because I am masochistic or that I love affliction, but because I've tasted the joy of living in the promises of God. I am learning that the darkest times can be turned into the most rewarding days my soul has ever known. We can't achieve patience without tribulation. We can't achieve a close walk with God without His loving discipline. Thank God for His discipline!

VI.

OUR AMAZING MISSION

WHY DID JESUS COME?
LUKE 19:10, JOHN 17:18, 20:21

Over Christmas vacation Lyn worked in a department store. Her boss was the most difficult human being. She was hard to please and would criticize and royally chew the salesperson out in front of the customers. Nothing Lyn did seemed to please her boss. Lyn cried out to the Lord, "I can't go back." God seemed to be saying to Lyn: "You will go back tomorrow morning, and you will stay there. You will love Miss Alma." "Impossible," cried Lyn. "I cannot love that woman." "You're right, you can't love her," the Lord plainly said. "But, I can. In fact, I already love her. I died for her."

Lyn thought going back would be impossible, but it wasn't. Now she saw Miss Alma in a different light—as someone who needed the Lord. I began to learn what it meant to turn the situation over to Jesus and let Him work through her. Her boss was just as nasty, but Lyn had changed. Now when Lyn was corrected, she smiled and thanked her boss for correcting her.

Lyn never tried to excuse her behavior. The other employees couldn't understand how Lyn could take all the guff. Lyn had the opportunity to witness to every woman in that department. Slowly Miss Alma's attitude changed. She invited Lyn to come back and work for her full time in her department.

Lyn said, "In my own strength I couldn't have done it. Even the stock boy was amazed. I got a chance to witness to him. I learned to love people as Jesus commanded us to love."

Jim Morgan writes: "Our passion for the Lord should be evident to all those around us. . . . Our faith should pour out through every fiber of our being. That passion should extend to a sincere concern for those who don't know the Lord. The fate awaiting those dying without Christ should compel Christians to set off on a rescue mission – to bring their family, friends, neighbors and coworkers toward Christ before it's too late. That sense of urgency should drive us to risk our reputation, even our lives for the sake of sharing something we value with those at such great risk."

If you found a doctor or a mechanic you could trust or even if you found a terrific diet, you would be glad to tell your friends. Since you've found Jesus who forgives sin and provides everlasting life, you will want to share, you will be compelled to share what Jesus has done for you.

Don't be discouraged if people don't respond immediately. Build a relationship with many people. It usually takes a variety of contacts before a person comes to Jesus. I worked with Marilyn for many months. She would promise to come to church again and again. I offered to mow her yard. I sensed she wanted to come but on Sunday morning other things took priority. Today she is an influential member encouraging others to walk with Jesus. Hearing her share her testimony with the congregation is something I will carry in my heart until the Lord calls me home.

Fifty times[2] in the Gospels we are told why Jesus came and how he spent his time.

Jesus came to seek and save those who are lost. (Luke 19:10 CEV).

His very name, Jesus, means "The Lord saves" (Matthew 1:21 NIV footnote).

Jesus came not to condemn the world but to save it. (John 3:17).

Jesus came to give sight to the blind and to show those who think they see that they are blind.(John 9:39b and 12:47-48).

Jesus says, "I have not come to call the righteous, but sinners" (Mark 2:17).

"The Spirit of the Lord . . . has anointed me to preach good news to the poor. He has sent me to proclaim freedom for the prisoners and recovery of sight to the blind, to release the oppressed, to proclaim the year of the Lord's favor" (Luke 4:18-19).

"Jesus had great pity for the crowds that came, because their

____

2. See my book, *Share the Irresistible Story of Jesus*, Chapters 1 & 2.

problems were so great and they didn't know where to go for help" (Matthew 9:36). "As he approached Jerusalem and saw the city, he wept over it" (Luke 19:41).

Jesus said, "We must go on to other towns as well, and I will preach to them, too, because that is why I came" (Mark 1:38 NLT).

Jesus said, "Don't say, 'Four months more and then the harvest.' The harvest is now. Open your eyes, the fields are ripe" (John 4:35)

Luke sums up Jesus' activities: ". . . He went around doing good and healing all who were under the power of the devil, because God was with him" (Acts 10:38).

It's clear Jesus came to save the lost and minister to the needs of those who were marginalized. Since He sends us just as the Father sent Him, we don't need to wonder about our assignment. (John 17:18 and 20:21).

If you have a passion for Jesus to use you as His representative, He will give you opportunities to share the Good News every day. You may not have opportunity to share the plan of salvation every day but you will have the opportunity to make comments that will help people become more aware of God. "He has committed to us the message of reconciliation. We are therefore Christ's ambassadors, as though God were making his appeal through us" (II Corinthians 5:19-20). "Make use of every opportunity because the days are evil" (Ephesians 5:16). "Be wise in the way you act toward outsiders, make the most of every opportunity" (Colossians 4:5). We are commanded to be courageous, (I Corinthians 16:13), and to be as bold as lions. (Proverbs 28:1).

Lord Jesus open my eyes and heart to see the opportunities You give me and to trust Your Holy Spirit to empower me and speak through me. I desire with all my heart to be a faithful disciple and to spontaneously witness for You. Amen.

FOLLOW ME
MATTHEW 4:19, JOHN 21:17

Two thousand years ago a couple of fishermen were going about their own business casting nets in the Sea of Galilee in hopes of their next big catch. Andrew and Peter were following their father's footsteps, casting their nets with expertise. Life was routine but demanding. They had no intention of beginning a new business or starting a new life.

But their life abruptly changed. A man of Galilee stood on the shore. They had heard about Jesus and to their surprise Jesus came walking toward them. He looked them in the eye and said in a clear voice of invitation, "Come follow me and I will send you out to fish for people" (Matthew 4:19). If you consider yourself a follower of Jesus you will be a fisher of people. Someone said, "If you are not fishing for people, I don't know whom you are following, but you are not following Jesus."

They immediately left their nets and followed Jesus. In one sense, in the three years of following Jesus, Peter heard those words, "follow me," many times. Jesus didn't say, "Listen to me or believe in me." He said, "Follow me." To follow Jesus, we must give up everything and lay our lives on the line for Him.

When the rich young ruler who claimed to keep all the commandments asked Jesus what he must do to have eternal life Jesus said, "One thing you lack, go sell everything you have and give to the poor, and you will have treasure in heaven. Then come, follow me" (Mark 10:21). After he walked away Jesus said, "How hard it is for the rich to enter the kingdom of heaven." The disciples were amazed. Peter said, "We have left everything to follow you!" Jesus replied, "No one who has left home or brothers or sisters or mother or father or children or fields for me and the gospel will fail to receive a hundred times as much in this present age: homes, brother, sisters, mothers, children and fields – along with persecutions – and in the age to come eternal life" (Mark 10:28-30).

To be a follower of Jesus we must obey His teaching. His teachings, especially those on the Sermon of the Mount (Matthew 5-7), are impossible to keep without the supernatural empowerment of the Holy Spirit. Many today dismiss Matthew 5-7 believing they are not for today but for a time following our Lord's return. They say it is impractical to love our enemies, not to lust or covet, to never worry, or to rejoice when we are persecuted. Has Jesus placed the bar so high that we can't obtain it?

Jesus never said it would be easy. His words come at a cost. But obeying His invitation is worth it. God still expects us to leave our nets. We hurt the church by trying to tell people you can be a Christian, just believe in Jesus; you can decide later if you want to become His disciple. Being a Christian makes all the difference in the world.

Jesus wants us to be hot or cold, not lukewarm. Those who are lukewarm He will vomit out of His mouth. They will be cut off from His Kingdom. (Revelation 3:16).

In Luke 9:57-62, Jesus further explains what it means to leave our nets. As they were walking along someone said to Jesus, "Lord I'll follow you wherever you go." Jesus said, Foxes have dens, birds have nests but if you follow me you may not have a place to call home. You will be in for some major adjustment in your lifestyle.

Jesus said to another person, "Follow me." But the man responded, "Let me first go and bury my father." Jesus said, "Let the dead bury their own dead, but you go and preach the kingdom of God." Very likely the father was in the midst of life but the son wanted to take care of getting a nest egg for his family to live, get his house mortgage paid off or to increase his 401K. I don't believe Jesus was saying he couldn't go to his father's funeral.

I was working with a pastor in his 50's. He had a clear vision that his church should move just a couple hundred yards from a back road to a main highway. But his father had a business that was dependent to a large extent on the pastor's expertise. I strongly encouraged him to move ahead telling him he will come to the end of life regretting his indecision. He decided to wait until his high school daughters would finish college then he would have more resources to make the move. He never did make the move. The church has suffered greatly.

Put Jesus first and all these things—all the material things will fall into their proper place because God who takes care of the birds and decorates the wildflowers will take care of you. Trust him! (Matthew 6).

When senior citizens were asked to evaluate their life 84% said they regret that they did not do what they would have liked to do. They failed to follow God's vision. Everything in life has a crucial moment. If we miss our opportunity, if we put it off by making excuses like this pastor, we may never do what Jesus wants us to do. How often have you felt you needed to make a phone call, send an email, or say a word of encouragement but you put it off until tomorrow and it never got done? Later when it is too late, you said, "If only I would have seized the opportunity." We all live with regrets. What are you putting off? Don't grieve the Holy Spirit. God didn't call you to make you comfortable, He called you to walk in obedience to His commands. Once you recognize your mistake confess it, receive God's forgiveness, put it behind you and move on vowing to be obedient.

Another individual said, "Lord, I'll follow you, but, [whenever you hear that word "but" perk up your ears], let me first go and say good-bye to my family and friends." Jesus said, "'No one having put his hand to the plow and looking back is fit for service in the kingdom of God'" (Luke 9:62).

Jesus was not releasing us of our family duties. He was saying, hand over your plans. Trust God to do what is best for you. Stop looking over your shoulder. Perhaps this man knew he had to make some wrong things right before he would be comfortable following Jesus. Get all your past under the blood of Jesus. Stop beating yourself with "if onlys." If only I would have not done this, or if only I would have said that. Jesus paid for all your "if onlys!"

When Jesus' call comes, drop your nets just like Peter and Andrew, and walk with Jesus, surrender your past, present and future. Hand your past over to Jesus. Trust Him to lead you. Oswald Chambers says, "Our motivation for surrender should not be for any personal gain. We have become so self-centered that we go to God only for something from him, and not for God himself. . . . I want to be on display in your showcase so I can say, 'This is what God has done for me.' Genuine total surrender is to make a personal sovereign preference for Jesus Christ himself."

You will be amazed at what He will do when you surrender your life to Him. No matter where you are God can use your smile, your joyful attitude and loving spirit to encourage others. He is not finished with you. You are here for a purpose. Furthermore, you have a fantastic future in heaven, which far outweighs the troubles of this life. (II Corinthians 4:17 and Romans 8:18).

Are you stuck? Have you dropped anchor where you are? Jesus said to Peter, "Feed my sheep" (John 21:17). Some sheep are pushy, difficult, and even cantankerous. That's part of what it means to be sent by Jesus. Take up you cross. Read your Bible—open the door of your heart—prepare to drop your own personal nets, catch the wind of God's Holy Spirit and like Peter and Andrew say, "Yes, I'll follow without reservations!"

Prayer: Father, we confess too often we have been lazy, putting off what we know You want us to do. Forgive us. Give us the courage to take up our cross and follow You. Amen.

THE AROMA OF CHRIST
II CORINTHIANS 2:14-16

Multitudes of Christians live in fear. Hospital psychiatric wards are overflowing. One in five adults experience mental illness each year and one in six youth (ages 6-17) experience mental health issues. The Apostle John writes, "The one who fears is not made perfect, (complete or mature) in God's love . . ." (I John 4:18). God's love removes fear.

Oswald Chambers says, "If you see Jesus when he says, 'let not your heart be troubled, I defy you to worry.' Jesus said, 'My peace I give you,' – a peace which brings confidence and covers you completely from the top of your head to the soles of your feet. Your life is hidden with Christ in God and the peace of Jesus that cannot be disturbed has been imparted to you."

The love chapter of the Bible lists 16 characteristics of God's self-sacrificing agape love. Practicing these characteristics will go a long way to help remove fear and mental illness. "Love is patient, love is kind. It does not envy or boast, it is not proud. It is not rude, it is not self-seeking, it is not easily angered, it keeps no record of wrongs. Love does not delight in evil but rejoices with the truth. It always protects, always trusts, always hopes, always perseveres. Love never fails" (I Corinthians 13:4-8).

This love is superior to all the gifts of the Spirit. God's love can heal all our sins and hurts. "If I have the gift of faith that can move mountains, but do not have love, I am nothing. If I have the gift of giving and give all I possess to the poor and give my body to be burned, but do not have love I gain nothing" (I Corinthians 13:1-3).

God's love is different than the world's love. God's love is other-centered. The world's love is self-centered. The world's love, loves you for what you can give and takes what it wants and then moves on. God's love is patient, kind, and constant. We don't need to work to earn it. No matter how bad the news or how impossible our situation looks: love always wins (I Corinthians 13:8). It wins even if it takes our physical life. (Romans 8:38).

God's love took Jesus' physical life—it took Jesus to the cross. It will take us there as well. Jesus made it clear we are to take up our cross daily. (Luke 9:23). You choose to pick up the cross. Your cross is not necessarily physical limitations we all experience. Your cross is choosing to go the second mile, i.e. choosing to do what you know

Jesus wants you to do even though you don't feel comfortable doing it. You will never grow unless you move out of your comfort zone. Ask yourself, what am I choosing to do that I don't particularly want to do but I know Jesus wants me to do it, so I choose to do it? That's the path to growth and good mental health.

People will never come to Jesus unless Christians move out of their comfort zone. Jesus calls us to be fishers of people. Many Christians seem to have forgotten we are to be calling people to Jesus. "Thanks be to God, who always leads us as captives in Christ's triumphal procession and uses us to spread the aroma of the knowledge of Him everywhere. For we are God's aroma of Christ among those who are being saved and those who are perishing. To the ones who are perishing we are the smell of death; to the other, the fragrance of life" (II Corinthians 2:14-16).

My wife, Helen, had just received a discouraging report from her doctor. She prayed, "My life is in your hands, Lord. I choose to rejoice in you." On the way home we stopped at the grocery to pick up an item. She walked up to the checkout counter with no customers waiting. The clerk said, "What's the name of the fragrance you are wearing?" She said, "I'm allergic to fragrances." "But it's such a mild pleasing scent," she said. Out of Helen's mouth came the words, "Maybe it is the essence of Jesus." The clerk smiled and said, "That would be a pleasing scent." Together they rejoiced in the Lord along with the bagger who had overheard their conversation.

Make Jesus attractive by how you live today so others will want to become His disciple. I pray as I walk that I can be a fragrance of Christ to everyone I meet, that He will give me the words to say in the tone of voice that communicates God's love.

Jim grew up in a home without love. Pushed around, beaten and at times penned in an attic. His anger grew. He vowed no one would ever push him around again. He became a boxer, using his pent-up anger to defeat his opponents. Coupled with various additions, he feared his vicious anger might kill an opponent. Helen and I spent hours at our house counseling and praying with Jim. Others gave a loving ear and helping hand. Today Jim is walking with Jesus and is a powerful witness for our Lord.

"The early Christians rescued abandoned babies from trash heaps and ransoming slaves and prostitutes. Medieval Christians preserved literacy, founded universities, and built hospitals. Christians in recent centuries are working to abolish slavery, championing civil rights, and are taking the compassion and salvation of Christ to some of the darkest corners of the world . . .

"The Plague of Cyprian (251-266 AD) reportedly killed as many as 5,000 people per day for almost 20 years. On Easter Sunday in 260, Bishop Dionysius of Corinth said: 'Most of our brother Christians, . . . never sparing themselves, and thinking only of one another . . . took charge of the sick, attending to their every need and ministering to them in Christ, and with them departed this life serenely happy; for they were infected by others with the disease . . . cheerfully accepting their pains.'" (Adapted from Jim Denison's blog, 12/5/19).

Since we are the salt and light in a decaying, dark world, we are responsible to take the transforming light of Christ to those around us. Jesus calls on you, He is counting on you to love as He loved you. He equipped you with gifts to share His love. If you keep them to yourself you will lose them.

Pray for your unsaved friends. Pray for your children and grandchildren. Do you have faith to believe your prayers will bring people to Jesus—even people in other nations? Don't forget to pray for the two billion people who have never heard the name of Jesus. Prayer is the most effective weapon we have. Jesus modeled prayer as He often withdrew and went alone to pray. Our world would be different if Christians would pray as Jesus prayed. Ask God to give you a burning desire to pray. He will do it.

Paul writes: "I have made myself a servant to everyone to win as many as possible. When I am with the Jews, I become one of them so that I can bring them to Christ. When I am with the Gentiles, I fit in with them as much as I can; in this way, I gain their confidence and bring them to Christ. When I am with those who are oppressed or who are complaining, I share their oppression so that I might bring them to Christ" (I Corinthians 9:20-23).

When people mention a problem; this is an open door for you to listen and pray for them. Share how Jesus has helped you. When I ask people if I can pray for them, no one has ever said no.

When someone thanks you, you might say, "God has been good to me. I enjoy helping others." Perhaps the easiest door to open a conversation is to talk about the weather. "Isn't God good to send the sunshine today." It's challenging to move the conversation from God to Jesus. Most people don't mind you mentioning God, but Jesus said, "All men will hate you because of me." The cross demands a response. Let's take up our cross.

Prayer: Lord Jesus, help me to be an aroma that brings people to You. Amen.

DOES GOD HELP THOSE WHO HELP THEMSELVES? MATTHEW 25:34-46, I JOHN 3:16-18

Many believe the statement: God helps those who help themselves. This phrase says if we help ourselves and employ our own natural efforts then God will help us. That's not the way it works. J. I. Packer says, "We do not make friends with God, God makes friends with us bringing us to know him by making his love known to us." We are not self-sufficient; we are God-dependent. God always takes the initiative. "We love because he first loved us" (I John 4:19). "Jesus came to seek and save all who are lost" (Luke 19:10). "God so greatly loved and dearly prized the world that he [even] gave up his only-begotten (unique) Son" (John 3:16 AMP).

We didn't seek God; He sought us. "He is the hound of heaven." Jesus said, "People can't come to me unless the father . . . draws them to me" (John 6:44). "For God did not send his Son into the world to judge the world; but that the world might find salvation and be made safe and sound – through him" (John 3:17 AMP).

We are not able to help ourselves. David writes, "The steps of a [good] man are directed and established of the Lord" (Psalm 37:23 AMP). "Trust in the Lord with all your heart and lean not on your own understanding; in all your ways acknowledge him and he will make your paths straight. Do not be wise in your own eyes; fear the Lord and shun evil" (Proverbs 3:5-7). "He lifted me out of the pit of despair, out of the mud and the mire. He set my feet on solid ground and steadied me as I walked along" (Psalm 40:2 NLT).

God provides the air we breathe, the rain and the sun to grow our food. He enables our heart to beat and gives us strength. "Apart from him we can do nothing" (John 15:5). Nothing is less than zero. Self-reliance keeps us from Spirit-reliance, which results in spiritual suicide. It turns us from God to self when we need God most. Our first response must be to repent: "Lord I need You! I can't make it without You." Repentance is an absolute must.

Paul explains why the phrase, "The Lord helps those who help themselves," is not appropriate. "Work out – cultivate, carry out to the goal and fully complete – your own salvation with reverence and awe and trembling, . . . [Not in your own strength] for it is God who is all the while effectually at work in you – energizing and creating in you the power and desire both to will and to work for his good pleasure and satisfaction and delight" (Philippians 2:12-13 AMP). We can do all things through Christ – with His strength. (Philippians 4:13).

There is no room for self-sufficiency. Self-sufficiency is pride. Even Jesus said, "I tell you the truth, the Son can do nothing by himself, he can do only what he sees the Father doing because whatever the Father does the Son also does" (John 5:19).

It's God who gives you the desire, the will and the power to do His will and work. When we line up our will with God's will, we will sense His pleasure. We cannot do what God does—save ourselves— and God will not do what we can do. He has chosen to limit Himself to our willingness to be His instruments to carry out His will. We are that important. We must form good habits. We must work out our own salvation, which God has worked in us. "I labor [unto weariness], striving with all the superhuman energy which he so mightily enkindles and works within me" (Colossians 1:29 AMP).

We labor with enthusiasm and energy knowing this is only possible because Christ gives us the desire to labor and the energy to work. He must receive all the glory. "God chose the weak things of the world to shame the strong. He chose the lowly and the despised things . . . so that no one may boast before him. It is because of him that you are in Christ Jesus, who has become for us wisdom from God – that is our righteousness, holiness and redemption. Therefore, as it is written: 'Let him who boasts boast in the Lord'" (I Corinthians 1:27-31).

"Pew Research Center reports that 56 percent of Americans say it is not necessary to believe in God in order to be moral and have good values. Hell ranks sixty-fourth on our list of fears. Eighty-five percent of us believe we'll go to heaven (including, ironically, 77 percent of nonreligious people), it is clear that most people don't think we need God to avoid hell or as they might say, i.e. "If there is a hell."

The majority of Americans are depending on their good works for entrance into heaven. Ask people if they are ready to meet God. They often say, "I'm a good person. I'm kind to my neighbor. When he was sick, I mowed his yard. I don't steal or murder. I try to help people. I provide for my wife and children as best I can. I try to obey the law. Occasionally I give to the scouts, Little League and the Red Cross.

I think I'll make it to heaven. God and I are on good terms." Works religion started in the Garden of Eden and it permeates our world and our life from birth.

There is an apocryphal story of a man who came to the gates of heaven. At the gate there was a sign that said, "2000 Points to Enter." Peter asked the man, "Why should I let you into heaven?"He replied, "I went to Sunday School most every Sunday of my life." Peter said, "That's one point." He said, "I gave money most every Sunday in the offering plate." Peter said, "That's one point." He said, "I provided for my family and loved my children." Peter said, "That's one point."In anguish the man realized he could not make the grade. In desperation he threw himself at Peter's feet and said, "I guess I'll just have to come to the cross and ask Jesus for His mercy."Peter said, "Come in!"

"All our righteous acts are like filthy rage; they all shrivel up like a leaf, and like the wind our sins sweep us away" (Isaiah 64:6). "There is no one righteous, not even one; there is no one who understands, no one who seeks God. All have turned away, they have together become worthless; there is no one who does good, not even one" (Romans 3:10-12). "The heart is deceitful above all things, and beyond cure" (Jeremiah 17:9). David writes: "I was sinful at birth, sinful from the time my mother conceived me" (Psalm 51:5).

"God saved us because of his mercy, and not because of any good things (works) that we have done. God washed us by the power of the Holy Spirit. He gave us new birth and a fresh beginning. God sent Jesus Christ, our Savior to give us the Spirit. Jesus treats us much better than we deserve. He makes us acceptable to God and gives us the hope of eternal life . . . Insist that the people follow these teachings so that all who have faith in God will be sure to do good deeds" (Titus 3:5-8 CEV).

No amount of good works can compensate for our sins or bring us into a right relationship with God. Only Jesus can forgive our sins and give us eternal life. We cannot do good (godly) works without God. We cannot do godly deeds unless we are His child who has been forgiven of our sins and transformed our unbelieving heart to one that is hungry for His righteousness. (Matthew 5:6).

Why can't our good works meet God's requirements? Because our self-centered nature makes it impossible to have pure and God-like motives. "When you ask, you do not receive, because you ask with wrong motives, that you may spend what you get on your pleasures" (James 4:3). "The plowing of the wicked is sin" (Proverbs 21:4). That's because it is not done to the glory of God. "Whether you eat or drink or whatever you do, do it all for the glory of God" (I Corinthians 10:31). "Whatever you do, whether in word or deed, do it all in the name of the Lord Jesus, giving thanks to God the Father through him" (Colossians 3:17). The ungodly man does what is necessary and innocent but it is not done for the glory of God. He may help people but his motives cannot be 100% for God's glory. His soul is infected deeply with sin. There is nothing holy to the unbeliever. "To the pure all things are pure, but to those who are corrupted and do not believe, nothing is pure. In fact, both their minds and consciences are corrupted" (I Titus 1:15).

Our motive for doing good works is to serve Jesus. When we encounter those who are hungry, thirsty, in need of clothes and shelter, those in prison or those who are sick and we care for them we are ministering to Jesus. Jesus continues: "I was hungry and you gave me nothing to eat, I was thirsty and you gave me nothing to drink, I was a stranger and you did not invite me in, I needed clothes and you did not clothe me, I was sick and in prison and you did not look after me ... Truly I tell you, whatever you did not do for one of the least of these, you did not do for me. Then they will go away to eternal punishment but the righteous to eternal life" (Matthew 25:42-46).

"Praise be to the God and Father of our Lord Jesus Christ! In his great mercy he has given us new birth (a new nature) into a living hope through the resurrection of Jesus Christ from the dead and into an inheritance that can never perish, spoil or fade" (I Peter 1:3-4). We receive a new nature, a new heart, when we are born from above. (John 3:3). God doesn't want our good works; He wants our heart. If He has our heart, He has all the good works we can do. The same is true with my relationship with my wife. My wife doesn't want all the things I might provide for her like a new car or my paycheck; she wants my heart, my loyalty, my love, then, of course, she will have all I have—it's all hers.

Doing good works will not get us to heaven. Jesus said, "This is the way to have eternal life – to know you, the only true God, and Jesus Christ, the one you sent to earth" (John 17:3). "Not everyone who says to me, 'Lord, Lord,' will enter the kingdom of heaven, but only he who does the will of my Father who is in heaven. Many will say to me on that day, 'Lord, Lord, did we not prophesy in your name, and in your name drive out demons and perform many miracles?' Then I will tell them plainly, 'I never knew you. Away from me, you evildoers!'" (Matthew 7:21-23).

The "good works gospel" leads us away from grace. "God saved you by his grace when you believed (trusted) him. And you can't take credit for this; it is a gift from God. Salvation is not a reward for the good things (good works) we have done, so none of us can boast about it. For we are God's masterpiece. He has created us anew in Christ Jesus, so we can do the good things (good works) he planned for long ago" (Ephesians 2:8-10).

Good words are important. After we know (experience) Jesus, after we have invited Him to rule our life then we are able to do the good works that God planned for us long ago. "God is not unjust; he will not forget your work and the love you have shown him as you have helped his people and continue to help them" (Hebrews 6:10). Paul writes, "We remember . . . your work produced by faith" (I Thessalonians 1:3).

James explains: "What good is it . . . if you claim to have faith but have no deeds? Can such faith save you? Suppose a brother or sister is without clothes and daily food. If one of you says to him 'Go, I wish you well, keep warm and well fed,' but does nothing about his physical needs, what good it is? In the same way, faith by itself, if it is not accompanied by actions, is dead" (James 2:14-17).

At the judgment day we will be rewarded for our good deeds. "God will repay each person according to what they have done. To those who by persistence in doing good seek glory, honor and immortality he will give eternal life. But those who are self-seeking and who reject the truth and follow evil, there will be wrath and anger. There will be trouble and distress for every human being who does evil . . . but glory, honor and peace for everyone who does good" (Romans 2:6-10). Each person sooner or later receives what he/she deserves—if not here, then hereafter. "God will judge you according to what you do. So, you must live in reverent fear of him during your time as foreigners in the land" (I Peter 1:17 NLT). Jesus says, "Look, I am coming soon! My reward is with me, and I will give to each person according to what they have done" (Revelation 22:12). We anticipate Jesus' return and so we purify ourselves, as He is pure. (I John 3:3). Purification comes as we obey the truth. (I Peter 1:22).

I had a motto in my room as a child that had a great effect on me. It read: "Your life will soon be past. Only what is done for Christ will last." This motto would be greatly improved if it read: "Your life will soon be past, only what's done with Christ will last." Working for Christ our motives are often on rewards and we grow weary and burn out. Working with Jesus, yoking up with Him, our efforts are not a burden but a joy. We will find it easy to thank God for all He is doing through us. (Matthew 11:28-30).

Love God, know God and serve Him with every ounce of energy He gives you and you will be rewarded greatly. We are saved by God's grace, i.e. God's undeserved gift to us, not by our good works. However, after we are saved and ignore the needs of others, we are in danger of being separated from our Lord for eternity in everlasting destruction. "This is how we know what love is: Jesus Christ laid down his life for us. And we ought to lay down our lives for our brothers and sisters. If anyone has material possessions and sees a brother or sister in need but has no pity on them, how can the love of God be in that person? Dear children, let us not love with words or speech but with actions and in truth" (I John 3:16-18).

HOLY FEAR
MATTHEW 10:28-30

Jesus said, "Do not be afraid of those who kill the body and after that can do no more. But I will show you whom you should fear: Fear him who after your body has been killed, has authority to throw you into hell. Yes, I tell you, fear him. Are not five sparrows sold for two pennies? Yet not one of them is forgotten by God. Indeed, the very hairs of your head are all numbered. Don't be afraid; you are worth more than many sparrows" (Matthew 10:28-30). "Do not fear what the people fear, and do not dread it. The Lord Almighty is the one you are to regard as holy, he is the one you are to fear, he is the one you are to dread" (Isaiah 8:12-13).

Today, one in eight Christians around the world are in danger of imminent persecution. In the book, *Hearts of Fire, Eight Women in the Underground Church and Their Stories of Costly Faith,* (Thomas Nelson Publishing), there are accounts of eight women from eight different nations where they suffered horrific persecution. They did not fear because after they were finally released from prison, they continued to give a bold witness for Jesus and because of their witness they continued to suffer greatly.

Why are we afraid of being a witness for Jesus? Are we ashamed of Jesus? Joe worked side-by-side with Jim for nearly fifteen years.

They both liked to play golf. Joe said to Jim, "Go with me golfing Sunday morning." Jim said, "You know I go to church every Sunday." Joe responded, "You don't believe that stuff." "What do you mean by that?" asked Jim. Joe said, "I have worked with you for fifteen years and you never invited me to church. I think your Bible says I am going to hell when I die. You don't believe the Bible or you would have invited me to church." Are you like Jim, afraid you will offend your neighbor if you talk about your love for Jesus?

It is sad that most Christians in America, like Jim, don't believe in hell. Not only do they not believe but most resent the Christians who give verbal witness to their faith. They have no intention of sharing the Good News with their lost neighbor. They don't believe that their neighbors who volunteer as an ambulance driver, or help the special-ed teacher, or who mows your lawn when you are sick, will go to hell. After all, they are such good neighbors doing such good deeds.

Jesus commissioned us giving us all His authority and promised He will be with us every day until He returns. He has given us His Holy Spirit to empower us to witness. (Matthew 28:18-20; Acts 1:8). Jesus said, "As the Father has sent me, I am sending you" (John 17:18; 20:21). It's obvious why our churches are decreasing. Perhaps this is a good thing. As our culture becomes more and more pagan the fully devoted disciples of Jesus will stand out from the others who neither were saved or they have experienced salvation but lost their first love. (Revelation 2:4, James 5:19).

I pray every morning that I will make use of every opportunity to share Jesus. If a day goes by where I feel I have not moved anyone closer to Jesus or at least made him or her aware of God, I feel I need to repent and ask God to forgive me for overlooking an opportunity. I try to pray when I am walking that as I meet people God will give me words to say from His Holy Spirit. It's thrilling to see how God answers that prayer. Paul writes: "Be very careful how you live. Make the most of every opportunity, because the days are evil" (Ephesians 4:15). He repeats the same message to the Colossians: "Be wise in the way you act toward outsiders, make the most of every opportunity" (Colossians 4:5). There is no greater joy than to experience the Holy Spirit flowing through you as you share Jesus with others.

If you are fearful to speak for Jesus, first, pray earnestly for God to give you a passion for the lost. Confess that you don't have passion like Paul who could wish his name were blotted out of the book of life for the sake of his brothers and sister who did not know Jesus if that would mean salvation for them. (Romans 9:1-3). Next, I suggest you share your faith with others who are already saved—even such comments as simple as "Isn't God good to us to send the bright sunshine after all those cloudy days?" This sounds simple but many Christians feel uncomfortable talking about God. Next ask Him to move your witness from God to Jesus. You will find it is more difficult to talk about Jesus. Even those who claim to be atheists may not be offended if you mention God, which to them is a generic term. Jesus said that all people will be offended by His name. (Mark 13:13). The reason they are offended by Jesus' name is they know intuitively a day is coming when every knee will bow and every tongue confess that Jesus is Lord. (Philippians 2:10-11).

To whom does the Lord want you to speak about Him today?

ENCOUNTERING WOLVES
LUKE 10:3-4, 19

I received a phone call on my birthday. The wife was desperate as her husband was threatening to kill her with a knife. By the time I got there he had left. In another situation a woman who was not married was living with an alcoholic. They were showing interest in Christ and church. Different times when he was drunk, she begged me to get him out of the house. Responding to her desperate plea another brother and I moved him to the WMCA. However, the next morning she was irate with me for moving her man. That was years ago. Some lessons I learned the hard way. On other occasions I battled with bed bugs and threatening looks, etc. When we help people, we encounter many kinds of "wolves."

Jesus says to the 70 disciples, "Go now, and remember that I am sending you out as lambs among wolves. Don't take along any money, or a traveler's bag, or even an extra pair of sandals" (Luke 10:3-4 NLT). Then Jesus says in verse 19, "I have given you authority over all the power of the enemy, and you can walk among snakes and scorpions and crush them. Nothing will harm you." A Christian facing martyrdom said, "I am near death, but I'm not in danger." This is what Jesus meant when He said that nothing can harm you. (v. 19).

What do wolves do with lambs? Devour them! Jesus sends you but that does not mean you will find it comfortable and easy. He sent the disciples in a boat and a furious storm terrified them. (Matthew 8:23-27). Jesus was driven by the Spirit into the wilderness and was severely tempted. (Luke 4:1). Just because Jesus promised to be with us every day until He returns does not mean our life will be spared. (Matthew 28:20). It is estimated there were one million martyrs the first one hundred years following the Crucifixion of our Lord. Jesus sends us out, but He did not promise we would return safely. (John 20:21). Someone said, "Wherever Paul went there was either revival or riot."

Why do we think God wants to send us to safe places? When God called Jonah to go to Nineveh he ran the opposite direction—he ran from the wolves. The Ninevites were fierce and powerful warriors. God had to take Jonah to the depths before he repented and went where God told him to go. The revival spared the nation for the next 100 years. All the prophets encountered wolves: Tradition says Jeremiah was killed by his own people; Isaiah was sawed in two; it's believed Amos was killed by the son of Amaziah, priest of Bethel, etc. All the disciples were martyred except John.

When we make Christ lord of our life, we die to self; we have no more claim to our life than a dead person does. "A century ago, a band of brave souls became known as one-way missionaries. They purchased single tickets to the mission field without the return half. Instead of suitcases, they packed their few earthly belongings into coffins. As they sailed out of port, they waved goodbye to everyone they loved, everything they knew. They knew they'd never return home. A. W. Milne was one of them. He set sail for the New Hebrides in the South Pacific, knowing full well that the headhunters who lived there had martyred every missionary before him. Milne did not fear for his life, because he had already died to himself. His coffin was packed. For thirty-five years, he lived among that tribe and loved them. When he died, tribe members buried him in the middle of their village and inscribed their epitaph on his tombstone: 'When he came there was no light. When he left there was no darkness.'" (Mark Batterson, *All In*, Zondervan, p. 13).

When God called three young women in 1947 to pioneer a province in China with the Gospel they said, "We may not reach our destination, we may die on the way, but we are willing to shed our blood on the highway to Mount Zion." (Paul Hattaway, *Back to Jerusalem*, p. 29). He adds: (p. 106), "Thousands have been sent out with nobody to rely on except God himself . . . We have become soldiers of steel, tempered in the furnace of affliction. We do not fear what people can do to us." The Chinese church experienced the greatest revival in Christian history.

Do you believe your security is in Christ even though the wolves may eat you alive? Jesus said, "Do not be afraid of those who kill the body but cannot kill the soul. Rather, be afraid of the One who can destroy both the soul and body in hell" (Matthew 10:28). Are you at peace with the thought of going home to be with Jesus even though it involves suffering? If you hesitate because of unfinished business with others then make peace now. If your hesitancy is because you believe your work on earth is not finished then tell God and let the decision in His hands.

King Herod had Peter's companion, James, killed with the sword. Peter knew he was next in line. But he slept in peace. (Acts 12:1-6). Paul writes, "To me, living is for Christ, and dying is even better. Yet if I live, that means fruitful service for Christ . . . I'm torn between two desires: Sometimes I want to live, and sometimes I long to go and be with Christ. That would be far better for me, but it is better for you that I live . . . I will continue with you so that you will grow and experience the joy of your faith" (Philippians 1:21-25 NLT).

Pastor Brother Yun says, "One day I may be killed for the sake of the gospel in a Muslim or Buddhist nation. If you hear this news, please don't grieve for me, but grieve for the millions of precious souls who are enslaved by Satan, without any gospel witness. Death is not the end for a servant of God; it is just the start of indescribable ever-lasting life in the presence of Jesus." (Paul Hattaway, *Back to Jerusalem*, p. 61).

Thomas Chisholm understood God's faithfulness and gave us the hymn: "Great is Thy faithfulness, O God my Father; There is no shadow of turning with Thee; Thou changest not, Thy compassions, they fail not; As Thou hast been, Thou forever will be. Pardon for sin and a peace that endureth, Thy own dear presence to cheer and to guide; strength for today and bright hope for tomorrow, blessings all mine, with ten thousand beside! Great is thy faithfulness; Lord unto me."

Lord, enable me to be faithful so that one day I will hear: "Well done, good and faithful servant, enter into the joy of the Lord." Amen.

WHERE IS OUR PASSION?
ROMANS 9:2-3, ACTS 20:24

Many who claim to be followers of Jesus would rather have a root canal than share Jesus. When Christ is our life, sharing the Good News is as natural as breathing. If all that you gained from your salvation in Christ is something that you could hold to without passing it on then it is not good news. Because of what the Good News is, it will make you share it with others. History shows us that when revival comes to a community Christians who seldom or never share Jesus receive a new boldness to share the Good News of Jesus.

John Piper writes: "What should we be doing? It's simple—not complicated at all. Tell people the good news of Christ from a heart of love and a life of service! That's it!" The majority of followers of Christ, and even many unbelievers, agree with two-thirds of this statement. They agree it's good to have a heart of love along with a life of service, but they do not agree on what "tell" means. Most would say you can "tell" without opening your mouth. This results in a lukewarm, or even a "Dead Sea" Christianity.

"If you declare with your mouth, 'Jesus is Lord,' and believe in your heart that God raised him from the dead, you will be saved . . . It is with your mouth that you profess your faith and are saved" (Romans 10:9-10).

If we knew the solution to curing cancer and didn't share it, we would be guilty of a criminal offense. We have the answer to life's problems. It is not right to withhold good news from those who, according to Jesus, are going to hell without faith in Him. (Luke 13:24-29). Only six percent of Christians make an effort to share their faith! What is holding us back? Could our "closed mouth" be indifference or cowardice? (Mark 8:38).

Lois, a vivacious second-grade teacher, who was just baptized, said, "I can talk about everything in the teachers' lounge but when it comes to sharing Jesus, I am tongue-tied. Why is that?" Our culture has taught us that religion is an individual matter. We are not impolite when we share what our best friend, Jesus, is doing in our daily life. The devil will do all he can to keep us quiet. The cross is offensive to all who believe they are good people and have no need to confess sin. Today most people do not believe there is such a thing as "sin," which means they will likely be offended.

As a church consultant I always prayed before I spoke, "Lord, You have blessed me with growing churches, help me when I speak not to come across as a braggart, or as one who has all the answers." As I was praying one night at two in the morning the Lord said to me to check in *Strong's Concordance* the number of times we are told to be bold and the number of times we are told to be humble. We are told to be bold more often than we are told to be humble. "The righteous are as bold as lions" (Proverbs 28:1).

Peter and John said, "We cannot help but speak about what we have seen and heard" (Acts 4:19-20). Paul writes, "I have great sorrow and unceasing anguish in my heart. For I could wish that I myself were cursed and cut off from Christ for the sake of my people" (Romans 9:2-3). "I consider my life worth nothing to me, my only aim is to finish the race and complete the task the Lord Jesus has given me – the task of testifying to the good news of God's grace" (Acts 20:24).

No person is a fully devoted follower of Jesus unless they are reaching out to bring others into the joyful presence of Jesus. (Psalm 16:11). We neglect to share Jesus because Jesus is not our life and breath. (Colossians 3:1-3). We have lost our first love. (Revelation 2:4).

Our TV, iPhones, cars, sports, and vacations are more important than the mandate of the Great Commission. People move to get a better job but seldom do we hear of people moving because God called them to help a struggling church or help plant another church. We say we love Jesus but we must ask, "How can we love him and not keep his command to share him?" (Matthew 28:18-20). Jesus said we are to overflow with streams of living water but there is no overflow for anyone who does not share Jesus. (John 7:38).

When we are not overflowing Oswald Chambers writes: "Keep paying attention to the source, and God will either take you around the obstacle or remove it. The river of the Spirit of God overcomes all obstacles. Never focus your eyes on the obstacle or the difficulty. The obstacle will be a matter of total indifference to the river that will flow steadily through you if you will simply remember to stay focused on the source." When we are filled with the Living Water, we have a song in our hearts, and a thankful spirit that people notice. (Ephesians 5:18-19).

Our grandson lived in Morocco for a time. Whenever he went outside people greeted him and asked if he was a Muslim. When he replied that he was a Christian they immediately said, "Why aren't you a Muslim?" What a contrast from our American culture! In our culture we usually need to build a relationship first before we share our faith.

Jesus built relationships as He asked more than 200 questions. Jesus will help us learn to ask questions as He did.

Sharing Jesus is all about showing God's love. His love comes with wisdom, with sensitivity to the person's needs and feelings. We fish, we urge, we compel, we invite under the leading of the Holy Spirit. Jesus compels by His extravagant love and we can do no less. He had an agenda and we must have one, too.

Imagine your Muslim friend invites you to the mosque. What is your gut reaction? Would you be embarrassed because you don't know what to expect or do? Where does my wife go during the service? Do I kneel when the other men kneel? Our secular friends have no idea what goes on inside a church building. This means it often works better to discover their interests and relate to them first on that level and discern when the Spirit opens the door to relate Jesus.

Building a relationship does not take as much time as you think. Most things we are doing we can keep on doing but we do them with pre-believers. When you help clean up after a storm or hurricane take them with you. Most pre-believers will be glad to help. When you go to a ballgame, shop, play golf, bowl, bike ride, or attend a school concert, invite your pre-believer friends to go with you. Invite them to your backyard barbeque along with a few church friends. If they enjoy sports invite them over to watch a game on TV. Build relationships and share the Good News from a heart of love and a life of service.

We come up with many excuses for not sharing Jesus. Some people don't share the Good News because they believe people don't want to hear it. Jesus reminds us that some seed will fall on good soil and bring a bountiful harvest. (Mark 4). We are Jesus' ambassadors, His fellow workers. Jesus said we are to compel them or make them come to the heavenly banquet. (Luke 14:23).

When we moved to a new community my wife, Helen, spent time with our neighbor showing love and sharing the difference Jesus makes in her life. However, she felt checked by the Holy Spirit that now was not the time to confront one neighbor concerning her relationship with God. My wife discovered later that a person had knocked on our neighbor's door and asked if she was a Christian. She said, "No." He told her she was going to hell. She said, "When I heard that a preacher was moving across the street, I was angry. But Helen you are different. No matter what I say or do, you just accept me. Maybe Jesus will accept me, too." Over the next months she and her family accepted Jesus and worshipped with us.

Like our neighbor sometimes we are rightly turned off by the way people witness, telling ourselves we never want to be like that. However, can you name one person who has come to Christ by those who think it's not cool or politically correct to share your faith in Jesus?

The only obstacle people should experience in coming to Christ is the offense of the cross. The cross demands that we swallow our pride and say, "Yes, I believe Jesus is the Son of God and that He died for my sin." Pride is the president of hell. Repentance is the most difficult exercise we will ever do or ask others to do.

The Gospel message doesn't resonate for people for whom life is providing their basic needs as well as many of their wants. Most in America are enjoying some success and pleasures of a wealthy culture. Even when there is a crisis as a job loss, divorce, or a major illness including serious accidents, they believe that somehow the safety net will be there so they shrug it off and go on. When there is a crisis, they blame the government, their employer, everyone or everything but "me." Jesus told us in the final days that hardness of heart will increase. Only the Holy Spirit can soften the heart. Ask God to help you be aware of hearts He is softening.

Studies show that 56% of evangelical Christians believe that there are many ways to heaven. If that's so there is little need to share the Good News and make disciples. Jesus made it clear that He is the only way. Jesus said in John 14:6, "I am the way and the truth and the life; No one comes to the Father except through me." Peter and Paul state clearly, "Salvation is found in no one else, for there is no other name under heaven given to men by which we must be saved" (Acts 4:12). "God . . . wants all people to be saved and to come to a knowledge of the truth. For there is one God and one mediator between God and man, the man Christ Jesus" (I Timothy 2:5).

Many say there is no day of reckoning. Craig Groesche writes, "I believe one of the main reasons people don't share their faith is that they don't really believe in hell . . . Research shows that while almost three out of four people believe in heaven, less than half believe in hell . . . If hell didn't exist, unbelievers would easily reject Christ with no fear of God whatsoever, and believers would be unmotivated to share their faith with nonbelievers . . . God has created a universe with a heaven—and a hell . . . We are here to help others come to terms with reality . . . When was the last time you were so burdened for someone far from God that you spent the whole day or night praying on their behalf? How many people have you brought with you to church?

. . . When was the last time you had a non-Christian in your home? Is there someone in your family who doesn't know Christ . . . an old friend, a neighbor, or someone at work? . . .

"If we truly understood what hell was like, we'd be much more motivated to help people avoid going there. Hell is a place of unspeakable suffering. Jesus says in Matthew 5:29, 'If your right eye causes you to sin, gouge it out and throw it away. It is better for you to lose one part of your body than for your whole body to be thrown into hell.' Can you imagine gouging out your own eye? According to Jesus as horrible as it would be, digging your eye out would be far better than being punished for your sins in hell. . . . The Bible calls hell a fiery furnace, a place of burning sulfur, the outer darkness, and a place where there is weeping and gnashing of teeth."

William Booth, the founder of the Salvation Army, took a group through an extensive training course lasting several weeks. His final statement may cause us to question his approach, but we see the results of his efforts around the world today. When he finished the course, he said to his apprentices, "I'm sorry our training took so long. If I could take you to hell for five minutes, none of what I've taught you would be necessary."

Some say, I don't share Jesus because I don't want to be a hypocrite. No one is perfect. Be humble and confess that you fall short many times. Unbelievers will understand and respect you if you are honest with them about your walk with Jesus. Confess any hypocrisy and don't hide behind your inconsistencies.

Do you fear rejection? Think of what Jesus went through and realize your "persecution" is nothing compared to His suffering for you. The sufferings of this life are not worth comparing to the rewards of heaven. (Romans 8:18). You are responsible to share the Good News in a humble, respectful way. You are not responsible for other people's reaction to Jesus or to yourself. Let the Holy Spirit work with them.

Don't use your shyness and being uncomfortable as an excuse for not sharing your faith. Such excuses didn't work for Moses or Jeremiah. (Exodus 3:11; Jeremiah 1:6). If sharing the Good News is new to you it will be uncomfortable at first. That will change. You will experience people who sincerely thank you for caring enough to share your faith with them. The Holy Spirit is a spirit of power and courage and he lives in you. (II Timothy 1:7).

David Platt writes: "We take Jesus' command to make disciples . . . and say, 'That means other people.' But we look at Jesus' command in Matthew 11:28, 'Come to me, all you who are weary and burdened, and I will give you rest,' and we say, 'Now, that means me.' We take Jesus' promise in Acts 1:8 that the Spirit will lead us to the ends of the earth, and we say, 'That means some people.' But we take Jesus' promise in John 10:10 that we will have abundant life, and we say, 'That means me.'" Don't be guilty of claiming Jesus' promises selectively. There are multitudes all around you who need Jesus so don't spend all your time with those who continually reject you. Move on. You will find the good soil. God's Word will never return void or empty. (Isaiah 55:11).

We must have an all-consuming passion for the lost. Jesus' compassion has to be imparted by the Holy Spirit. Go to God in full repentance to plead for an impartation of His heartbeat for the lost. God is patient toward us (the believers), not willing that any (of the unbelievers) should perish, but that all should come to repentance. (II Peter 3:9).

A professed atheist wrote: "The New Testament offers a picture of a God who does not sound at all vague to me. He has sent his son to earth. He has distinct plans both for his son and for mankind. He knows each of us personally and can communicate directly with us. We are capable of forming a direct relationship. We are told this can be done only through his son. And we are offered the prospect of eternal life – an afterlife of happy, blissful, or glorious circumstances . . . Friends, if I believe that, or even a tenth of that . . . I would drop my job, sell my house, throw away my possessions, leave my acquaintances and set out into the world burning with the desire to know more and when, I had found out more, to act upon it and tell others."

The secret of removing the fear and hesitancy of sharing Jesus is to ask God to give you His passion for the lost just as the Father gave Jesus His passion for humanity. This passion took Him to His death. It's a matter of life or death.

COMPEL THEM TO COME
LUKE 14:15-24, MARK 2:1-12

Someone said to Jesus it would be great to share in God's Kingdom. In response Jesus gave this illustration: "A man prepared a great feast and sent out many invitations. When all was ready, he sent his servant to notify the guests that it was time to come. They all began making excuses. One said, he had just bought a field and wanted to inspect it. Another said he had just bought five pair of oxen and wanted to try them out. Another had just been married, so he said he couldn't come. The servant returned and told the master what they said. The master was angry and said, 'Go quickly into the streets and alleys of the city and invite the poor, the crippled, the lame and the blind.' After the servant had done this, he reported, 'There is still room for more.' So, his master said, 'Go out into the country lanes and behind the hedges and compel anyone you find to come, so that my house will be full. For none of those I invited will get even the smallest taste of what I had prepared for them'" (Luke 14:15-24 NLT).

The Greek word for "compel or make" in verse 23 means "this is an absolute necessity." I checked 19 versions or translations: six said, "make them come in," six "compel," four "urge," two "force," and one "drag them in." How do we make/compel/force people to come to the heavenly banquet? We do it just like Jesus did—by giving His life, denying Himself, loving sacrificially, giving His time, money, energy, and even to the point of dying. We are called to do no less, i.e. take up our cross daily. (Luke 9:23). Is this why there are few disciples?

In Mark 2 when Jesus came to His hometown the people packed out the house where He was. Four men brought a paralytic on a stretcher for Jesus to heal him. Because of the crowd they were unable to get to Jesus so they went up on the roof, removed the tiles and lowered the man down in front of Jesus.

Imagine going to your neighbor's house and taking off part of the roof! These men meant business! They had faith that Jesus would heal this man. They were determined to have him meet Jesus. How determined are we to have our neighbors meet Jesus? Jesus said we are to compel them to come to the heavenly banquet. After all, Jesus suffered on the cross to make it possible for us to come to Him for healing, both spiritually and physically. Do you have this kind of passion? Ask Jesus to give you the passion and the faith of these four men who brought the paralytic to Jesus.

God's call comes to us in many different ways: He used the burning bush to call Moses, the donkey to direct Balaam, the fish to vomit up Jonah, a vision to call Isaiah, a verbal message to call Jeremiah. When our son served as a missionary in Columbia, South America, the Lord spoke to him in His spirit and told him to plant a church in Ohio. Two days later he received a letter signed by several pastors in Ohio to come plant a church.

Do you know Jesus calls you and sends you? Jesus said to His disciples before He ascended to heaven, "Peace be with you! As the Father has sent me, I am sending you" (John 20:21). As He was praying, He said to the Father, "As you sent me into the world, I am sending them into the world" (John 17:18 NLT). Jesus' prayer includes you and me. Notice the word "as." Just as Jesus was sent, He sends us. This implies that there is no difference between the Father sending Jesus and Jesus sending us. Does that mean we have the same authority? "He breathed on them and said, 'Receive the Holy Spirit. If you forgive anyone his sins, they are forgiven, if you do not forgive them, they are not forgiven'" (John 20:22-23).

Where does Jesus send us? "Into the world!" Forty-five of Jesus' parables were given in the marketplace and all but ten of His conversations were outside the temple. Jesus made it a point to intentionally move among people in the marketplace or the town square. Where is your marketplace—where you work, shop or . . . ? He urges us to let our light shine brightly in the world—in our homes, across the street and the ends of the earth.

As the Holy Spirit leads you, you will have opportunities to invite your friends to receive the forgiveness that Jesus has already provided for them. You don't condemn them for what they are doing but when the Spirit guides you, you can ask them if they would like to receive the forgiveness and joy Jesus has provided. You might say, "I receive Jesus' forgiveness every day. It's great to live with no condemnation for my thoughts and actions that are not in line with God's will. Sometimes I have thoughts or actions of pride, jealousy, envy, irritability, lust or hate. God says these are all sins. He forgives me when I sincerely ask Him. The Bible says, 'If we say we have no sin, we are only fooling ourselves and refusing to accept the truth. But if we confess our sins to Him, He is faithful and just to forgive us and to cleanse us from every wrong. If we claim we have not sinned, we are calling God a liar'" (I John 1:8-9 NLT).

When Elwood, a new believer, went to a church conference someone asked him why he started coming to church. He said, "Because Pastor Dave kept inviting me; he wouldn't give up." I had gone to his home and visited with him and his family many times. I called occasionally and prompted others in the church to do the same. This is one way we "compel" them to come.

When you see a real estate sign pray for the family that will move into that home. When they move stop by and welcome them to your community and tell them you have been praying for them. This opens the door to eventually discover their openness to the Gospel. Often those on the margins of society need transportation. I have spent many years picking up people for church. Be alert to those going through a major adjustment i.e., auto accident, divorce, loss of a job, illness, etc., see how you might help and hopefully form a relationship that will give you an opportunity to share Jesus. As Paul said, "I have become all things to all people so that by all possible means I might save some" (I Corinthians 9:22).

A chorus I have sung since I was a youth and one that has stayed with me throughout my life is: "Lord, lay some soul upon my heart and love that soul through me. And may I ever do my part to win that soul for thee." Will you make that your prayer today?

WHOM DO WE COMPEL TO COME?
MATTHEW 22:1-14

"The kingdom of heaven is like a king who prepared a wedding banquet for his son. He sent his servants to those who had been invited to the banquet to tell them to come but they refused to come. Then he sent some more servants and said, 'Tell those who have been invited that I have prepared my dinner: My oxen and fattened cattle have been butchered and everything is ready. Come to the wedding banquet.' But they paid no attention and went off – one to his field, another to his business. The rest seized his servants, mistreated them and killed them. The king was enraged. He sent his army and destroyed those murderers and burned their city . . .

"Then he said to his servants. 'The wedding banquet is ready, but those I invited do not deserve to come. So, go to the street corners and invite to the banquet anyone you find.' So the servants went out into the streets and gathered all the people they could find, the bad as well as the good, and the wedding hall was filled with guests. But when the king came in to see the guests, he noticed a man there who was not wearing wedding clothes. He asked, 'How did you get in here without wedding clothes, friend.' The man was speechless. Then the king told the attendants, 'Tie him hand and foot, and throw him outside into the darkness, where there will be weeping and gnashing of teeth. For many are invited, but few are chosen'" (Matthew 22:1-14). The phrase "few are chosen" can be interpreted "few chose to come."

Notice the servants were to invite all the people they could find, both good and bad. The word "bad" used here in verse 10 is frequently translated, "wicked or evil." We Christians tend to look at people as good and bad. We have an image of ourselves as being good or better than the people of the world, or those in prison, who we see as bad. As Christians we must not make distinctions that suggest we are the "good people" and those are the "bad people," rather, it's a matter of knowing Jesus or not knowing Jesus, which is the difference between life and death. We all have sinned and come short of God's standard. (Romans 3:1-10, 23). We all inherited the sin nature from Adam and Eve. Some children grow up with parents who fail to discipline them and often end up in our prisons. What about the drug addicts, the homeless, those who are on parole from prison? Do we want them as our friends in our churches?

Ron, who was married seven times, moved to our community. I received his name through a new movers list. (www.newmovers.org). Ron's mother told him she never wanted him. He left home and eventually found a good job. However, his pain of rejection affected his relationships. His seventh wife was physically and emotionally abused as a child, locked in a room for days without adequate food. Their hygiene left a lot to be desired. Helen and I worked with this couple for months and years. They have made progress. Ron gives witness of God's love to most everyone he meets. We will share eternity in heaven with them.

A minister read a long list of sins from Galatians 5:19-21 and said, "I want everyone here to stand up if you have committed any of these sins." One man stood then another and another until nearly everyone stood. A man attending the church for the first time said, "These are my kind of people. I will be at home here." He gave his life to the Lord.

Many have been spiritually crippled because of self-centered, insensitive and sinful parenting. They can be healed. Sally, born out of wedlock, was a great embarrassment to her parents. For the first thirteen years of her life whenever family members came, she was locked in the closet until they left! She did not know most of her relatives until she was well into her adult life. Needless to say, Sally had many problems. God in His kindness has transformed her into a trophy of grace. Today, thanks to a supportive and accepting church, Sally ministers effectively to many children and adults. Oh, the depth of the richness of the mercy and grace of our Lord! (Romans 11:33).

Paul calls the people in the church in Corinth, "saints." However, even after eighteen months of instruction many of them were carnal and still baby Christians. (Acts 18:11). Many were practicing a lifestyle that was obviously depraved. He describes them: "But you were washed, you were sanctified, you were justified . . . by the Spirit of our God" (I Corinthians 6:11). When Paul leaves them and then plans to return, he writes: "I fear that there may be discord, jealousy, fits of rage, selfish ambition, slander, gossip, arrogance and disorder . . . I am afraid I will be grieved over many who have sinned earlier and have not repented of the impurity, sexual sin and the debauchery in which they had indulged" (II Corinthians 12:20-21).

Hurting people tend to hurt others. No matter how offensive one's actions, we all need God's mercy. I have experienced more of God's love than many who were not raised in a Christian family. Therefore, I have more responsibility to show God's love and mercy to those who have not experienced His love to the extent I have. This helps me see myself on the same level as those whose actions and motives seem more overtly evil than mine. By God's grace I have been forgiven, but I have the same sin issues as everyone else. No matter how repulsive their sin, my sin is just as repulsive to God as theirs, maybe even more so, since I should have grown in my walk with the Lord over many years. Furthermore, my sin costs Jesus just as much pain as theirs. When we critically judge others, it points to a lack of understanding of our own sin nature. We lack faith in the marvelous transformation God's Spirit will provide for all of us.

There is freedom in letting the judging to God and simply holding up the grace of Jesus. "God so loved the world that he gave his only Son, so that everyone who believes in him will not perish but have eternal life. God did not send his Son into the world to condemn it, but to save it" (John 3:16-17 NLT). He who has the Son has life, those who do not believe or trust in Jesus the wrath of God abides on them. (John 3:36).

VII.

OUR AMAZING FUTURE

WHAT WILL HEAVEN BE LIKE?
I CORINTHIANS 2:9

"What no eye has seen, what no ear has heard, and what no human mind has conceived – the things that God has prepared for those who love him" (I Corinthians 2:9). What will heaven be like? Artists have pictured heaven as people becoming angels who float around on clouds playing harps. Let me assure you the Bible gives a different picture. Heaven will not be boring. Heaven's grandeur is beyond description.

Our pastor asked the congregation, "What's the first thing you think of when you think of heaven?" Then we were to share with the people seated around us what came to our mind. Most people mentioned meeting loved ones. Helen, my wife, had a better answer: J-e-s-u-s! She's looking forward to seeing Jesus. David said, "In your presence is fullness of joy and at your right hand are pleasures from evermore" (Psalm 16:11 KJV). Our joy will be full or complete as we live in the presence of God and fellowship with each other.

Hebrews 12:22-23 is a picture of rich friendship. "You have come to Mount Zion, . . . the heavenly Jerusalem, to thousands upon thousands of angels in joyful assembly, to the church of the firstborn, whose names are written in heaven. You have come to God the Judge of all, to the spirits of the righteous made perfect, to Jesus the mediator of a new covenant." Wow! We will all be perfect and live in continual joy. No room for monotony or boredom there!

Can you imagine having all the time you want to talk with God, with His angels, with the Old and New Testament saints, and with Christians through all the ages? As someone has said, "There will be no misunderstandings or tension among us. Our relationships will be so much healthier in heaven than here. Here we have problems even with closest friends. Someone says something to you, and you aren't sure how to interpret it. You react to it—perhaps overreact. You say to yourself, 'I wonder what he meant by that? I wonder why she said that?' In heaven our relationships will be open, honest, interesting, loving, and uncomplicated by sin. We will live in perfect compatibility and refreshing intimacy.'"

Heaven will be full of exciting activity. "His servants shall serve him" (Revelation 22:3). We will be joyfully serving in the fullest expression of the capacity God has given us. We will discover new gifts, new interests, and new pursuits. We will have new responsibilities and exercise positions of authority. When we get to heaven, everything we do will bring us perfect satisfaction and lasting reward. We will never again engage in anything that will leave us feeling even a tad empty— our joy will be full. We'll be home!

To those who used the talents they were given Jesus said, "Well done, good and faithful servant; thou hast been faithful over a few things, I will make thee ruler over many things: enter thou into the joy of thy lord" (Matthew 25:21, 23 KJV). In God's presence is fullness of joy. (Psalm 16:11). There is rejoicing in heaven when sinners repent. (Luke 15:7, 10, 24).

We all have a longing for home. Ecclesiastes 3:11 tells us God has placed eternity in our hearts. He created us with a space in our souls that can't be satisfied by anything except things of everlasting duration. We need permanence. We need transcendence. Here we try to cram temporal things in the empty space of our heart. "We know that the whole creation groans and labors with birth pangs together until now. Not only that, but we also who have the firstfruits of the Spirit, even we ourselves groan within ourselves, eagerly waiting for the adoption, the redemption of our body" (Romans 8:22-23).

We will have a resurrected body like Jesus' body. (I Corinthians 15:49, Philippians 3:21). "The body that is sown is perishable, it is raised imperishable; it is sown in dishonor, it is raised in glory; it is sown in weakness, it is raised in power; it is sown a natural body, it is raised a spiritual body" (I Corinthians 15:42-44). Jesus' resurrection body enables Him to eat, demonstrating that He was not merely a spirit as His disciples thought. (Luke 24:37-43). His resurrected body is capable of entering rooms even when the doors are locked. (John 20:19).

Why didn't God tell us more about heaven? Paul was not permitted to tell his experience of being caught up to the third heaven. (II Corinthians 12:2-4). I believe if we knew more about heaven, we would focus on the gift rather than the giver. Worship in the book of Revelation is focused on Jesus. (Revelation 4 & 5). It's easy for me to focus on the aspects of heaven rather than on Jesus. For example, light travels at 186,000 miles a second. That means in one second light goes around the earth seven times. When we get to heaven we may even travel at the speed of thought, but that is nothing compared to God who is everywhere present at all times. My imagination goes wild, and that takes my mind off of Jesus. Heaven is all about Him and being with Him.

There is a song by Charles J. Butler, "Where Jesus Is, Tis Heaven There." Jesus is everywhere. He is omnipresent. Therefore, don't picture heaven so far away. "Am I only a God nearby, and not a God far away? Who can hide in the secret places so that I cannot see them? Do not I fill heaven and earth?" (Jeremiah 23:23-24). We will be seated with Jesus in the heavenly realms. (Ephesians 2:6). The heavenly realms can be near or far, we'll just have to wait and see.

Joni Eareckson Tada gives this illustration: When a baby is in its mother's womb we might say, "You are going to be born into a great new world full of mountains, rivers, fresh air and a sun and a moon. In fact, you are in that world now." The baby might say, "My world is the one surrounding me. It's soft, warm and all my needs are being met. I don't want to leave." Just as an unborn baby can't imagine its future world so we can't imagine how wonderful heaven will be.

There is a hunger with all creation. It's a yearning and anticipation for the coming day of ultimate redemption. The redemption process unleashed at Calvary isn't finished. God won't be finished until all creation is redeemed. We yearn for that day. The decaying world around us will be replaced at the end of time by the new heaven and the new earth and the city of New Jerusalem. That's what we truly crave. I can't wait!

PERFECT CHURCH,
PERFECT PEOPLE, PERFECT HEAVEN
EPHESIANS 5:25-32

How often have your heard, "You won't find a perfect church and if you do and you join it, it will no longer be perfect." The church is often sick and is known to have hurt people. A frequent criticism is: "The church is full of hypocrites."

Paul spent considerable time ministering to the church at Corinth but he says: "I fear that there may be discord, jealousy, fits of rage, selfish ambition, slander, gossip, arrogance and disorder. I am afraid that when I come again . . . I will be grieved over many who have sinned earlier and have not repented or their impurity, sexual sin and debauchery in which they have indulged" (II Corinthians 12:20-21).

While the church is far from perfect it is the best we have. The government will not bring healing to our world, the best educational institutions and philosophers will not bring peace, the military will not bring wholeness to the nations, the medical profession, the humanitarian efforts, not even the Salvation Army and its wonderful ministry to the hurting of our world can bring freedom from the ills of our society.

"Christ loved the church and gave himself up for her to make her holy, cleansing her by the washing with water through the word, and to present her to himself as a radiant church, without stain or wrinkle or any other blemish, but holy and blameless" (Ephesians 5:25-27). Just as we feed and care for our body, Christ feeds and cares for the church of which we are members. (Ephesians 5:29-30).

How can Christ present a church to the Father that is radiant and perfect? Christ's death on the cross sanctifies and cleanses the church. He cleanses us from sin and sets us apart for His service. "You are made clean through the words I have spoken unto you" (John 15:3). "Blessed are those who wash their robes that they may have the right to the tree of life and may go through the gates into the (heavenly) city" (Revelation 22:14). Just as Jesus cleanses us, He cleanses the church.

God chose us in Christ before the creation of the world to be holy and blameless in His sight. (Ephesians 1:4). We are far from blameless in our sight but God sees us through His Son who tore the veil of the temple so we can enter into His the Holy of Holies and come boldly to His throne of grace. (Matthew 27:51). How wonderful!

We can never thank God enough for His plan, which redeems us from sin and death making us perfect in His sight. Jesus suffered outside the city gate, a place of shame, to make us holy. (Hebrews 13:12). Hebrews 10:29 reminds us that Christ gave His blood to sanctify or make us holy. That's how much He loves us. Consider yourself as holy—that's the way God sees you. Seeing yourself as God sees you will be most helpful in living victorious.

Just as God sees us as pure and holy, He sees the church through Jesus' sacrifice as pure, holy without spot or blemish. The realization of this will take place when Jesus returns and presents us as members of His church to the Father. Then we will reign with Him throughout eternity! Eternity will be perfect: "Nothing impure (or defiled) will ever enter heaven, nor will anyone who does what is shameful or deceitful, but only those whose names are written in the Lamb's book of life" (Revelation 21:27).

Jesus' brother Jude describes the indescribable: "To Jesus who is able to keep you from stumbling and to present you before his glorious presence without fault and with great joy – to the only God our Savior be glory, majesty, power and authority, through Jesus Christ our Lord, before all ages, now and forevermore! Amen" (Jude 24-25). Imagine Jesus joyfully presenting us to the Father and giving us everlasting joy. Just as He presents us to the Father, He will present His church in the same way. What a future! Heaven will be perfect in every way we can imagine.

NO NIGHT THERE
REVELATION 22:5

"There will be no more night. They, (those in heaven), will not need the light of a lamp or the light of the sun, for the Lord God will give them light. And they will reign for ever and ever" (Revelation 22:5). "The city does not need the sun or the moon to shine on it, for the glory of God gives it light, and the Lamb is its lamp" (Revelation 21:23). "In Christ there is no darkness at all" (I John 1:5). Jesus is the light who gives light to everyone in the world. The darkness or evil cannot overcome the light of Christ (John 1:4-9). Jesus said, "I am the light of the world. Whoever follows me will never walk in darkness, but will have the light of life" (John 8:12). As Jesus hung on the cross, darkness came over the land from noon to three in the afternoon. When Jesus shouted, "It is finished!" the darkness left. At that point the veil of the temple tore from top to bottom enabling God's children to enter into the light of the Holy of Holies. (Matthew 27:51).

Satan's weapon is to blind people so they cannot see the light of the Gospel. (II Corinthians 4:4). "Light has come into the world, but people loved darkness instead of light because their deeds were evil" (John 3:19). Darkness is frequently an indication of judgment. One of the ten plagues God brought upon the Egyptians was darkness. (Exodus 10:21-22). The sun and the moon will be darkened, and the stars no longer shine when the Lord appears again. (Joel 3:15). Hell is a place of darkness. (Matthew 8:12). Since light exposes evil anyone who does not live in Jesus' light will not be at home in His presence here or in heaven. They would be miserable, living as guilty hypocrites in the light of Jesus.

Light and the "color" white are often associated together. On the Mount of Transfiguration, when Jesus was transfigured before Peter, James and John, Jesus' face shone like the sun, and His clothes became as white as the light. (Matthew 17:2). Angels appear both in heaven and on earth dressed in white. On Resurrection morning, the angel's appearance "was like lightning and his clothes were white as snow" (Matthew 28:3).

The overcomers of their evil culture will be given a white stone with a new name. (Revelation 2:17). In the Roman world a white stone was a ticket into an event. Might this be our ticket? The new name is given us because we now are a new person in Christ Jesus. (II Corinthians 5:17). "Dear friends, now we are children of God, and what we will be has not yet been made known. But we know that when Christ appears, we shall be like him, for we shall see him as he is" (I John 3:2).

While at Capital Christian Fellowship, a family came regularly for months participating in church activities. I was unable to get them to join our church in a formal way. When I asked them why they were unwilling to join they said, "We can't decide on our new name, especially for our children." In their native context when a person is baptized, they are given a new name. Would it help you to be more faithful to Jesus if you needed to choose a new name when you became a follower of Jesus? What name would you choose for yourself? I think that would be a meaningful exercise—maybe something we could try in our small discipleship groups.

Light and purity are also often associated in scripture. "Though your sins are like scarlet, they shall be as white as snow, though they are red like crimson, they shall be like wool" (Isaiah 1:18). David prayed, "Purify me from my sins, and I will be clean; wash me, and I will be whiter than snow" (Psalm 51:7 NLT). James Nicholson's beautiful hymn "Whiter Than Snow" dramatizes this theme. The first stanza reads: "Lord Jesus, I long to be perfectly whole; I want Thee forever to live in my soul; Break down every idol, cast out every foe – Now wash me, and I shall be whiter than snow." The refrain: "Whiter than snow, yes, whiter than snow, Now wash me, and I shall be whiter than snow."

Unfortunately, the Caucasian race at times has been insensitive and blind to how this song appears to persons of other races. We often naively and perhaps unintentionally believe Jesus was Caucasian. What was Jesus' skin color? Jesus likely had a darker complexion than we imagine, not unlike the olive skin common among Middle Easterners today. According to the Internet most scholars believe Jesus was dark brown and sun-tanned, perhaps with an oriental cast.

A young married couple came to Capital Christian Fellowship for the first time. He was white and she was black. Our Capital Christian congregation consists of twenty or more nationalities. The worship team is integrated. Our worship team leader was white and married to a black partner. The Sunday when they came the worship team leader led us in James Nicholson's beautiful hymn "Whiter Than Snow." I could tell they were not pleased with our worship but I did not know why, so I visited in their home that evening. They were irate that I would allow the church to sing this hymn. As you might suspect they never returned.

We need to be sensitive to how our language affects others. In heaven we will not have this problem. One of the most wonderful promises in scripture is given by John: "I looked, and there before me was a great multitude that no one could count from every nation, tribe, people and language standing before the throne and before the Lamb. They were wearing white robes and were holding palm branches in their hands. And they cried out in a loud voice: 'Salvation belongs to our God who sits on the throne, and to the Lamb'" (Revelation 7:9-10, 5:9).

Anti-Semitism, the hatred of God's special people, has been a constant problem throughout history and even more recently throughout the world. That persistent prejudice will finally be put to rest when we get to heaven. Do all you can to make friends with persons of different nations. After pastoring Capital Christian Fellowship with twenty or more nationalities I can assure you it is like a foretaste of heaven.

REJOICE IN HOPE
ROMANS 15:13, EPHESIANS 2:12

A Christian's hope includes waiting with expectancy. "Those who wait (hope) on the Lord will find new strength" (Isaiah 40:31 NLT). We usually think of hope as wishing for something to happen. A believer knows that their hope is solid, concrete evidence because it is grounded in the Word of God. We know that God cannot lie. (Hebrews 6:18). Biblical hope is an indication of certainty therefore we "rejoice in hope" (Romans 12:12). Hope and joy are couplets. "May the God of hope fill you with all joy and peace as you trust in him, so that you may overflow with hope by the power of the Holy Spirit" (Romans 15:13). We boast in the hope or in the certainty of the glory of God. (Romans 5:2).

"Remember – you were separated from Christ, without hope and without God in this world" (Ephesians 2:2). If you were raised in a Christian home where the Bible was read, prayers were prayed and church was the most important activity of the week you may find it a bit difficult to remember being without God. Even though I was raised in a Christian home, I clearly remember as an elementary school child being convicted of my sin and my need for a savior. Jesus came into my life and gave me a peace that made a big difference. Since then I have been growing in the certainty of God's promise that my sins are forgiven and I have new life in Christ. My hope is secure. I rejoice in hope. "The eyes of the Lord are on those who fear him, on those whose hope is in his unfailing love" (Psalm 33:18).

Sarah Young in her devotional book, *Jesus Today*, writes as though Jesus is speaking personally to us: "To enjoy abundant life, it is essential for you to have hope. However, many people indulge in false hopes and find themselves increasingly disillusioned as the years go by. So, I urge you to choose well the object of your hope. The best choice is my unfailing love . . .

"When you follow my divine guidelines, you can enjoy the Peace of my Presence, I am everywhere and I see everything, but my eyes are especially on those who are putting their hope in me. Such people are ever so precious to me, and I watch over them vigilantly. This does not mean I shield them from all adversity. It means I bless them with my nearness in good times, in hard times — at all times."

Edward Mote was born in London in January 1797. Edward's parents managed a pub and often left Edward to his own devices playing in the street. Speaking of these childhood years he said, "So ignorant was I that I did not know that there was a God."

Edward came to know God and became a pastor and songwriter. He wrote the hymn: "My hope is built on nothing less than Jesus' blood and righteousness; I dare not trust the sweetest frame but wholly lean on Jesus' name. When darkness veils His lovely face, I rest on His unchanging grace; In every high and stormy gale, my anchor holds within the vale. His oath, his covenant, his blood support me in the whelming flood; when all around my soul gives way, he then is all my hope and stay. When He shall come with trumpet sound; O may I then in him be found; Dressed in His righteousness alone, faultless to stand before the throne. On Christ the solid Rock I stand; all other ground is sinking sand. All other ground is sinking sand."

Build your life on Christ, the solid Rock. We have a bright future—think of standing before the Father's throne faultless, dressed in Jesus' robe of righteousness. I can't wait to wear that robe. A chorus that I have sung thousands of times in my heart is: "I'm covered over with the robe of righteousness that Jesus gives to me. I'm covered with the precious blood of Jesus and he lives in me. What a joy it is to know my heavenly Father loves me so and gives to me my Jesus. When he looks at me, he sees not what I used to be but he sees Jesus" (Isaiah 61:10). No wonder I can rejoice in hope.

Before he dies Paul encourages Titus to "look for the [fulfillment, the realization of our] blessed hope, even the glorious appearing of our great God and Savior Christ Jesus, the Messiah, the Anointed One" (Titus 2:13).

Paul prays that the eyes of those in Ephesis, "may be enlightened that they may know the hope to which he has called them . . . He continues to pray that we would experience the great power . . . that raised Christ from the dead and seated him in the heavenly realms beside the Father" (Ephesians 1:18-20). In 2:6 he says we are seated with Jesus—what a future!—no wonder Paul prays that their eyes would be open. Are your eyes open to the fact that you are seated with Jesus beside the Father?

When we are feeling discouraged and weighed down with problems and the cares of life, it is hard to continue to hope. David cries out in anguish: "Why are you in despair oh my soul? Why have you become disturbed within me? Hope in God, for I shall again praise him for the help of his presence" (Psalm 42:5).

When we take our eyes off of Jesus, we can easily become overwhelmed and discouraged. My wife, Helen, lives with five chronic incurable conditions including a rare form of blood cancer. She knows from experience that hope in Jesus is much more than a mere feeling; it is walking in peace and serenity. She says, "Daily I choose to praise Jesus regardless of my pain level or how I am feeling." Jesus promises never to leave and forsake us. He promises to provide all we need to live godly in Christ Jesus. (Philippians 4:19).

Quoting again from Sarah Young's devotional, "The day will come when you will spontaneously burst into songs of worship – joyously praising me for my glorious presence! However, when you rejoice in me during times of sadness, a marvelous thing happens; your words of hope and trust in me lift you above your circumstances. This sets your feet on an upward path of gratitude where joy increases step by step. This sacrifice of praise is most pleasing to me!"

"May the God of hope fill you with all joy and peace as you trust in him, so that you may overflow with hope by the power of the Holy Spirit" (Romans 15:13).

TORN BETWEEN NOW & HEAVEN – LIVE WITH ANTICIPATION
I CORINTHIANS 1:7

Paul prays that he will have sufficient courage that Christ will be exalted in his body, whether by life or by death. "For to me, to live is Christ and to die is gain. . . . I am **torn between the two**: I desire to depart and be with Christ which is better by far; but it is more necessary for you that I remain in the body. Convinced of this I know that I will remain, and I will continue, with you for your progress and joy in the faith, . . . so your joy in Jesus will overflow" (Philippians 1:21-26).

"Our citizenship is in heaven. We eagerly await a Savior from there, the Lord Jesus Christ, who, by the power that enables him to bring everything under his control will transform our lowly bodies so that they will be like his glorious body" (Philippians 3:20-21). There is no comparison between the present hard times and the coming good times. The created world can hardly wait for what is coming next. Our joyful anticipation deepens. (Romans 8:18-21). Earth is temporal – soon to pass away. Heaven should be more real to us than earth. Why? Heaven is eternal.

Anticipation is healthy for everyone. As a child I anticipated Christmas, as a teen I anticipated getting a driver's license. I anticipated graduating from high school and college. Later I anticipated getting married to my beautiful bride. Today I have a much greater anticipation. Most every day my wife Helen and I talk about our great future awaiting us in heaven. On her daily walks or when we are driving in the car, she will see a beautiful cloud and say, "Wouldn't it be great for Jesus to appear through those clouds?" "Every cloud is a flag to God's faithfulness" (Psalm 8:4 Msg.).

When Jesus ascended through the clouds two angels appeared. They said, "This same Jesus, who has been taken from you into heaven will come back in the same way you have seen him go into heaven" (Acts 2:11). The heavens will reveal our Lord. Let's look with anticipation. We are so preoccupied with earthly things that we forget to set our hearts and minds on things above, where Christ is seated at the right hand of God, not on things of the earth. (Colossians 3:1-2).

New Testament Christians lived with great anticipation of heaven. The Corinthians were eagerly waiting for the Lord Jesus Christ to be revealed. (I Corinthians 1:7). "No eye has seen, nor ear has heard, no mind has conceived what God has prepared for those who love him" (I Corinthians 2:9). "I will create new heavens and a new earth. The former things will not be remembered, nor will they come to mind" (Isaiah 65:17).

We live by faith, not by sight. We are confident, and would prefer to be away from the body and at home with the Lord. So, we make it our goal to please him, whether we are at home in the body or away from it. (II Corinthians 5:7-9). "Though outwardly we're wasting away, yet inwardly we are being renewed day by day. For our light and momentary troubles are achieving for us an eternal glory that far outweighs them all" (II Corinthians 4:16-18). Again, Paul writes: "I consider that our present sufferings are not worth comparing with the glory that will be revealed in us" (Romans 8:18).

Abraham walked in faith not knowing where God was calling

him to live because he was longing for a better country – a heavenly one. (Hebrews 11:16). Paul instructs Titus to look for the glorious appearing of the Savior Christ Jesus, the Messiah. (Titus 2:13).

When we read how John the Revelator describes our future it will make our anticipation peak, "These are they who have come out of the great tribulation; they have washed their robes and made them white in the blood of the Lamb. Therefore, they are before the throne of God and serve him day and night in his temple; and he who sits on the throne will spread his tent over them. Never again will they hunger, never again will they thirst. The sun will not beat upon them, nor any scorching heat. For the Lamb at the center of the throne will be their shepherd; he will lead them to springs of living water. And God will wipe away every tear from their eyes" (Revelation 7:14-17).

Fannie Crosby expresses it in these words: "When my life work is ended and I cross the swelling tide, when the bright and glorious morning I shall see; I shall know my redeemed when I reach the other side, and his smile will be the first to welcome me. Oh, the soul thrilling rapture when I view his blessed face, and the luster of his kindly beaming eye; how my heart will praise him for his mercy, love and grace that prepares for me a mansion in the sky. Through the gates to the city in a robe of spotless white, he will lead me where no tears shall ever fall; in the glad song of ages I shall mingle with delight; but I long to meet my Savior first of all."

"I heard a loud shout from the throne, saying, 'Look, the home of God is now among his people! He will live with them, and they will be his people. God himself will be with them. He will remove all of their sorrows and there will be no more death or sorrow or crying or pain for the old world and its evils are gone forever.' And the one sitting on the throne said, 'I am making all things new! . . . To all who are thirsty I will give the springs of the water of life without charge! All who are victorious will inherit all these blessings, and I will be their God, and they will be my children. But cowards who turn away from me, and unbelievers, and the corrupt and murderers, and the immoral, and those who practice witchcraft, and idol worshipers, and all liars – their doom is in the lake that burns with fire and sulfur'" (Revelation 21:3-8).

"Then the angel showed me the Water-of-Life River, crystal bright. It flowed from the Throne of God and the Lamb, right down the middle of the street. The Tree of Life was planted on each side of the River, producing twelve kinds of fruit, a ripe fruit each month. The leaves of the Tree are for healing the nations. Never again will anything be cursed. The Throne of God and of the Lamb is at the center. His servants will offer God service – worshiping, they'll look on his face, their foreheads mirroring God. Never again will there be any night. No one will need lamplight or sunlight. The shining of God, the Master, is all the light anyone needs. And they will rule with him age after age after age" (Revelation 22:1-5 Msg.).

"Our final home will hear no 'goodbyes.' Gone forever. Let that promise change you: from sagging to seeking, from mournful to helpful, from dwellers in the land of goodbyes to a heaven of hellos!" (Max Lucado). D. L. Moody said, "Someday you will read in the papers that D. L. Moody is dead. Don't you believe a word of it! At that moment I shall be more alive than I am now; I shall have gone ... into a house that is immortal – a body that death cannot touch, that sin cannot taint; a body fashioned like unto his glorious body."

How blessed we are to live with assurance of our great future. Live with anticipation!

REIGNING WITH CHRIST
REVELATION 2:26, 22:5

"To the one who is victorious and does my will to the end, I will give authority over the nations" (Revelation 2:26). "To the one who is victorious, I will give the right to sit with me on my throne, just as I was victorious and sat down with my father on his throne" (Revelation 3:21). "There will be no more night . . . For the Lord God will give them light. And they will reign forever and forever" (Revelation 22:5). Those surrounding Jesus' throne sang a new song: "You are worthy to take the scroll and to open its seals, because you were slain, and with your blood you purchased for God, persons from every tribe and language and people and nation. You have made them to be a kingdom of priests to serve our God, and they will reign on the earth" (Revelation 5:9-10). Some manuscripts read, "they reign" instead of "will reign." We can't imagine the authority and power God not only gives now, (Matthew 28:18-20) but throughout eternity.

"If we died with Jesus, we will also live with him, if we endure, we will also reign with him, if we disown him, he will also disown us, if we are faithless, he remains faithful, for he cannot disown himself" (II Timothy 2:11-13). We are "a royal priesthood, a holy nation, God's special possession, that we may declare the praises of Christ who called them out of darkness into his wonderful light" (I Peter 2:9).

Blessed and holy are those who share in the first resurrection. (The first resurrection refers to the new birth.) The second death (the second death refers to a spiritual death) – everlasting separation from God – (Revelation 21:8) has no power over them, but they will be priests of God and of Christ and will reign with Him for a thousand years. (Revelation 20:6).

In the parable of the King's ten servants Jesus says, "Because you have been trustworthy in a very small matter, take charge of ten cities" (Luke 19:17). "The saints of the Most High shall receive the kingdom, and possess the kingdom forever, even forever and ever" (Daniel 7:18).

God says to Jesus and since we are in Jesus, He says to us as well, "Ask me, and I will make the nations your inheritance, and the ends of the earth your possessions" (Psalm 2:8). Since we are in Jesus and reigning with Him, we need to pray with authority for the Gospel to push back the gates of hell and bring captive in every country of the world those who are open to the Good News. When we do our job of intercession for workers to take the Gospel to the ends of the earth Jesus promised: "And this gospel of the kingdom will be preached in the whole world as a testimony to all nations and then the end will come" (Matthew 24:14). May the Lord raise up an army of prayer warriors to see that the Kingdom of our Lord overcomes the kingdoms of this world.

God limits Himself to the intercession of His people. "I looked for someone among them who would build up the wall and stand before me in the gap on behalf of the land so I would not have to destroy it, but I found no one. So I will pour out my wrath on them and consume them with my fierce anger, bringing down on their own heads all they have done, declares the Sovereign Lord" (Ezekiel 22:30-31). God wanted to spare His people from judgment but Jeremiah reports He could not find one honest man. "Go up and down the streets of Jerusalem, look around and consider, . . . If you can find but one person who deals honestly and seeks the truth, I will forgive this city" (Jeremiah 5:1). Pray for God to raise up intercessors. Be sure you are an intercessor. Your intercession will help bring many from destruction and enable many to come to glory.

We have access to the mighty power that raised Christ from the dead. "I pray that the eyes of your heart may be enlightened in order that you may know the hope to which he has called you, the riches of his glorious inheritance in his holy people, and his incomparably great power for us who believe. That power is the same as the mighty strength he exerted when he raised Christ from the dead and seated him at his right hand in the heavenly realms, far above all rule and authority, power and dominion, and every name that is invoked, not only in the present age but also I the one to come" (Ephesians 1:17-21). May God enlighten our hearts to His resurrection power!

We have the power to bind the strong man. Jesus said, "How can anyone enter a strong man's house and carry off his possessions unless he first ties up the strong man? Then he can plunder his house" (Matthew 12:29). If we will learn through intercessory prayer to bind Satan, then we will see the Holy Spirit break the yoke of slavery that is keeping our unsaved friends from becoming followers of Jesus.

"Do you not know that the saints will judge the world? And if the world will be judged by you, are you unworthy to judge the smallest matters? Do you not know that we shall judge angels? How much more things that pertain to this life?" (I Corinthians 6:2-3). "Whoever can be trusted with very little can also be trusted with much" (Luke 16:10).

We can't fully understand these promises but they are included in God's Word not just to take up space. They are there to encourage us to take up our cross and follow Him, (Matthew 16:24), in this "wicked and adulterous generation" (Matthew 16:4). These promises are there to remind us that we are to endure, to be trustworthy and victorious. Jesus never calls us to do or be anything other than what He equips us to fulfill. We are more than conquerors through Christ who loved us. (Romans 8:37).

"I will give power over the nations to everyone who wins the victory and keeps on obeying me until the end. I will give each of them the same power that my Father has given me" (Revelation 2:26 CEV). God has granted us a greater authority than we can imagine but we must possess it by prayers of faith. Jesus said, "I will give you the keys of the kingdom of heaven; whatever you bind on earth will be bound in heaven, and whatever you loose on earth will be loosed in heaven" (Matthew 16:19). Even so come Lord Jesus!